AF352320

Studies of the Americas

edited by

James Dunkerley

Institute for the Study of the Americas

University of London

School of Advanced Study

Titles in this series are multi-disciplinary studies of aspects of the societies of the hemisphere, particularly in the areas of politics, economics, history, anthropology, sociology, and the environment. The series covers a comparative perspective across the Americas, including Canada and the Caribbean as well as the United States and Latin America.

Titles in this series published by Palgrave Macmillan:

Cuba's Military 1990–2005: Revolutionary Soldiers during Counter-Revolutionary Times
By Hal Klepak

The Judicialization of Politics in Latin America
Edited by Rachel Sieder, Line Schjolden, and Alan Angell

Latin America: A New Interpretation
By Laurence Whitehead

Appropriation as Practice: Art and Identity in Argentina
By Arnd Schneider

America and Enlightenment Constitutionalism
Edited by Gary L. McDowell and Johnathan O'Neill

Vargas and Brazil: New Perspectives
Edited by Jens R. Hentschke

When Was Latin America Modern?
Edited by Nicola Miller and Stephen Hart

Debating Cuban Exceptionalism
Edited by Bert Hoffman and Laurence Whitehead

Caribbean Land and Development Revisited
Edited by Jean Besson and Janet Momsen

Cultures of the Lusophone Black Atlantic
Edited by Nancy Priscilla Naro, Roger Sansi-Roca and David H. Treece

Democratization, Development, and Legality: Chile, 1831–1973
By Julio Faundez

The Hispanic World and American Intellectual Life, 1820–1880
By Iván Jaksić

The Role of Mexico's Plural *in Latin American Literary and Political Culture: From Tlatelolco to the "Philanthropic Ogre"*
By John King

Faith and Impiety in Revolutionary Mexico
Edited by Matthew Butler

Reinventing Modernity in Latin America: Intellectuals Imagine the Future, 1900–1930
By Nicola Miller

The Federal Nation

Perspectives on American Federalism

Edited by
Iwan W. Morgan and Philip J. Davies

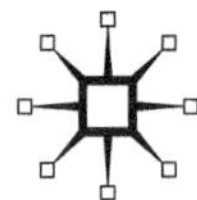

First published in 2008 by
PALGRAVE MACMILLAN®
in the United States—a division of St. Martin's Press LLC,
175 Fifth Avenue, New York, NY 10010.

Where this book is distributed in the UK, Europe and the rest of the world,
this is by Palgrave Macmillan, a division of Macmillan Publishers Limited,
registered in England, company number 785998, of Houndmills,
Basingstoke, Hampshire RG21 6XS.

Palgrave Macmillan is the global academic imprint of the above companies
and has companies and representatives throughout the world.

Palgrave® and Macmillan® are registered trademarks in the United States,
the United Kingdom, Europe and other countries.

ISBN-13: 978–0–230–60940–2
ISBN-10: 0–230–60940–6

Library of Congress Cataloging-in-Publication Data

The federal nation : perspectives on American federalism / edited by
Iwan W. Morgan and Philip J. Davies.
    p. cm.—(Studies of the Americas)
Includes bibliographical references and index.
ISBN 0–230–60940–6
    1. Bush, George W. (George Walker), 1946– 2. United States—Politics
and government—2001– 3. Federal government—United States—
History—21st century. I. Morgan, Iwan W. II. Davies, Philip.

E902.F43 2008
973.931—dc22   2008021288

A catalogue record of the book is available from the British Library.

Design by Newgen Imaging Systems (P) Ltd., Chennai, India.

First edition: December 2008

10 9 8 7 6 5 4 3 2 1

Printed in the United States of America.

Contents

Part I   U.S. Federalism in National and Comparative Perspective

Part II   Intergovernmental Strategies in Contemporary Federalism

Part III Inequality and Federalism

Part IV Uniformity and Diversity in Federalism

List of Figures

List of Tables

Contributors

Joel D. Aberbach is Professor of Political Science and Public Policy at University of California, Los Angeles. He is the author and coauthor of many books on U.S. politics, the most recent of which is *The Executive Branch*.

Edward Ashbee is Associate Professor in the Copenhagen Business School. His most recent publication is *The Bush Administration, Sex and the Moral Agenda*.

Christopher J. Bailey is Professor of U.S. Politics at Keele University. Among his publications are *Congress and Air Pollution* and *The Republican Party in the U.S. Senate 1974–1984*.

Timothy J. Conlan is Professor of Government and Politics at George Mason University. He is the author of more than fifty studies on federalism and public policy, including *New Federalism: Intergovernmental Reform from Nixon to Reagan* and *Taxing Choices: The Politics of Tax Reform*.

Andrew Davies is a graduate student in criminal justice at State University of New York, Albany.

Philip J. Davies is Director of the Eccles Centre for American Studies at the British Library and Professor of U.S. Studies at de Montfort University. Among his numerous publications are *Elections USA* and *New Challenges for the American Presidency*.

Christopher Dunn is Professor of Political Science at memorial University, Newfoundland. Among his many publications are *The Handbook of Canadian Public Administration* and *Canadian Political Debates: Opposing Views on Issues That Divide Canadians*.

Douglas Jaenicke was formerly Senior Lecturer in Government at the University of Manchester. He has published extensively on U.S. social policy, including (with Alex Waddan) "President Bush and Social Policy" in *Political Science Quarterly*.

Kimberley S. Johnson is Assistant Professor of Political Science at Barnard College, Columbia University. She is the author of *Governing the American State: Congress and the New Federalism, 1877–1929*.

John Kincaid is Professor of Government and Public Service at Lafayette College. He is coeditor of *Publius: The Journal of Federalism* and author of many studies on federalism and intergovernmental relations.

Robert McKeever is Professor of Politics and Dean of Law, Governance and International Relations at London Metropolitan University. He has published widely on U.S. politics, notably on the Supreme Court, including *Raw Judicial Power.*

Iwan W. Morgan is Professor of U.S. Studies at the Institute for the Study of the Americas, University of London. He has published extensively on the politics of U.S. economic policy.

Jonathan Parker is Lecturer in U.S. Politics at the University of Keele. A specialist on education policy, he has published articles in this field.

Gillian Peele is a fellow of St Margaret's Hall, Oxford University. She has published extensively on U.S. politics, including *Revival and Reaction: The Right in Contemporary America.*

Carl W. Stenberg is professor of Public Administration and Government at University of North Carolina, Chapel Hill. He is the author of many works on federalism and on public policy, including *America's Future Work Force*

Alex Waddan is Senior Lecturer in American Politics at Leicester University. He has published widely on the politics of U.S. social policy and his latest book is *Clinton's Legacy: A New Democrat in Governance.*

Alissa Pollitz Worden is Associate Professor of Criminal Justice at State University of New York, Albany. She has published many articles and papers on judicial, criminal justice and criminology issues.

Joseph F. Zimmerman is Professor of Political Science at State University of New York, Albany. He is the author of more than twenty-five books on politics and public policy, including *The Referendum: The People Decide Public Policy* and *Contemporary American Federalism.*

Introduction

Iwan W. Morgan

Whatever its complexity in practice, federalism can be defined quite simply as the organizational mechanism through which different levels of government manage and share power. It is a process for dividing the responsibilities of collective governance between national and subnational units of authority. As Joseph Zimmerman, one of the contributors to this volume, has written, in a federal system "all exercisable governmental powers are divided between a national government and several … state governments with the exception of the concurrent powers exercisable by either plane of government."[1] Federalism as a term appears nowhere in the U.S. Constitution of 1787 but it was the singularly American invention of that document. Adopted and adapted by other nations in modern times, this system has been hailed as "the greatest of American contributions to the art of government."[2] Arguably, however, the real triumph of America's experiment in federalism was not its launch but its endurance. The survival of this structure of government largely intact for more than two hundred years as the nation underwent immense political, social, and economic changes has been remarkable. Crucial to the longevity of American federalism was the balance that the constitutional founders struck between firmness of principle and flexibility of detail. As constitutional scholar Michael Kammen observed, they settled for establishing a workable form of shared powers between national and state governments but left resolution of contentious jurisdictional issues to be worked out in light of operational experience and historical change.[3]

The constitutional settlement bequeathed a legacy of conflict and consensus for American federalism. With the notable exception of the Civil War crisis, the operational system of government represented by federalism has commanded broad acceptance and support within the American polity since its inception. On the other hand, the long history of American federalism is littered with contestations of jurisdictional authority between different levels of government. Such disputes found expression in competing interpretations of the Constitution's intent regarding the relative powers of the federal government and the states. Nevertheless, they were also rooted in disagreement about the legitimate functions of government in American society, regardless of whether exercised at national or subnational level.

According to E. E. Schattschneider, the American system of federalism has entailed a "socialization of conflict" because it has offered so many points of access for ideas and interests to compete for the attention of public policy-makers at whatever level of government was likely to respond to them.[4] To some critics, this resulted in an amorphous and confusing system character-ized by overlapping jurisdictions and ambiguous authority, one that worked more by default than design.[5] Whatever its virtue or vice in this regard, American federalism has provided a framework for different groups to con-test public policy outcomes. In the words of political scientist Aaron Wildavsky, "the operational meaning of federalism is found in the degree to which the constituent units disagree about what should be done, who should do it, and how it should be carried out. In a word, federalism is about conflict."[6]

The chapters in this volume explore some of the conflicts that have been manifest with regard to three particular issues in recent American federal-ism. The first of these concerns the vertical tensions over the distribution of authority between national and subnational government. The second relates to the tensions between the national government's role as the instrument of policy uniformity throughout the nation and the inclination of the states to take different approaches to similar issues in light of their particular political and social values. The third concerns the changing political context of feder-alism in the more conservative climate of the late twentieth and, particularly, early twenty-first centuries.

Contested authority between the national government and the states is as old as the Constitution, but the balance of power swung inexorably toward the former in the twentieth century and beyond. More often than not, the major political, social, and economic issues that have confronted modern America have been national ones that required national solutions. The fed-eral government has increasingly become the dominant actor in a diverse range of policy domains that were once considered outside the legitimate scope of any level of government. Even if they have not always marched in step, the three institutions of the federal government have all acted as agents of change to expand national power at the expense of the states. At different times, the Supreme Court has used its powers of judicial review, the presi-dency has employed its national agenda-setting capacity, and the Congress has wielded its legislative power to promote federal aggrandizement.

Also underlying the changing balance between national and state governments was the emergence of fiscal federalism. In the nineteenth century, the national government's fiscal capacity was entirely dependent on tariff revenues that did not provide a stable or reliable source of funds. In the second half of the twentieth century, by contrast, the expanding reach of federal income taxation provided national government with the financial clout to support its enlarged agenda. As political scientists Michael Reagan and John Sanzone observed, the ratification in 1913 of the

Sixteenth Amendment that legitimized federal income taxes was instrumental in bringing about the "drastic centralization of American federalism."[7]

The growth of national government power raised the corollary issue of uniformity or diversity in American federalism. Modern advocates of a strong national government see it as the best guarantor of the universality of public policy standards throughout the nation. To some, it is also an essential safeguard for democracy and equality to counter the centrifugal tendencies of the states to pursue different approaches regarding individual rights.[8] Others insist, conversely, that diversity is the lifeblood of a healthy body politic because the federal template cannot fit the preferences of all fifty states. In Ira Sharkansky's opinion, political cultures necessarily differ from one state and region to the next, and should be allowed to leave their imprint on public affairs.[9]

Despite the growing power of national government, few if any questions of public policy within federalism have been finally and wholly resolved in the modern era. Battles continue to be fought and refought over a range of issues and against a background of broader political change. The expansion of the federal government's role was broadly driven by the liberal thrust in national politics promoted by the New Deal in the 1930s and sustained in the postwar period through the 1960s. Since the 1980s, however, America has turned rightward, albeit in somewhat hesitant fashion that has fallen far short of a political counterrevolution.

Under Ronald Reagan, traditional conservative suspicion of big government found expression in efforts to deregulate federal involvement in state and local affairs. One such initiative was Executive Order 12612, issued in 1987, which deferred to the states interpretations of "national standards." This was later overridden in 1993 by Bill Clinton's Executive Order 13083 allowing federal agencies to limit the policymaking capabilities of state and local governments. Expectations of another turn of the pendulum in favor of the states under George W. Bush were not borne out. Instead, the 43rd president indulged in what some termed "big government conservatism" that has expanded federal authority in support of conservative rather than liberal ends.

In addressing these interrelated features of American federalism, the contributions to this book are divided into four sections that examine the U.S. system in national and comparative perspective, intergovernmental strategies in contemporary federalism, inequality and federalism, and issues of uniformity and diversity in federalism.

In "Federalism, the Bush Administration, and the Evolution of American Politics," Timothy J. Conlan examines George W. Bush's advancement of policies that increased federal spending, preempted state authority, and centralized decision making in areas of traditional state and local concern. In his assessment, this development reflects the willingness of contemporary conservatives to use federal authority to achieve their social and economic objectives in the manner liberals once employed it for their ends. As such, intergovernmental policy under the Bush administration becomes a useful lens for viewing the broader evolution of American politics.

In "What a Difference a Few Decades Make: The Conservative Movement, Executive Power, and the Constitution in the United States," Joel D. Aberbach and Gillian Peele place the development of federalism into the context of broader constitutional changes under George W. Bush. Reviewing traditional Republican doctrine, they demonstrate how far Bush has departed from Madisonian orthodoxy in pursuit of his political agenda. In addition, they explore the resultant tensions and divisions generated within the wider conservative coalition and consider the extent to which Bush has undermined the intellectual credibility of the conservative approach to constitutional issues.

In "Canada's 'Open Federalism': Past, Present, and Future," Christopher Dunn places the Bush-era changes in U.S. federalism in sharp relief by exploring the different direction taken by federalism in Canada since the coming to power of Stephen Harper's Conservative national government in 2006. Under Harper, so-called Open Federalism—particularly its fiscal elements—appeared to repudiate the longstanding nation-building emphasis of intergovernmental policies, pursued by previous Liberal governments, in favor of a more flexible approach to the provinces. To date, however, the policy has focused primarily on Quebec, which raises questions about the significance of its broader impact on Canadian federalism.

In "Three Faces of Contemporary American Federalism," John Kincaid explores continuity and change in contemporary federalism in which he identifies the new element of coercive federalism coexisting alongside cooperative federalism and the continuing vitality of the reserved powers of the states. In his assessment, coercive federalism itself is not a twenty-first-century phenomenon but was increasingly operational from the late 1960s onward. Though currently associated with George W. Bush's imposition of federal dictates to achieve conservative ends, it has a bipartisan pedigree that makes it likely to endure under a new administration of whatever stripe. For Kincaid, the most characteristic element of coercive federalism is not its ideological applications but its shift of focus in federal policymaking from the interests of places (namely, state and local governments) to the interests of persons (namely, voters and interest groups).

In "Fragmented Structures and Blurred Boundaries," Carl W. Stenberg moves the focus from vertical to horizontal federalism to consider whether the fragmented structure of local government prevents many communities from tackling complex and costly problems that spill across boundary lines. In his assessment, local experience indicates that new strategies for regional governance are essential but racial divisiveness, local official parochialism, suburban resistance and citizen distrust of big government stand as impediments to their development.

In "Congressional Devolution of Power," Joseph F. Zimmerman reviews the constitutional delegation to Congress of broad regulatory powers that can (with one exception) be devolved to the states. He demonstrates that

Congress has generally enacted devolution and preemption statutes in a conceptual vacuum and ad hoc problem-solving basis. In his assessment, publication of codes governing such statues would reduce citizen confusion about their use and counter the democratic deficit they currently engender.

In "Hurricane Katrina, Racial Federalism, and the American State: A Tale Foretold?" Kimberley S. Johnson uses a "path dependency" model to link the Hurricane Katrina disaster to the persistence of racially structured federalism, defined as a power-sharing arrangement between constituent levels of government based on acceptance of racial hierarchy. Reviewing the development of racially structured federalism from the "bargain" struck by the constitutional founders in 1787 through the nineteenth and twentieth centuries to 2005, she attributes the public-policy response to the disaster to structural issues of racism that had far deeper roots than individual ones.

In "The Politics and Policy of the State Children's Health Insurance Program" (SCHIP), Alex Waddan and Douglas Jaenicke consider the politics leading to the enactment of the SCHIP. They demonstrate its deviation from the recent norm in its promotion of federal assistance directly to states rather than individuals. Nevertheless, their assessment concludes that it is unlikely to become a model for future healthcare policymaking partly because of the substantial state-level variations that characterized its operation and the partisan conflict over its reauthorization.

In "Criminal Justice Policy Across the United States: Due Process in the Punitive Turn," Andrew Davies and Alissa Pollitz Worden undertake an empirical analysis of diversity within federalism pertaining to criminal justice. Focusing on state practices across the dimensions of punitiveness and due process, they consider whether there has been a "punitive turn" to harsher policies in recent years. However, they find no evidence that states are possessed of a generalized orientation to due process issues or policy matters. In their assessment, the "punitive turn" as a paradigmatic approach to understanding and characterizing criminal justice policy development over the last thirty years is limited in its descriptive generalizability.

In "Gay Rights, the Federal Marriage Amendment, and the States," Edward Ashbee considers another issue of diversity within federalism in a conservative era. He examines Republican efforts to secure a Marriage Protection Amendment to the Constitution to define marriage as a heterosexual institution and prohibit gay marriage across the nation. This approach stands at variance to traditional conservative preferences to facilitate state differences, but the issue was a critical one for consolidation of Christian Right support of the GOP in the tight electoral environment of the Bush era.

In "Clearing the Air: The New Politics of Public Smoking," Christopher J. Bailey ascribes growing support for a ban on smoking in public places to popular acceptance that public smoking is a health hazard. Despite this, regulatory activity to control public smoking has been stronger at state and local than national levels, with the consequence of considerable variation in laws and ordinances. Different populations across the nation have therefore received varying degrees of health protection. This raises the important normative question at the heart of federalism—namely whether disparities in the provision of such an important public good as health care should be tolerated.

In "Abortion, the Judiciary and Federalism in North America," Robert McKeever examines the empirical issue of how federalism impacted on abortion policy in the United States and Canada; and the normative one of whether federalism is a desirable mechanism for policy formulation and implementation of constitutionally protected rights. His empirical review demonstrates that the right of abortion is enjoyed very unevenly across class and geographical location in both countries because states and provinces have succeeded in restricting its scope within their borders. In normative terms, however, he argues that the judicial compromises underlying these restraints constitute a justifiable refusal to sacrifice wholly one core constitutional principle (diversity within federalism) on the altar of another (individual rights).

Finally, in "No Child Left Behind: Federalism and Education Policy," Jonathan Parker analyses the signatory domestic reform of the Bush Presidency. He concludes that the No Child Left Behind (NCLB) Act of 2001 represents something of a revolution in national education policy through its success in placing standards and accountability at the core of the agenda. In contrast, it is not a revolution in federalism since it continues the late twentieth-century trend of using prescriptive financial assistance to compel state and local governments to do the federal government's bidding. Moreover, Parker concludes that NCLP exemplifies federal "overreach" because the measure cannot achieve its ends no matter how strictly enforced.

The chapters in this book are based on presentations made at a conference on *The Federal Nations of North America*, held at the British Library in March 2007 and co-organized by the University of London's Institute for the Study of the Americas and the British Library's Eccles Centre for American Studies. The coeditors of this volume, also the co-organizers of that conference, record their gratitude to their respective institutions and the United States Embassy for financial support to bring together participants from the United States and the United Kingdom, and to their colleagues who rendered always cheerful and efficient administrative support for the project (Olga Jimenez and Karen Perkins at ISA, Kate Bateman and Jean Petrovic at the Eccles Centre). They hope that the book that has emerged from this venture testifies to the enduring capacity of federalism to rank among the most significant and fascinating aspects of American politics.

The book is dedicated to Ros Davies, wife of coeditor Philip J. Davies and mother of contributor Andrew Davies. Ros lost her long fight with cancer as the manuscript was coming to completion. Philip and his children, Andrew and Carolyn, also record their thanks to Philip's mother, Iris Davies, and her partner, Ralph Joyce, for all their help and support in the last months of Ros's life.

Notes

1. Joseph Zimmerman, *Contemporary American Federalism* (Westport, CT: Praeger, 1992), 4–5.
2. Leslie Lipson, *The Democratic Civilization* (New York: Oxford University Press, 1964), 143.
3. Michael Kammen, ed., The Origin of the American Constitution: A Documentary History (New York: Penguin, 1986), xix–xx.
4. E. E. Schattschneider, *The Semi-Sovereign People* (New York: Holt, Rinehart and Winston, 1966), 7.
5. See, for example, G. Ross Stephens and Nelson Wikstrom, *American Intergovernmental Relations: A Fragmented Federal Polity* (New York: Oxford University Press, 2007).
6. Quoted in David Schleicher and Brendon Swedlow, eds., *Federalism and Political Culture* (New Brunswick, NJ: Transaction Publishers, 1998), 17.
7. Michael Reagan and John Sanzone, *The New Federalism*, 2nd ed. (New York: Oxford University Press, 1981), 38.
8. See, for example, William Hudson, *American Democracy in Peril*, 3rd ed. (New York: Chatham House, 2001), 221.
9. Ira Sharkansky, *The Maligned States*, 2nd ed. (New York: McGraw Hill, 1978).

Part I

U.S. Federalism in National and Comparative Perspective

Chapter 1

Federalism, the Bush Administration and the Evolution of American Politics*

Timothy J. Conlan

"The era of big government is over." That dramatic pronouncement by Bill Clinton was the catch phrase of his 1996 State of the Union address. Coming in the wake of Ronald Reagan's efforts to devolve power back to state governments, and uttered in the midst of Clinton's battles with an assertive Republican Congress, this proclamation appeared to mark a turning point in the evolution of American federalism

In hindsight, it is now clear that the obituary for big government was premature. Government spending resumed its growth trajectory during Clinton's second term, and the rate of growth accelerated significantly during George Bush's first term. Spending increases were supplemented with significant new federal mandates, new federal preemptions, the creation of a huge new cabinet department of Homeland Security, and the largest expansion of federal entitlement programs since Lyndon Johnson's Great Society. Consequently, Bush is now routinely described—and on the right he is often denounced—as a "big government conservative."[1]

This development was wholly unexpected, given traditional Republican values and rhetoric favoring smaller government and states' rights, as well as Bush's own background as a governor. Republicans, moreover, were in control of the White House and Congress for the first time in nearly fifty years. Consequently, the rise of big-government conservatism is an important development with implications for American federalism, for American politics and governance more generally, and for conservative ideology in the United States. These developments and their broader implications are the focus of the following analysis.

Government Growth under George W. Bush

Federal government spending grew substantially during the George W. Bush administration, and that growth—especially the component generated by Bush's education and health care initiatives—underlay conservative's complaints about Bush's big-government tendencies. Measured in current dollars, total federal outlays increased 49 percent between fiscal years 2001 and 2007, from $1.86 trillion to $2.78 trillion. That was almost twice as fast as the rate of growth in federal spending under President Bill Clinton. Measured in constant dollars, the increase was still substantial at 18 percent, rising from $1.62 trillion to $1.79 trillion.[2] This compares to an 11 percent increase in real spending over the eight years of the Clinton administration.[3]

A similar story was repeated in federal aid to state and local governments. Because federal grants can distort state and local spending priorities, generate dependence on continued federal assistance, and come with significant strings attached, the level of federal aid is often taken as one indicator of the degree of centralization in the federal system. In FY 2005, federal spending on grants-in-aid, as measured in constant dollars, reached a record high of $374 billion, almost $90 billion more than its peak in 2000 under Bill Clinton (see figure 1.1). This was partly a reflection of continued rapid growth in intergovernmental health care spending, under the Medicaid program. In addition, however, federal grants for services and institutional support, such as education, homeland security, and antirecession fiscal assistance, increased by nearly 40 percent between 2000 and 2005—from $54.6 billion to $93.3 billion.[4]

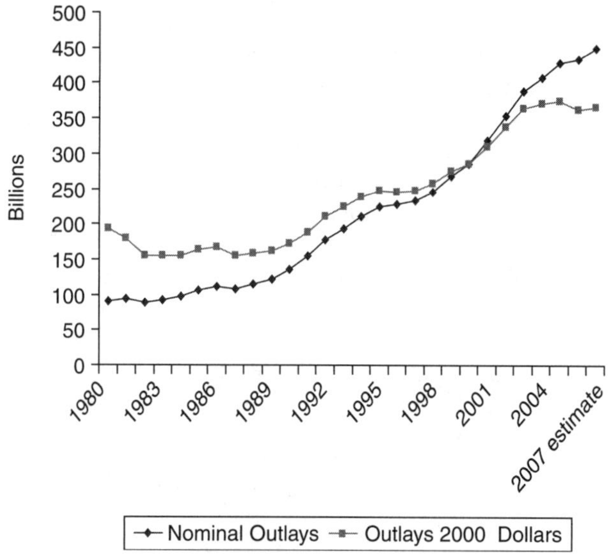

Figure 1.1   Federal grants to state and local governments, 1980–2007

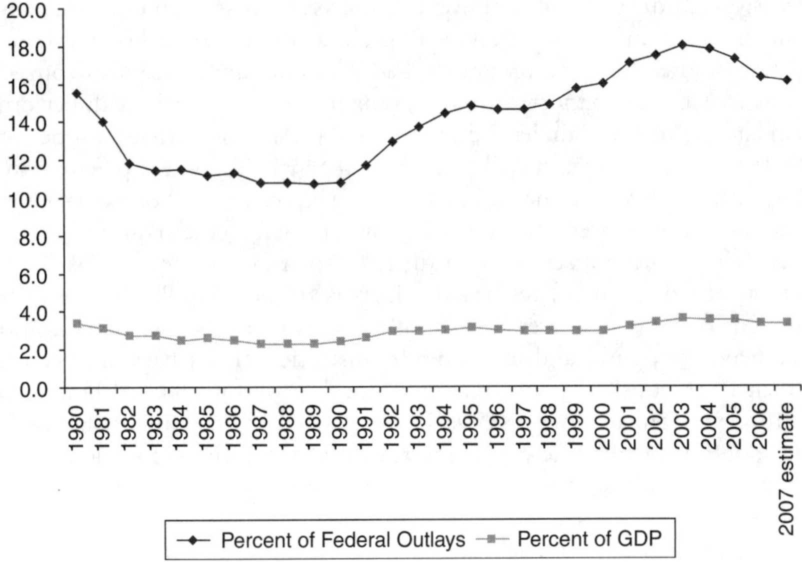

Figure 1.2   Federal grants to state and local governments, relative measures, 1980–2007

Consequently, relative measures of federal grants-in-aid expenditures also showed considerable growth during the Bush era. Federal aid to states and localities as a percent of total federal outlays reached a record high of 18 percent in 2003, exceeding the previous peak of 17.8 percent in 1978 (see figure 1.2). Although this declined to 16.3 percent in 2006—partly due to rapid increase in spending on non-grant expenditures, such as the war in Iraq and the Medicare prescription drug program—grants-in-aid still constituted a greater percentage of total federal spending in 2006 than during any year between 1980 and 2000. Similarly, grant spending totaled 24.4 percent of all domestic outlays in 2005 and 24.3 percent of state–local expenditures—levels last seen in the 1970s period of "big government" that was challenged by Ronald Reagan.

Mandates and Preemption

The expansion of federal grants-in-aid to state and local governments is only one dimension of federal policy influence in the intergovernmental system. Indeed, contemporary U.S. federalism is characterized by the proliferation of more coercive instruments of federal control to such an extent that the system has been dubbed "regulatory federalism" or "coercive federalism."[5] State and local governments in the United States know that the national government does not just show up at their doorstep like a kindly Uncle Sam handing out gifts of federal aid. All grants-in-aid come with strings attached, although they differ in their intrusiveness. For some programs, strings consist only of routine grant conditions, which are meant to assure fiscal and programmatic accountability in the use of federal funds. Other conditions of aid are more intrusive and difficult to circumvent, however, such as conditions that apply to many or all grants or sanctions that cut across program boundaries and apply to more than one program.[6] Federal policy influence also comes in forms that are unconnected to any grant funds at all, such as direct order mandates, which contain legal directives and prescriptions that must be complied with under threat of civil and criminal penalties, and the preemption of state authority—where the national government claims full or partial constitutional authority over a field of policy hitherto left to the states.

Although the impact is more difficult to measure with precision, the burden of federal mandates has also increased under the Bush administration. Major new mandates have been adopted in fields such as education, emergency response, and election administration that have long been the principal responsibility of state and local governments. Although the Unfunded Mandates Act of 1995 has succeeded in deterring or modifying the adoption of some new intergovernmental regulations, loopholes in the law and political support for policy nationalization in Washington have limited the effects of the law.

Among the new mandates adopted during the Bush era, the No Child Left Behind (NCLB) Act of 2001 has received the most attention, and for good reason. This measure was one of the signature domestic initiatives of George W. Bush. It provided substantial new funding for education, but it also intruded into aspects of elementary and secondary education that have long been reserved to states and localities. As Patrick McGuinn observed: "NCLB contains a large number of prescriptive mandates that reach into every major area of education policy and will require states and districts to fundamentally change the way they run their public schools."[7] Indeed, the statute's annual testing requirements and mandatory corrective actions for schools and districts that fail to meet their testing targets had the potential to significantly restructure education delivery in future, including state takeovers of local schools, school-supported private tutoring, curriculum changes, and expanded use of charter schools.

Outside of education, the Help America Vote Act sets standards for voting systems and mandates that states establish statewide voter databases. Voters must be allowed to correct voter registration errors and to cast provisional ballots when mistakes are found. By specifying new requirements for statewide voter databases and uniform voter definitions, the law entails significant new centralization of the registration and elections process at the state level.[8] Although Congress provided $3 billion in funding for implementing the new law, to help pay for modernizing voting machines, federal funds were still estimated to fall short of the actual costs of implementing the new law.[9]

In homeland security, new national standards are being developed for emergency preparedness, communications, and response. In addition, the Real ID Act of 2005 established new standards for issuing state drivers licenses, with document validation requirements that would impose up to $11 billion in compliance costs.[10] The new Medicare Prescription Drug

Improvement and Modernization Act of 2003 contained a "clawback" provision that was estimated to cost states $6 billion in 2006. The clawback was designed to prevent state fiscal windfalls from reduced Medicaid costs for "dual eligible" participants (those who receive both Medicare and Medicaid benefits), but was imposed in a unilateral fashion that may overestimate state savings.[11] Finally, unilateral federal actions in tax policy, particularly the elimination of the federal estate tax and changes in federal rules governing depreciation and dividends, have had major fiscal implications for states that couple their tax systems to federal tax law.

Federal preemption of state authority has also increased during the Bush administration. According to a compilation by Joseph Zimmerman, a total of sixty-four new preemptions were adopted in the first five years of the Bush administration.[12] As Zimmerman notes, many of these were modest restrictions of state authority that did not significantly alter the balance of power in the federal system. On the other hand, a handful of new preemptions substantially restricted state authority to raise revenues or regulate behavior, such as the limitation on state taxation of internet access and removal from state courts of liability lawsuits against firearms manufacturers. Moreover, the Bush administration vigorously sought but failed to pass legislation preempting state authority over medical liability torts and to permit gay marriage.

Most important from an institutional and evolutionary perspective, the velocity of preemption has increased under George W. Bush. The sixty-four new preemptions adopted during Bush's first five years, as tabulated by Zimmerman, yielded an annual average of 12.8 per year. This is a higher adoption rate than under Ronald Reagan, George H. W. Bush, or Bill Clinton.[13] Moreover, a downward trend from Reagan to Clinton in the rate of annual preemption adoptions was reversed under George W. Bush and the Republican Congress. Such trends should be interpreted cautiously because all preemptions are not created equal. The 1960s and 1970s saw the adoption of many more expansive preemptions of state authority than during the Bush era. Nevertheless, few would have predicted such an active pace of federal preemption or mandating during the first period of Republican control of the White House and Congress in almost fifty years.

Implications for American Politics

The Bush presidency has clearly affected the contours of American federalism, but do these developments have significance for American government and politics more generally? This chapter argues that they do, because of what they tell us about the changing nature of American conservatism, about the current state of American politics, and about the nature of contemporary governance.

Big Government Conservatism

First, the Bush administration's approach to intergovernmental policy issues has implications for the evolving character of conservatism in the United

States. President Bush has never enunciated a coherent and well-developed philosophy of governance in the style of President Ronald Reagan, or a systematic approach to reforming American federalism as did Richard Nixon. We are forced to infer the outlines of his public philosophy from his statements and decisions and from the actions of his administration more generally. When we do, it is evident that the Bush administration has embodied a distinctive brand of conservatism, quite different from his Republican presidential predecessors, with important implications for federalism and intergovernmental relations.

There are several different strains of conservatism in the United States, and four somewhat overlapping strains are especially relevant to contemporary issues of federalism and the vertical distribution of power. The relative significance of these different strands of thought, and the ways in which they are woven together, has changed over time, and such changes are important for understanding the design of administration policies and their implications for federalism.

The strain of conservative thought most conducive to decentralized governance is what might be termed *institutional conservatism*, which aims to preserve traditional governmental roles and norms of behavior in the federal system. This is a historically prevalent form of American conservatism, and it is a principal reason why we have come to expect conservatives to support states' rights and a constricted role for the federal government—limited to a relatively narrow interpretation of Congress's enumerated powers under the Constitution. Indeed, given its respect for the norms and traditions of the past, this strain of conservatism resembles an American variant of Edmund Burke's philosophy. Finally, when change seems inevitable, this brand of conservatism places a premium on incrementalism to modulate the effects of change.

Perhaps the most prominent proponents of this strain of conservative thought in recent years have been justices on the U.S. Supreme Court—particularly Sandra Day O'Connor and the late William Rehnquist. They animated efforts by the Court to show greater deference to the traditional, institutional roles of state governments within the federal system, through such doctrines as "anti-commandeering" and state sovereign immunity.[14] When present in the elected branches of government, institutional conservatives are the most apt to sacrifice their preferred policy outcomes out of deference to the institution of federalism.[15]

Economic conservatives are classical liberals, advocating smaller government, free markets, and libertarian values. They tend to assume contingent positions on federalism-related issues, depending on how state and federal policies will advance or retard their ideological goals. Thus, their commitment to a small public sector often generates a preference for decentralization, partly out of an (empirically fragile) belief that interstate competition will hold down state tax levels and discourage regulatory activism. Since the ultimate goal is smaller government and unencumbered markets, however, economic conservatives will happily support the heavy-handed federal preemption of activist state policies that interfere with national or global markets.[16] Ignoring the intergovernmental consequences of the estate tax elimination, abolishing federal deductions for payment of state taxes, and preemption of state tax sources are other nationalist positions held by most economic conservatives.

Social conservatives, in contrast, are willing to support active government policies that promote traditional social norms and roles. As Gary Bauer, a former Reagan aide and presidential candidate, puts it: "The question is not whether you legislate morality. The question is whose morality you're going to legislate."[17] Needless to say, libertarian-oriented economic conservatives, such as Michael Tanner, are appalled by that formulation. Yet such reasoning leads social conservatives to favor policies ranging from federal restrictions on gay marriage and abortion to limits on welfare and faith-based social services. Since the stakes of public policy may involve matters of deep conviction, this form of conservatism can also favor centralization or decentralization, contingent on who controls the levers of power in Washington and the states. The bottom line for social conservatives is the policy outcome, not the implications for federalism.

Finally, *neoconservatism* overlaps with social conservatism in its dim view of post-1960s cultural liberalism. However, its advocates have historically tended to be more conscious of the limits of government power—at least domestically—given its partial origins in critiques of Great Society era "social engineering."[18] In recent years, at least, neoconservatism has also been identified with an active and interventionist approach to foreign policy.

Given these multiple strands of thought, there are many potential combinations that can result. However, the center of gravity in American conservatism—and certainly in the Bush administration—has been shifting in ways that have diminished federalism as a conservative value. Institutional conservatism has been on the decline, and the rise of other strains has made conservatives much more open to activist federal policies in pursuit of their ideological goals.

Bush, in particular, has placed a higher priority than his predecessors on social conservatism, beginning with his formulation of "compassionate conservatism" and his heavy emphasis on religious themes and mobilization of the Christian right. Programmatically this emphasis has been evident in the President's faith-based initiative, his support for school vouchers, and his policies toward abortion, gay marriage, and stem cell research. Accordingly, he has been far more disposed to tolerate a stronger, larger, and more active national government across a range of policy issues. He has married this social conservatism to the tax cutting and regulatory preemption goals of economic conservatives. Add to this the neocon war president, and you have the formula for a much more muscular, assertive, nationalistic conservatism.

Given the inherent tensions between libertarian economic conservatism and paternalistic social conservatism, advocates of both strains have voiced disappointment with Bush's policies and with each other. Bush has been called an imposter, a hypocrite, and an architect of leviathan by disgruntled economic and social conservatives.[19] Nonetheless, the President has attempted a new synthesis of conservative ideology that explains much about his administration's indifference to traditional views about federalism.

Bush's Federalism and Partisan Politics

The President's role as party leader has also had an important influence on the Bush administration's policy agenda. One of President Bush's long-term goals has been to build a permanent Republican majority, both in Congress and in the country at large. As congressional election specialist Gary Jacobson has argued: "Creating the basis for a durable Republican majority was one of the major purposes of the administration's policy agenda. I don't think these guys do anything without weighing the potential partisan consequences and are particularly attracted to policies that might increase the Republican coalition."[20] Although this goal was compromised by the effects of the Iraq war, it shaped the design of the administration's domestic agenda for at least the first five years.

Such purposes can be seen informing Bush's proposal to partially "privatize" Social Security accounts, for example. As former Republican National Committee chairman Ken Mehlman put it: individual accounts under Social Security "would produce a generation of voters less reliant on government as distributor of benefits, and more ready to identify with the Republican Party."[21]

This strategy was also apparent in administration proposals with more obvious intergovernmental ramifications. Administration-backed proposals for Medical Liability Tort Reform would preempt state laws in this area and choke off income to trial lawyers, who are among the biggest contributors to the Democratic party. Similarly, the administration's strong push for drug coverage in Medicare Part D was driven in large part by partisan motives. As many fiscal conservatives have complained, the Bush Administration engineered the largest expansion of a federal entitlement program since 1965 in order to deny Democrats a popular election issue, build party loyalty among senior citizens, and shape a reform structure beneficial to financial backers in the pharmaceutical industry.[22]

More broadly, Bush and his top political advisor Karl Rove (until his resignation in 2007) tried to use policies like No Child Left Behind and "faith based" social services to redefine American politics on their new conservative terms. There has been long-term ambivalence in American politics between what Lloyd Free and Hadley Cantril once called philosophical conservatism and operational liberalism.[23] Large majorities of the public identify with conservative nostrums of small government in the abstract, but they support the operational manifestations of big government—spending and action on almost every major domestic issue or problem. Bill Clinton tried to solve the paradox with his New Democrat formula. Bush and Rove have done so by embracing big new spending programs for education, social services, and Medicare. As former RNC (Republican National Committee) chairman Ed Gillespie told conservative newspaper editors: "The public wants an expanded federal role in these areas, and the Republican Party at the highest levels has decided to give the public what it wants."[24] But they have done it in a way that is intended to promote conservative policy ends— restructuring education, social services, and health care by incorporating more consumer choice, competition, and religious involvement.

In short, President Bush has proved remarkably willing to sacrifice state and local policy interests and, if necessary, substantially expand the federal government's fiscal and functional profile in order to construct and cement a new political majority—especially if it can be done by undermining the social policy props of the Democratic party.

Federalism, Governance, and War

President Bush's approach to the presidency has also had significant intergovernmental implications, including his role as a wartime president and his business oriented managerial style. The President and Vice President entered office determined to increase presidential prerogatives and reverse a perceived loss of authority to Congress since the 1970s. The terrorist attack on September 11, 2001, the subsequent military invasions of Afghanistan and Iraq, increased attention of matters of homeland security, and prosecution of a "global war on terrorism" all greatly reinforced these initial proclivities.

Historically, wartime presidents have tended to exert centralizing effects on American government and public policy.[25] Major growth periods of central government power also have been associated with wartime, with an enlarged national role often persisting after the cessation of hostilities.[26] These effects extend well beyond issues of federalism, but the contemporary war on terror has had significant implications for the U.S. federal system. This is most clearly evident in the enormous expansion and consolidation of federal authority in homeland security. During the past six years, the president and Congress have created a new Department of Homeland Security, established expansive new programs of federal aid for state and local emergency preparedness and response, and established new areas of federal regulatory authority over aspects of homeland security. The latter includes efforts to transform state drivers' licenses into a proxy national identification card and to standardize police and fire communications. The federal government has also stimulated efforts to deepen both vertical and horizontal collaboration among state and local police, fire, emergency response, and public health authorities. Thus, functions such as law enforcement and fire protection—which traditionally ranked among the most local of government functions—have experienced a significant expansion of federal involvement, regulation, and spending as a result of wartime policies under the Bush administration.

In addition to homeland security, the war presidency has further enhanced federal control over the National Guard and expanded national security operations in domestic governance. National Guard units have become such integral components of the nation's war fighting capacity that state units increasingly have been unavailable for traditional duties during domestic emergencies—such as Hurricane Katrina. In 2006, the president sought new authority to nationalize the Guard for domestic duty without a state governor's consent. In addition, laws such as the USA Patriot Act of 2001 and the president's claim of authority for domestic surveillance further expanded federal authority in terrorism-related domestic activities.

Finally, President Bush has advanced an expansive theory of presidential authority that may establish a precedent for further broadening of national authority in the future. His endorsement of the so-called unitary executive theory, although aimed at expanding the president's authority vis-à-vis Congress and the Judiciary rather than the states, creates such an expansive interpretation of presidential powers that it inevitably entails intergovernmental effects. Thus, when Congress established the Institute of Education Sciences (IES) as part of the Education Sciences Reform Act of 2002, it explicitly intended to insulate the collection, preparation, and publication of educational analysis and data from the Secretary of Education.[27] Bush's signing statement explicitly rejected that element of the law and insisted that the IES director would be subject to the Secretary of Education's supervision.[28]

Beyond national security, other aspects of George W. Bush's management style have affected both his presidency and intergovernmental relations. Soon after his election, Bush was widely hailed as America's first "MBA president."[29] In addition to earning a business degree at Harvard University, he had executive experience in the oil industry and with the Texas Rangers baseball team prior to embarking on his political career. Once elected, he surrounded himself with close advisors who also came with business, as well as political, experience. Vice President Dick Cheney spent the 1990s in business as CEO of Haliburton. Chief of Staff Andrew Card and Secretary of Defense Donald Rumsfeld also came to the administration with considerable private sector experience, complementing their earlier experience in government.

This background had implications for the administration's approach to policy-making. The Bush White House became known for a "corporate style" of management, characterized by secrecy, hierarchy, and control.[30] The President viewed his role as establishing parameters and principles of policy and then delegating heavily to his staff.[31] Within the broader administration, power was centralized in the White House and agency officials were expected to stay on message. This predilection for centralization was replicated in intergovernmental affairs as well.

For example, the President's Management Agenda was a major Office of Management and Budget (OMB) initiative designed to incorporate a greater degree of businesslike practices and performance-related management into federal budgeting and administrative processes.[32] It included efforts to rate agencies' management performance with color-coded scorecards, establish "lines of business" for grants management, financial management, human resources, and other fields, and implement the Performance Assessment

Rating Tool (PART) process in OMB, in order to assess the effectiveness of federal programs and integrate the results into budget decisions.

As Beryl Radin argued, the performance government movement often lends itself to centralization of authority in intergovernmental programs:

> "The federal efforts dealing with performance ... move against the devolution tide. Efforts to hold federal government agencies accountable for the way that programs are implemented actually assume that these agencies have legitimate authority to enforce the requirements that are included in performance measures."[33]

The performance management approach also meshes poorly with more collaborative methods of network and third-party governance.[34] Hence, it is no surprise that grants to state and local governments often rate poorly when assessed under the PART process. Their longer implementation chains, dispersion of public authority, melding of resources from multiple levels of government, and often contested goals and purposes make it difficult to ascribe clear program objectives and assess progress toward achieving them.[35] Such difficulties are especially pronounced with federal block grant programs. Not surprisingly, OMB deemed block grants among the least effective of all types of federal programs, a judgment that underlay administration efforts to reduce funding for programs like Community Development Block Grants.[36] Ironically, these grants, which provide considerably more flexibility for state and local recipients, were among the policy hallmarks of earlier Republican administrations.

Implications for American Federalism

What does all of this say about American federalism? Clearly its political foundations are shifting. Its status in conservative thought and the political underpinnings of the institution are in flux. This chapter has focused only on the national level—especially the Bush administration—but there are other very interesting developments going on at the state level as well. These include a flurry of state initiatives on issues such as global warming, consumer protection, and health care expansion. Moreover, Democrats have their own policy agendas with implications for the federal system. All of these developments and more need to be examined to gain a full portrait of contemporary U.S. federalism.

Overall, however, Bush's philosophy and policies are consistent with a broader pattern of what can be called "opportunistic federalism."[37] Policy entrepreneurs throughout the intergovernmental system now have opportunities—and incentives—to pursue their individual political and policy interests with little regard for the institutional or collective consequences. Mandates, policy preemptions, and prescriptive grant conditions all appeal to opportunistic federal policy-makers who seek to advance their own policy goals regardless of traditional norms of behavior or institutional boundaries. Old-fashioned dual federalism legally and politically constrained such behavior. Later, cooperative federalism encouraged shared intergovernmental goals and vertical professional integration. More recently, however, changes in the U.S. party system, in congressional incentive structures, and now in conservative philosophy are promoting a more co-optive style of intergovernmental politics, and the Bush administration has contributed to, rather than resisted, this transformation.

Notes

*A version of portions of this chapter appeared in Tim Conlan and John Dinan, "Federalism, the Bush Administration, and the Transformation of American Conservatism," *Publius: The Journal of Federalism* 37 (Summer 2007): 279–303.

1. See Michael D. Tanner, *Leviathan on the Right: How Big Government Conservatism Brought Down the Republican Revolution* (Washington: Cato Institute, 2007); and Bruce Bartlett, *Impostor: How George W. Bush Bankrupted America and Betrayed the Reagan Legacy* (New York: Doubleday, 2006).
2. Office of Management and Budget, *Historical Tables, Budget of the United States Government, Fiscal Year 2008*, 25–26.
3. Ibid.
4. Office of Management and Budget, *Analytical Perspectives, Budget of the United States Government, Fiscal Year 2008*, 107.
5. See U.S. Advisory Commission on Intergovernmental Relations (ACIR), *Regulatory Federalism: Policy, Process, Impact and Reform* (Washington, DC: Advisory Commission on Intergovernmental Relations, 1984); and John Kincaid, "From Cooperative to Coercive Federalism," *Annals of the American Academy of Political and Social Science* 509 (May 1990): 139–152.
6. ACIR, *Regulatory Federalism*, 7–10.
7. Patrick J. McGuinn, *No Child Left Behind and the Transformation of Federal Education Policy, 1965–2005* (Lawrence, KS: University of Kansas Press, 2006), 182.
8. Sarah F. Liebschutz and Daniel J. Palazzolo, "HAVA and the States," *Publius: The Journal of Federalism* 35 (Fall 2005): 497–514.
9. Congressional Research Service, *Election Reform: The Help American Vote Act and Issues for Congress*, (Washington, DC: CRS, 2004).
10. *The Real ID Act: National Impact Analysis*, Report Prepared by the National Governors Association, National Conference of State Legislatures, and American Association of Motor Vehicle Administrators (Washington: September 2006).
11. Martha Derthick, "Going Federal: The Launch of Medicare Part D Compared to SSI," *Publius: The Journal of Federalism* 37 (Summer 2007): 351–370.
12. Joseph F. Zimmerman, "Congressional Preemption During the George W. Bush Administration," *Publius: The Journal of Federalism* 37 (Summer 2007): 432–452.
13. Based on data provided by Zimmerman, the corresponding rates are 11.5 new preemptions per year under Reagan, 8.5 per year under George H.W. Bush, and 8 new preemptions annually under Bill Clinton. Ibid., 443, 444.

14. See, among others, such cases as *New York v. United States,* 112 S.Ct. 2408; *Printz v. United States,* 521 U.S. 98 1997; *Seminole Tribe of Florida v. Florida, et al.,* 517 U.S. 44, 1996; and *Alden, et al. v. Maine,* 119 S.Ct. 2240, 1999.

15. For some examples in the Reagan administration, see Timothy J. Conlan, "Federalism and Competing Values in the Reagan Administration," *Publius: The Journal of Federalism* (Winter 1986): 29–47.

16. See, for example, Michael S. Greve, "Federalism's Frontier," *Texas Review of Law & Politics* 93 (2002): 93–126.

17. Quoted in Tanner, *Leviathan on the Right,* 48.

18. See, for example, Francis Fukuyama, *America at the Crossroads: Democracy, Power, and the Neoconservative Legacy* (New Haven: Yale University Press, 2006), chap. 2.

19. For a libertarian critique, see Bartlett, *Imposter;* social conservative complaints of Bush Administration hypocrisy can be found in David Kuo, *Tempting Faith* (New York: The Free Press, 2006).

20. Quoted in Thomas B Edsall and John F Harris, "Bush Aims to Forge a GOP Legacy: Second-term Plans Look to Undercut Democratic Pillars," *The Washington Post,* January 30, 2005, A1.

21. Ibid.

22. Andrea Louise Campbell and Kimberley Morgan, "The Medicare Modernization Act and the New Politics of Medicare," Paper Prepared for the American Political Science Association Annual Meeting, Philadelphia, PA, August 31–September 3, 2006.

23. Lloyd Free and Hadley Cantril, *The Political Beliefs of Americans: A Study of Public Opinion* (New Brunswick, NJ: Rutgers University Press, 1967).

24. Quoted in Tanner, *Leviathan on the Right,* 6.

25. Arthur Schlesinger, Jr., *The Imperial Presidency* (Boston: Houghton Mifflin, 1973).

26. Advisory Commission on Intergovernmental Relations, *The Condition of Contemporary Federalism: Conflicting Theories and Collapsing Constraints,* A-78 (Washington: ACIR, 1981), 224–226.

27. HR 3801, sec. 186 (a).

28. President George W. Bush, "Statement on **Signing** Legislation to Provide for Improvement of Federal **Education** Research, Statistics, Evaluation, Information, and Dissemination, and for Other Purposes," *Weekly Compilation of Presidential Documents* (November 8, 2002), 1995. See also Charlie Savage, "Bush Challenges Hundreds of Laws: President Cites Powers of His Office," *The Boston Globe,* April 30, 2006. Accessed online at www. boston.com/news/nation/articles/2006/04/30/bush_challenges_ hundreds_of_laws/

29. James Pfiffner, "The First MBA President: George W. Bush as Public Administrator," *Public Administration Review* 67 (January/February 2007): 6–20.

30. See, for example, "Of the CEOs, by the CEOs, for the CEOs," *The American Prospect* (August 12, 2002): 6; and Lexington, " The CEO presidency," *The Economist* (June 15, 2002), 50.

31. Kenneth T. Walsh, "Falling Stock: George Bush Wants to Run His Presidency Like a Business, but Critics Say the Bottom Line Is Not Encouraging," *U.S. News and World Report* (April 3, 2006), 31–33.

32. See Office of Management and Budget, *The President's Management Agenda, Fiscal Year 2002* at http://www.whitehouse.gov/omb/budget/fy2002/mgmt.pdf; and http://www.whitehouse.gov/results/.

33. Beryl Radin, "Performance Management and Intergovernmental Relations," in *Intergovernmental Management for the 21st Century*, ed. Paul Posner and Timothy Conlan (Washington, DC: Brookings Institution Press, forthcoming).

34. H. George Frederickson, "When Accountability Meets Collaboration," *PA Times* (February 2007), 11.

35. Paul L. Posner, "Accountability Challenges of Third Party Government," in Lester M. Salamon, *The Tools of Government* (New York: Oxford University Press, 2002), 523–551.

36. Office of Management and Budget, *Analytical Perspectives, Fiscal Year 2008*, 105–106.

37. Tim Conlan, "From Cooperative to Opportunistic Federalism," *Public Administration Review* 66 (September/October 2006): 663–676.

Chapter 2

What a Difference a Few Decades Make: The Conservative Movement, Executive Power, and the Constitution in the United States

Joel D. Aberbach and Gillian Peele

This study approaches the topic of American federalism from an explicitly oblique angle. It seeks to understand the pressures on the contemporary federal system by placing them in the context of two broader interlinked themes: the impact of the Bush presidency on the American constitution and the interaction between the Bush presidency and the contemporary conservative movement. It explores those themes by focusing on the constitutional designs and statecraft of George W. Bush. We argue that in relation to a number of key constitutional questions—most notably the scope of executive power and federalism, but also issues such as the role of the courts and the relationship between church and state—we have witnessed an approach that is radical and highly controversial. As we show, Bush's position had a divisive impact within the contemporary conservative movement.

The chapter is organized into three parts. First it briefly examines the traditional conservative and Republican attitudes to some key constitutional issues, especially the role of government and the relative powers of the presidency and Congress and the federal and state governments. It further highlights the transformation of the conservative movement that occurred in the 1970s. Finally it examines George W. Bush's constitutional statecraft.

Conservatives and the Constitution

Constitutional themes in general and executive power in particular have been defining issues for American conservatives across the country's history. Reflecting presidential scholar Edward Corwin's judgment that no clause of the Constitution was as ambiguously framed as Article 2, battle has raged about the scope of executive power from the debates at Philadelphia to our own day.[1] In the early controversies, those who feared a strong and tyrannical government were ranged against those who saw the need for the president to exercise leadership as well as a related requirement for "energy in the Executive," to quote Hamilton's famous dictum.

The institution of the presidency inevitably developed in response to the successive crises of the infant Republic and the agendas of those who held the office. In the first part of the twentieth century, both Republican and Democratic incumbents provided examples of a more assertive executive. Yet many saw the successful exercise of presidential leadership as an uphill battle for, as Harold Laski noted in 1939 in his pithy lectures on the presidency, each turn toward presidential power provoked, if not a backlash, a counteraction.[2] Laski's lectures were dedicated to Franklin Delano Roosevelt and indeed it was FDR's expansion of the presidency that mobilized a new bipartisan conservative coalition in Congress in opposition both to his dominance and the substantive policies associated with the New Deal. In his classic treatise on American conservatism, Clinton Rossiter observed, "As to the Presidency, even the sight of one of his own kind in this highest office has not allayed his suspicions of executive power. The yearning for Mr. Coolidge cannot be suppressed."[3]

It was hardly surprising that Roosevelt's presidency became the symbolic embodiment of everything conservatives disliked because it had made the expansive presidency in an expansive state an established part of American life. Political scientist Andrew Rudalevige notes that while "even before Franklin Roosevelt took office ... ambitious presidents could choose from an array of precedential actions that pushed against congressional power and, finding insufficient resistance, expanded the scope of presidential power. ... [F]rom FDR's time forward, these tools became expectations rather than possibilities."[4] Most scholars would concur that Roosevelt's initiatives marked a turning point in the country's governmental evolution.

Conservative opposition to a strengthened presidency and a vastly expanded role for federal government was naturally fuelled by the series of progressive policy changes promulgated under FDR. An enhanced presidential capacity was then inherently connected in the minds of many critics with the progressive interventionist policies and programs of the New Deal and retreat from laissez faire. This opposition to the New Deal brought together a diverse array of politicians. In Congress in particular, Republicans and Southern Democrats often made common cause against the New Deal in a coalition that would endure beyond the 1930s. Historian James Patterson wrote of this conservative coalition at its inception:

> Some of these men might be better termed reactionaries, others moderates. Many spoke the language of Social Darwinism; others were Burkean conservatives. Some were agrarian conservatives; others were spokesmen for urban business interests. But the unifying factor ... was opposition to most of the domestic program of the New Deal. By and large, the congressional conservatives by 1939 agreed in opposing the spread of federal power and bureaucracy, in denouncing deficit spending, in criticizing labor unions and in excoriating

most welfare programs. They sought to conserve an America which they believed to have existed before 1933.[5]

It is also important to note with Patterson the extent to which the conservative opposition to the New Deal had an institutional basis: Congress feared that executive enhancement would undermine its own independence and integrity and the balance of the constitution. It is also equally important to recognize the extent to which this "conservative coalition" within Congress was a bipartisan one, made up of Southern Democrats who liked elements of the New Deal's largesse, especially its agricultural price supports, but feared its other liberal policies, and conservative Republicans, who disliked almost everything about the New Deal.

It might be asked what kept Republicans and Southern Democrats apart in the period prior to the civil rights movement that eventually changed the political alignment of the South. Southern conservatism was, as Eugene Genovese has noted, a "special kind of conservatism" that had little in common with market-oriented bourgeois ideologies.[6] It was thus to some extent at odds with the spirit of capitalism that dominated the Republican Party. Historical memories and regional patriotism dating back to the Civil War era also played an important part in keeping Southern Democrats loyal to their party, while the South's leverage within the Democratic ranks remained sufficiently powerful even by the late 1930s to make defection to the GOP. unthinkable, especially in the light of the huge economic benefits the New Deal brought to the region. In addition, the military traditions of the South made Roosevelt's foreign policy more acceptable than much of his domestic agenda.

Despite the activity of conservative critics, opposition to the New Deal and its legacy remained very much a minority cause as liberal ideas about an extensive and positive role for government became intellectually dominant and as the New Deal was transformed by successive presidents into the policies of the Fair Deal and ultimately the New Frontier and the Great Society.

It was not merely on the domestic front that conservatives found themselves in opposition to an enhanced presidential role. Roosevelt's expansion of the presidency and the federal role at home was followed by an expansion of the American role abroad, and with this came a further enlargement of executive influence. From at least 1900, doubts about America's growing international role had drawn criticism from those who feared unhealthy domestic consequences in the form of a more powerful presidency. Indeed, political scientists Christopher Yoo and Steven Calabresi go so far as to say: "[Once] America became more imperial, her presidents took on an imperial persona as well."[7]

The cold war shifted power much more decisively to the executive as the "old battles of the balance of power intersected with the new logic of the nuclear age."[8] Conservatives were initially divided about the role of the United States abroad. By 1945, many prewar isolationists, who were suspicious of the

United Nations and indeed of American involvement in world affairs more generally, were motivated by fear that such involvement would undermine the country's domestic institutions and its economy. On the other hand, many conservatives were not only highly suspicious of communism but anxious to resist it at all costs, even if that meant an acceptance of entangling alliances and a strengthened executive role. Prewar isolationists of the stripe of Robert Taft and John W Bricker found their hold on the Republican Party contested by internationalists such as Dwight Eisenhower. While the latter became dominant at the presidential level, the former isolationist wing retained strength in Congress, and its anticommunism in the postwar period took on a much less moderate form than that of the Eisenhower wing. As opposition to communism became increasingly salient, conservatives in Congress shifted their ground somewhat so that, while remaining suspicious of executive initiative in foreign policy, they could join the battle against communism at home, in Europe, and in Asia. In the words of American historian Richard Abrams, American conservatives eagerly adopted a "limited sort of internationalism," one that made it "clear that the issue was Soviet communism and not any New Deal, do-gooder program for promoting prosperity and social welfare abroad."[9]

Conservative activism in the postwar Congress shifted to efforts to block the Fair Deal programs of Harry Truman and to curb the power of labor unions through such measures as the Taft-Hartley Act, but it also took the form of support for broad-based effort to reinvigorate the role of Congress. The Legislative Reorganization Act of 1946 called for greater congressional oversight of the vastly expanded federal government and its programs. Much of this strengthening was needed, but it also had an ugly side in the excesses of McCarthyism and corollary attempts to use oversight to undermine elements of the executive branch.

While many traditional conservatives were appalled by McCarthyism, they were nevertheless anxious to enhance congressional power, not only on constitutional grounds, but because they had greater leverage there due to the growing "conservative coalition." This remained their position for a quarter century after World War II. The excesses of the Nixon administration led Democrats and liberals to adopt it as well. At that juncture, however, conservatism was undergoing its own change of heart in the opposite direction. With the GOP looking more likely to control the presidency but not the Congress, many on the right began migrating to a position of strong endorsement of executive power, culminating in the fierce unilateralism of the Bush II administration.

Attitudes toward the aggrandizement of the federal government took longer to change. American conservatives had a powerful tradition of attachment to states rights and hostility toward the growth of federal power at the expense of local autonomy. During the New Deal period, conservatives argued against an expansion of federal government into novel areas, particularly those in which the states had previously reigned supreme. In the South, as Dewey Grantham observed, there was a tension between the urge to respond to constituent needs and a preference for balanced budgets, strong local government, and administrative efficiency. As he noted, "[S]tates rights in the Depression seemed less essential than national subsidies, and especially so since many of the New Deal programs benefitted the South more than other regions and since the benefits southerners received far surpassed their contributions to federal revenue collections."[10]

For Republicans, however, the orthodoxy of limited government continued after World War II despite the enormous shift toward Washington. Eisenhower came to power in 1953 after campaigning for the presidency on a platform of revitalizing of the authority of the states as a protection against federal centralization and autocracy. Yet he was unable to stem the New Deal–initiated trend toward bigger national government and indeed admitted his contribution to federal expansion.

In the early 1950s and 1960s, support for states' rights tended to be strongly associated with hostility to integration, rendering it a difficult cause to defend. Nevertheless some conservative Republicans made clear their opposition to federal activism and their support of states rights. Most notably, Senator Barry M. Goldwater of Arizona—who adopted a Southern strategy in his 1964 presidential campaign—called for the national government to "withdraw promptly and totally from every jurisdiction which the Constitution reserves to the States."[11]

As integration became a less dominant issue on the policy agenda, supporters of a greater role for the states acquired more legitimacy. From the Nixon period onward Republican and conservative opponents of federal activism championed greater autonomy for the states, including the transfer of some federal functions to their authority. Ronald Reagan's support for this cause influenced his selection of federal judges with a restrained view of national power and his unsuccessful efforts to promote the New Federalism plan to transfer fully responsibility for some welfare programs to the states. Restoring authority to the states remained a central tenet of conservatism in the final decade of the twentieth century and was a core principle of the Contract with America manifesto of House Republicans in the 1994 midterm elections.

Attitudes toward the Supreme Court constituted another important battle line for conservatives and Republicans. Having applauded this body's opposition to the early New Deal, they became increasingly critical of its judicial activism in the postwar era. Many of the federal initiatives that caused them most anguish from the mid-1950s to the early 1970s (school desegregation, electoral reapportionment, and the expansion of due process rights, for example) had been promulgated not so much by the executive or Congress as by the federal courts. Conservatives were especially appalled by the judicial policymaking on a range of civil and personal rights issues by the Supreme Court under Chief Justice Earl Warren.

Responding to this concern, Nixon attempted to move judicial appointments in a conservative direction. It was not until the Reagan administration, however, that a systematic attempt was made by conservatives to redress the liberal bias of the judiciary. This is not the place to rehearse all the details of that effort, but it is important to note three features of the new approach. First, it focused on the president's power to make judicial appointments and entailed a centralization of the appointments process. Second, it employed rigorous prescreening to select jurists who would not bend toward a more pragmatic view of their role and the conservative agenda. Belief in the gold standard of original intent became a popular criterion for assessing the credentials of a potential nominee, but so too did attitudes toward *Roe v. Wade,* the landmark Supreme Court decision that partially decriminalized abortion in 1973. Finally the new approach on judicial matters aimed to establish a network of conservative lawyers who could generate enthusiasm and legitimacy for conservative positions on legal and constitutional issues and provide suitable appointees at all levels from clerks to justices. What is interesting to note here is the blending of pragmatic and principled positions on the right. Many conservatives did believe in an objective standard of constitutional interpretation and bitterly criticized liberal jurists for distorting the constitution by extending its protections to women seeking abortion and homosexuals seeking gay rights. At the same time, they were prepared to use sophisticated and sometimes ruthless measures to ensure that their own appointees were put in place on the bench.

The Evolution of the American
Conservative Movement

From the New Deal to the late 1960s, American conservatism was very much an ideology in retreat, a political persuasion apparently doomed to minority status in a society wedded to an optimistic liberalism. However, the experience of the 1960s, especially failure in Vietnam and social unrest at home, created a backlash against liberalism. Paradoxically, the humiliation of Richard Nixon led to a new conservative resurgence initially outside the Republican Party but ultimately integrated into it.

The conservative movement that emerged in the 1970s had a very different quality from earlier conservative movements. Four elements gave it a novelty and dynamism previously lacking. The first was the intellectual vibrancy provided by the neoconservative intellectuals, richly described by Peter Steinfels.[12] Many of these public intellectuals were former Democrats who had moved right in response to the Vietnam War and the redistributive orientation of liberalism in the 1960s. The second distinctive feature of this new conservative movement was the growth of a number of think tanks and policy foundations that brought together conservative activists, academics, journalists, and politicians in a manner designed to maximize the spread of conservative influence. Some of these think tanks, such as American Enterprise Institute, were long established; others—such as the Heritage Foundation—were new creations. Many were Washington-based, but there were also important think tanks in other cities such as New York and San

Francisco. The think tanks provided new arenas for conservative ideas to be injected into the policy process.

This third dimension of the new conservatism can be seen in the emergence of pressure groups associated with the right during the 1970s and early 1980. They were commonly mobilized around social issues such as abortion, busing, and textbook content. Although many of these organizations had a single-issue focus, their leaders often planned their tactics in common and kept in close contact with like-minded organizations. They also brought to the conservative cause a resurgence of conservative activism at the grass roots.

Finally, and this particularly differentiated the conservative movement of the 1970 and beyond from its predecessors, the growing political involvement of conservative Christians became an important factor in the politics of the right.

The new conservative movement that appeared in the 1970s was very different in style, political assumptions, and agenda from the conservative movement of the preceding period. It was better funded, better organized and more ambitious. It had a new agenda on foreign policy, the domestic role of government, budgetary policy and taxation, and moral issues. It also represented a different political coalition. The old-line conservative coalition mixed northeastern Protestants (and the traditional finance establishment that was its cornerstone), Midwestern traditionalists, and many Westerners and Southern Democrats in a group that aimed to roll back some elements of the New Deal, but basically sought to contain further liberal change. It was eventually undermined by the effects of social changes in the United States in the postwar period, most notably those that gave rise to the civil rights movement but also by changing mores that were seen as a threat to so-called family values."

As the context of politics developed a greater socio-moral character, white southerners flocked to the Republican Party and brought with them the newly unleashed political activism of the evangelical churches. Rather than opposing change, these new elements in the conservative movement wanted to change government policy in areas like abortion and church–state relations. This entry of new groups into the GOP unsettled its traditional power structure. Religious groups and Southerners gained influence in the party at the expense of Northeastern and Midwestern Republicans. This in turn reinforced policy change within the party. While the GOP still aimed to roll back many of the liberal social initiatives of the 1960s, it did not shrink from employing federal activism in pursuit of its own ends, particularly in regard to protecting lifestyles and values and enforcing moral standards. Rather than a retrenchment of national government, this represented a potentially huge federal intrusion into the most intimate affairs of its citizens.

The Constitutional Designs of George W. Bush

Although the new conservatism that emerged in the 1970s was very much geared to issues and policies, it did have strong views on a number of constitutional issues. Most notably there was much interest in using the presidency to reduce the federal role in economic regulation, reestablish what it considered a proper balance between national and state government, and reassert a more traditional style of jurisprudence. The conservative movement was also keen to reinforce the role of religion in public life and employ federal power to enforce public and private morality.

The George W. Bush presidency took up and developed many of these themes. Traditional conservatives had wanted to see executive power controlled. From the Bricker Amendment limiting presidential authority in foreign affairs to efforts to limit federal rule-making power, conservatives favored checks on the president. Bush's embrace of the "unitary presidency" doctrine, his use of signing statements, and his claims of power flowing from the president's role as commander in chief were all efforts to make the president the central figure in the U.S. Government. In Bush's telling, if rather inelegant, expression: "I'm the decider."

We emphasize executive power because it goes to the core of the transformation of both conservative and Republican doctrine. Once upon a time, limited government was a key concept, perhaps *the key* concept, for most American conservatives. It fitted nicely with their ideas about individual rights and liberty, responsible fiscal policy, states rights, and an essentially isolationist foreign policy.

The New Deal challenged many traditional conservative doctrines, but none more strongly than its views on executive power. Roosevelt was unabashedly the central player in the political system. More importantly, he used both his position as president and the federal government as instruments of political change. He proposed, and Congress initially granted, a series of reforms that created a large national state, one endowed with federal agencies that held vast sway over the economy and over many facets of everyday life. The New Deal agencies (and their successors created by the Great Society programs of Lyndon Johnson) became both symbols of liberalism and, in the view of Republicans/conservatives, agents of the Democratic Party. The question was what to do about them.

One answer evolved in the administration of Richard Nixon. Frustrated by a Democratic Congress (and hungry for power), Nixon asserted the right of the president to use executive power to govern as he saw fit. An approach dubbed the "administrative presidency" in the political science literature,[13] its political core was best summarized—albeit in emotive terms—by Nixon speechwriter Pat Buchanan:

> When Richard M. Nixon looked upon his executive bureaucracy as a barricade manned by political enemies to frustrate the expressed will of the American people, he was right on the mark. And when he sought to seed that bureaucracy with political loyalists, his instincts were unerring. ...
>
> For a new Republican President to expect his handful of appointees to impose upon this savvy leftist bureaucracy a program of reduction, reorganization or reform is to send missionaries into the Central Highlands and Mekong Delta to convert the Viet Cong.[14]

In essence, Buchanan argued that executive power, its legitimacy based on a plebiscitary presidential election, was necessary for conservatives to transform a government whose legislature and, especially, bureaucracy were in the hands of its opponents. That doctrine was refined and extended during the administration of Ronald Reagan, even though Republicans controlled the Senate for six of his eight years of office. It reached full flower in the administration of George W. Bush despite GOP control of Congress for most of his first six years in office. Marching in lockstep with Bush, most Republicans in Congress and the party's constituent groups went along with a series of actions and doctrines asserting the primacy of the presidency. Bush has used signing statements in large numbers to assert his right to decide which elements of laws he signs will actually be enforced. He has declared that as Commander in Chief he can ignore provisions of laws like FISA (the Foreign Intelligence Surveillance Act) to decide when the government can wiretap. As Yoo and Calabresi observed, he contended that, as the embodiment of the "unitary executive," he should be free from impediments and in full control of the executive branch, with "all executive authority . . . centralized in the president." As a result of Bush's enhancement of his office, they concluded: "[T]he presidency now far surpasses any other governmental institution in terms of political leadership. . . . For better or worse, we have an imperial presidency now."[15]

Bush's ambitions have also had a profound impact on the practice of federalism. Traditional conservatives were opposed to an active government role, especially an active federal government role, in the economy and the social welfare sector generally. Government intervention was seen as morally corrupting in his creation of dependency, a threat to individual liberty, and a danger to free enterprise. Conservatives were appalled by the New Deal and aghast at the Great Society programs of President Lyndon Johnson. They were also disturbed about the administrative mechanisms used to implement these programs—large bureaucracies, regulations written by executive branch personnel to implement statutes written in general language, and national standards imposed on states and localities.

Contemporary conservatives, at least those in the Bush administration, favored a strong state role, even though they often used market-like mechanisms to implement it. From the hugely expensive Medicare drug benefit of 2003 (with its limitations on government bargaining for lower prices with the drug companies) to the interventionist No Child Left Behind (NCLB) law of 2001 (with its mandatory testing and federal government controls) to the enhancement of federal government powers to fight terrorism (with its new standards for the issuance of state driving licenses), Bush steadfastly pursued the enhancement of federal power. This was roundly criticized not merely by libertarian groups such as the Cato Institute but even at times by some congressional Republicans. David Boaz, the vice-president of Cato, in a 2005 article cited the No Child Left Behind Act as evidence of a general determination to use power in Washington to force uniform standards on the states.[16] He detected a similar dynamic in Bush's approach (backed by a conservative Congress) to class action suits and state-issued driving licenses and identification cards. Most of all, Boaz objected to the intervention of the federal government in moral issues, notably the Terry Schiavo case and gay marriages. In his assessment, the blame for much of this could in large part be attributed to liberals who "for decades scoffed at federalist arguments that the people of Wisconsin or Wyoming understood their own needs better than a distant Congress. ... Now those chickens have come home to roost. Republicans run Washington, and they're using federal power that liberals built in ways that liberals never envisioned."[17]

Increasing numbers of congressional Republicans seem to share some of Boaz's doubts as far as the No Child Left Behind Act is concerned. Following a steep increase in state and local resistance to NCLB during 2005, which included the filing of lawsuits against the measure, Republicans in Congress began to voice their opposition.[18] In March 2007 fifty members of the House and Senate (including sponsors of the original measure) introduced legislation that would weaken NCLB by allowing states to opt out of its testing mandates.[19]

Bush has also continued the court-centered strategy initiated by the Reagan administration. By the time he became president it was apparent how successful this tactic had been in reshaping the federal bench. Two decades of conservative activism (and long periods of Republican presidential power) had exerted a considerable impact on the composition of America's courts and on the law schools. The foundation of the Federalist Society in 1982 had also provided a vehicle for the conservative movement's legal and constitutional agenda and an effective network of lawyers who could furnish personnel for the Department of Justice, the White House Counsel's office, and indeed throughout the administration. This organization also helped in developing a reservoir of potential clerks and younger lawyers to form the basis of the next generation of judicial recruits. In George W. Bush's administration, its influence has replaced that of the American Bar Association (itself once a very conservative institution) in the rating of judicial nominees.

Nevertheless, Bush's pragmatic and executive-centered approach to constitutional issues did not fit easily with the Federalist Society's essentially Madisonian philosophy of limited federal government. On policy issues, it is closely associated with hostility to government intervention to prevent discrimination and views with suspicion the liberal civil rights agenda. At times there is evidence of an even more ambitious political agenda: for example, one of its conferences was entitled "Rolling Back the New Deal."

On the separation of church and state, the Federalist Society endorses a new accommodation. Its stance reflects conservative rejection of liberal secularism and the greater influence of religious organizations in the conservative movement. Since the 1970s, the Christian right had steadily increased its political clout within the Republican Party and the broader conservative movement. By the time Bush came to power, evangelicals and conservative Christians had become an influential part of the Republican constituency.

The Christian right has itself changed character since the early days of mobilization. Initially disparate groups had organized around key issues, targeting the Republican Party but also pursuing a policy agenda outside of it. Early groups such as the Moral Majority collapsed, but Ralph Reed's Christian Coalition provided a new model of political mobilization with greater clout within Republican ranks.[20] Some observers have noted a more assertive tendency within the conservative Christian movement, one that Sara Diamond among others have labelled "dominionism." Its adherents believe that Christians have a duty to try to control secular government rather than simply defending their values within a pluralist society.

Bush himself is a born-again Christian whose mind-set fitted well with that of the more fundamentalist elements of the Christian right. Early in his bid to become president, he lined up endorsements from key religious groups and, through his administration's policies and appointments and his rhetorical style, revealed the depth of his commitment to this faction of the conservative coalition. Although there were rumblings from former insiders such as David Kuo that his administration was exploiting the religious groups, their agenda and his, for the most part, meshed together closely.[21]

The agenda of the Christian right is extensive. At its core are traditional family values and opposition to constitutional rights to abortion or recognition of gay marriage. But its interests extend beyond these themes to include wider issues of domestic policy including education, welfare, and health, themes with strong implications for federalism. Some parts of the Christian right are also strongly committed to certain positions on foreign policy, notably the defense of Israel.

When the Bush administration came to power, the symbolism of his religious adherence was marked—both in the inauguration ceremonies and in the encouragement of prayer meetings and bible study in the White House. Bush has used his power of appointment to bring like-minded evangelical Christians into his administration, often after consultation with the religious right network. According to one commentator, Bush (aided by Karl Rove) made it a priority to address the neglect of the evangelical agenda by previous presidents through personnel changes:

> Karl Rove had cultivated the extensive network of religious right organizations, and they were consulted at every step of the way as the administration set up its policies on gays, AIDS, condoms, abstinence programs, creation and other matters that concerned evangelicals. All the evangelicals' resentments under previous presidents, including Republicans like Reagan and the first Bush, were now being addressed.[22]

Many members of Bush's inner circle were closely associated with evangelical Christianity and the movement to enhance its role in public life. These politicians included Kay Coles James, who became White House Head of Personnel ("an evangelical in charge of placing evangelicals throughout the bureaucracy");[23] Michael Gerson, a devout evangelical who became

Bush's speechwriter; Andrew Card, Bush's Chief of Staff until 2006; and Karen Hughes, a long term political adviser to Bush. The role of conservative Christians in the Bush administration at the Cabinet level was symbolized early on with the nomination of John Ashcroft as Attorney General. In office, Ashcroft moved to establish a religious rights division within the Department of Justice's Civil Rights Division. The Bush administration was also quick to establish a White House based Office of Faith Based Initiatives (OFBI), but this soon became highly contentious. Initially billed as a way of developing compassionate conservative measures for social problems, its supporters rapidly became disillusioned. John DeIulio, its first head, resigned after only a few months. Although the OFBI continued, critics charged that its mission had been undermined not just by explicit opposition to its goals from secular social organizations and their constituencies but also by underfunding and lack of backing within the administration.[24]

Bush's own Bible-based Christianity has allowed a widespread assault on mainstream science and official endorsement of right-wing evangelical/ fundamentalist ideas on topics such as "intelligent design" and global warming. Of particular concern have been the implications of a more fundamentalist approach to issues such as Aids research and stem cell research where Bush used his first veto. Not surprisingly, the religious right's hostility to abortion had an important impact on policy once Bush had become president. Indeed, Bush administration's responsiveness to ideas that would have seemed risible a generation ago has been a cause for alarm among academics and other critics who have talked about a "war on science."[25]

Conclusion

We have placed recent developments in federalism in the context of more general controversies about the constitution and issues of public policy in the United States. And we have related those controversies to some of the transformations of conservative thought and organization in the United States. We note that on domestic policy the shift from traditional conservatism to today's version has seen a movement away from limited government and laissez faire and toward an aggressive federal role. On foreign policy too the shift has been dramatic. Traditional conservatives were isolationist in the 1930s. There was great suspicion of international organizations and, initially, opposition to a large military establishment. They were little concerned with spreading democratic government beyond the borders of the United States, particularly through the projection of military power. Contemporary conservatism, again particularly of the neoconservative group that has had extensive influence in the Bush II administration, and which has been dubbed "the Vulcans," is assertively internationalist.[26] It endorses huge power for the president in foreign affairs, unilateral American action, the spreading of democracy through the use of American power—economic or military—and generally sees itself as making history rather than reacting to events.

The conservative movement of today, while much more complex than our brief description has necessarily made it sound, is at a crossroads. Its political coalition is fraying somewhat with the loss of many who were once traditional conservatives (or who might support traditional conservatism today), but who now feel uncomfortable in the Republican Party. Free marketeers are uncomfortable with big-state-role conservatives. Foreign policy moderates are uncomfortable with aggressive interventionists. Mainstream and liberal denominations are uncomfortable with evangelicals and fundamentalists. Balanced-budget traditionalists (and many bankers) fear the effects of huge deficits. And those who favor limited government—the bedrock of traditional conservatism—are faced with an administration that now endorses almost unchecked presidential power.

One can ascribe many of these changes to the demography of the new Republican coalition that has emerged, to the role of public intellectuals and organized think tanks that have developed neoconservative thought, and perhaps to a large extent to the willingness of Republican identifiers and politicians to approve the policies of Bush and his inner circle due to their often fierce party loyalty. Whether there will be future changes in the orientation of the conservative movement remains to be seen. It is clear that conservatives of the mid-twentieth century would not today recognize the political party that was once associated with their cause. But equally, there is strong reason to suggest that Bush' s persistently assertive approach to the use of government stands in stark contrast to many of the more sophisticated efforts to rebuild firm intellectual foundations for conservatism in the United States. How far the Republican Party or the conservative movement will remain locked into George W. Bush's legacy remains to be seen; it would be surprising if it could quickly be forgotten, especially if Republicans remain in control of the executive branch.

Notes

1. Edward S Corwin, *The President: Office and Powers 1787–1957* (London: London University Press).
2. Harold J .Laski, *The American Presidency: An Interpretation* (London: George Allen and Unwin, 1940).
3. Clinton Rossiter, *Conservatism in America*, 2nd rev. ed. (Cambridge, MA: Harvard University Press, 1982), 192.
4. Andrew Rudalevige, *The New Imperial Presidency: Renewing Presidential Power After Watergate* (Ann Arbor, MI: University of Michigan Press, 2005), 39–40.
5. James T .Patterson, *Congressional Conservatism and the New Deal: The Growth of the Conservative Coalition in Congress 1933–1939* (Lexington, KY: University of Kentucky Press , 1967), vii–viii.
6. Eugene D. Genovese, *The Southern Tradition: The Achievements and Limitations of an American Conservatism* (Cambridge, MA: Harvard University Press 1994), 2.

7. Christopher S. Yoo and Steven G. Calabrese, "The Unitary Executive During the Third Half-Century, 1889–1945," 8. Social Science Research Network Electronic Paper Collection (http://ssrn.com/abstract_id=558284).

8. Rudalevige, *The New Imperial Presidency*, 51.

9. Richard M Abrams, *America Transformed: Sixty Years of Revolutionary Change 1941–2001* (New York: Cambridge University Press, 2006), 67–68.

10. Dewey W Grantham, The *Life and Death of the Solid South: A Political History* (Lexington, KY: University of Kentucky Press, 1992), 104.

11. Barry M Goldwater, *Conscience of A Conservative* (Shepherdsville, KY: Victor Publishing, 1960), quoted in David Boaz "Does Anybody Believe in Federalism ?" *Cato Policy Report*, May/June 2005.

12. Peter Steinfels, *The Neoconservatives: The Men Who are Changing American Politics* (New York : Simon and Schuster, 1979).

13. Richard P. Nathan, *The Plot That Failed: Nixon and the Administrative Presidency* (New York: Wiley, 1975).

14. Pat Buchanan, "Nixon's Paranoia Justified," *Chicago Tribune*, August 17, 1976.

15. Christopher S. Yoo and Stephen G. Calabresi, "The Unitary Executive in the Modern Era, 1945–2001," 4, 11. Social Science Research Network Electronic Paper Collection (http://ssrn.com/abstract=558306).

16. David Boaz , "Does Anybody Believe in Federalism?" *Cato Policy Report*, May/June 2005.

17. Ibid.

18. John Dinan and Dale Krane "The State of American Federalism 2005" *Publius :The Journal of American Federalism* 36, 3 (2006): 327–374.

19. *Washington Post*, March 15, 2007.

20. Sara Diamond, *Roads to Dominion: Right Wing Movements and Political Power in the United States* (New York : Guilford Press, 1995).

21. David Kuo, *Tempting Faith: An Inside Story of Political Seduction* (New York: Free Press, 2006).

22. Garry Wills, "A Country Ruled by Faith," *The New York Review of Books*, November 16, 2006.

23. Ibid.

24. See especially Amy E Black, Douglas L. Koopman, and David Ryden, *Of Little Faith: The Politics of George W Bush's Faith Based-Initiatives* (Washington, DC: Georgetown University Press, 2004), chapter 5.

25. Chris Mooney, *The Republican War on Science* (New York: Basic Books, 2005).

26. James Mann, *The Vulcans: The History of Bush's War Cabinet* (London: Penguin Books, 2004).

Chapter 3

Canada's "Open Federalism": Past, Present, and Future

Christopher Dunn

This chapter explains the origins, meaning and likely future of the working theory of federalism adopted by Canada's Conservative Government elected in 2006 under the leadership of Stephen Harper. Called the "Open Federalism,"—and in recent federal documents the "federalism of openness," complete with small capitals—it is a collage of approaches and policies with deep roots in the debates regarding Canada's intergovernmental relations. Its origins lie in the coalitions that Conservative politicians have had to cobble together in order to take power away from the centrist Liberal Party. With some exceptions, the Harper Coalition is a coalition of outsiders, groups who have traditionally felt ignored on the intergovernmental and fiscal plane. Its present manifestation is in the two budgets that the Conservatives have issued since being elected as a minority government in 2006. Its future depends on whether the Government continues to be pragmatist instead of ideological. The indications so far are that pragmatism reigns and the Open Federalism is an important part of that pragmatism.

The Open Federalism designation is barely three years old, but its meaning evolves with every new pronouncement. As enunciated by Stephen Harper in 2004–2005 and the 2006 election platform, it meant a variety of things. These included a sense of mutualism, a long-term give-and-take attitude as opposed to a issue-based zero-sum approach; respect for the "federal principle" and the notion of strong provinces; abiding by the 1867 Constitution's division of powers—a kind of "strict constructionism"; a commitment to limit the federal spending power; reforms to address Quebec's needs; dedication to making the new provincial intergovernmental body, the Council of the Federation, work; rectification of the federal–provincial "fiscal imbalance" by a variety of instruments (equalization reform, tax room, tax transfers, increased transfers, use of sizable infrastructure spending, and so forth). The 2007 federal budget added some detail and specificity. It emphasized clarification of roles, tax reduction, targeting spending to federal jurisdiction, limiting the spending power, and transparency in future spending, this time under the rubric of "redressing fiscal balance." An overlooked but vitally important aspect of Open Federalism is also to provide a third option for Quebeckers between centralist federalism and separatism.

Most of these policies amount to a repudiation of the long-standing intergovernmental policies of successive Liberal Governments. Since 1945, Liberals have broadly adopted a nation-building stance that featured a substantial use of the federal spending power coupled with a vigorous resistance to efforts to limit it; reluctance to make significant changes to the federal–provincial division of powers, especially where Quebec was concerned; maintenance of a centralist "executive federalism" in preference to promoting provincial intergovernmentalism; sustaining federal primacy in fiscal relations, resisting provincial "opting-out" of shared-cost programs, especially opting out with compensation; and using some of the fiscal surplus for nation-building programs. Even provincial efforts to restrain the federal spending power did not markedly disturb the status quo, as can be seen in the Social Union Framework Agreement of 1999.[1]

Open Federalism is a fascinating development in Canadian Federalism in several respects. It comes from a prime minister who, judging from his past ("Calgary School" neoconservativism, Reform Party activist, stint in the anti-big-government interest group National Citizen's Coalition), might have been predicted to be against special treatment for Quebec and massive infrastructure and social policy spending. Moreover, the Liberal version of federalism paid handsome dividends in electoral support across the country for most of the postwar period and had become even more sophisticated in the new century, but Open Federalism has yet to produce comparable benefits for the Conservatives. Finally, it is counterintuitive to expect one level of government to advocate strengthening another level of government at the cost of its own fiscal and policy transcendence.

It is therefore important to consider the prospects of this risky and apparently daring departure from Canadian federal practice. The chapter reviews the successive waves of theories of Canadian federalism that influenced Open Federalism, the electoral calculus involved in modern Canadian intergovernmentalism, and other factors affecting the past, present, and future of the Open Federalism.

Theories of Canadian Federalism

Canada's Open Federalism cannot be understood without realizing that Canadians have a fascination with theories of federalism. One cannot take a stance vis-à-vis other levels of government without utilizing some set of guiding assumptions, and that is what these "theories" amount to. Many have emerged from the literature, often with different names but having essentially the same meanings. Political parties more often than not associate themselves with one or another theory and paint their opponents as exemplifying other approaches. As will be seen at the end of this section, the

Conservatives cherry-pick what they feel are the most attractive ones. Some of the most influential theories are as follows.

Centralist Federalism

As it was originally understood, this theory posited that the federal government should be the predominant level of government, and provinces should be the subordinate level. In the interests of nation-building, many powers were explicitly (or in some cases implicitly) accorded to the federal level in the 1867 constitution. Centralists originally held that these powers were meant to be taken literally.

In the modern era, some of the 1867 powers have become "dead letters" of the Constitution. Centralism now manifests itself as centrally led policy innovation that provincial governments are expected to follow. Federally designed cost-sharing agreements in areas of provincial jurisdiction are examples of this.

Cooperative (now Collaborative) Federalism

This accepts the continuance of the two orders of government as outlined in the Constitution, but it values rational policy and service to the public more than maintenance of jurisdictional sovereignty. Historically, it resulted from pressure for national standards in social programs and desire to end disparities between both socioeconomic classes and geographical regions. Cooperative federalism manifested itself after 1945 in the growth of federal–provincial conferences, the establishment of intergovernmental institutions, broad-ranging federal-provincial agreements, and lack of resistance to the use of the federal spending power.

Some analysts have seen a return of cooperative federalism in the frequent mentions of *"collaborative federalism"* in the 1990s. The Social Union Framework Agreement of 1999 (SUFA), considered a new charter of intergovernmental behavior, displayed collaborative themes. The federal authorities were to adhere to principles like due notice, partnership, collaboration, performance management, fact-finding, and mediation when considering the use of the spending power.

Intrastate Federalism

Intrastate federalism means federalism *within* federal institutions: making federal institutions reflect and represent provincial diversity. Two variants of intrastate federalism exist. *Provincialist intrastate federalism* aims to strengthen provincial government or provincial electorate representation in national institutions. *Centralist intrastate federalism* wants nongovernmental provincial interests represented in federal government institutions to make Ottawa more responsive and legitimate.

In both of the variants, there would be a qualitative change in federal institutions: they would now become truly "national" institutions. The "provincial" variant is more popular and was featured in the Charlottetown Accord's Triple-E (elected, equal, and effective) Senate design. Most provincialist reformers would have the provincial governments or provincial electors choosing who would represent them in the national institutions. Conversely, most centralist reformers would have the federal authorities choosing who would represent the provincial interests.

Asymmetrical Federalism

This is "a federalism that would not only recognize natural differences (such as size, population, history, etc.) among the units of a federation, but also formal differences in law among them either with respect to jurisdictional powers and duties, the shape of central institutions, or the application of national laws and programs. In part, this view of federalism seeks to know whether a federation can tolerate one or more forms of "special status" without the federation falling apart on the shoals of "provincial equality."[2]

However, some observers argue that asymmetrical federalism can also be achieved by informal means. Peter Russell differentiates between *hard asymmetrical federalism* and *soft asymmetrical federalism*. The former is the achievement of asymmetry through formal constitutional law, whereas the latter accords it in fact but not in constitutional form.[3] Working arrangements set up pursuant to the Labour Market Development Agreement (LMDA) reflect soft asymmetry: each province is free to establish unique relations with the federal government. The Canada-Newfoundland and Labrador Offshore Petroleum Board (C-NLOPB), a federal–provincial "co-management," is another asymmetrical model.

This review of theories is instructive in the Canadian context. In promoting his theoretical variant of federalism, Stephen Harper implicitly criticized other models, like centralist federalism, and subtly connected it with still others, like collaborative federalism and asymmetrical federalism. In labeling it anew, however, he disencumbered himself of the political and psychological baggage associated with older concepts. Prime Minister Martin, for instance, faced negative political fallout when he flirted with adopting the politically dangerous term "asymmetrical federalism" as a theme for his relations with the provinces.

The Evolution of Open Federalism

Open federalism is intentionally not easy to encapsulate in summary description. A concept that is an essential tool in the construction of a winning coalition needs to be flexible and multilayered. Over its evolution, therefore, there were different definitions and explanations given for the concept, many of which added nuances not seen before.

There were several iterations of the Open Federalism, culminating in perhaps its definitive explanation in the Federal Budget of 2007. This made Open Federalism essentially a nested concept, associated with a variety of other features deemed necessary in constructing the coalition, and reflecting the minority situation of the government. (In the 2006 general election the Conservatives garnered 124 seats, Liberals 103, the Bloc Québécois 51, New Democrats 29, and Independents one.)

In a *National Post* article, Harper initially used language redolent of Quebec nationalism themes.[4] He called for a renewed respect for the division of powers between the federal and provincial governments. This was associated with the need to investigate anew ideas that addressed Quebec's unique demands. There was a call for orderly intergovernmental relations and an end to the ad hoc arrangements characteristic of the chaotic intergovernmental meetings of the Martin era.

The Conservative National Policy Convention of March 19, 2005 later commented on a new notion of Open Federalism in the context of its founding *Policy Declaration*.[5] The Policy Declaration was intended to establish the founding principles and policy stances of the new Conservative Party formed two years earlier. As might be expected, federalism was not the only policy area dealt with, accounting for only one of the twenty-three sections.

However, the section on Open Federalism strategically targeted a new coalition, especially Quebeckers, Westerners, and middle-class taxpayers. Its policies committed a future Conservative Government to restore the constitutional balance between the federal and provincial and territorial governments; defend the notion of strong provinces within Canada and the federal principle; ensure that the use of the federal spending power in provincial jurisdictions is limited; advance specific reforms to respond to both Quebec's reluctance to sign the Constitution as well as western alienation; support the new interprovincial forum, the Council of the Federation (an idea initiated by Quebec); and fix the fiscal imbalance by various means, including increasing the amounts allocated to provincial transfers, by reducing taxes, or by transferring tax points to the provinces.

According to two scholarly analysts, these provisions reflect a sense of strict constructionism, that is, attentiveness to the original distribution of powers in the Constitution Act and support for disentangling the activities of the orders of government.[6] Perhaps more pertinently, however, they embody the constitutional and policy wishes of specific sectors of Canadian society.

The Conservative Party's Quebec platform speech of December 2005 made clear, by implication that the spending power provisions were meant to have special resonance in Quebec. Speaking to the Quebec Chamber of Commerce, Harper criticized the Liberals' use of the spending power as creating a domineering and paternalistic federalism and promised to monitor its use.

The Conservative Party's 2006 Quebec Platform (*For Real Change*) further reinforced the relevance of Open Federalism themes to Quebec nationalism and placed it, pointedly, as a midpoint between Liberal Party paternalism and the pointless obstructionism of the Bloc Québécois (BQ) (the federal party representing the separatist movement).[7] This made it a useful analogue for the policies of the Quebec Liberal Party (QLP). Despite its name, this is a coalition of federalist forces in the province and is not affiliated with the federal Liberals. It also attempts to situate itself as the nationalist alternative between the provincial separatists and Canadian centralist federalism tendencies. The platform mentioned matters covered in the main national campaign, but in particular added comments with appeal for Quebec voters: recognition and respect of provincial autonomy, particularly Quebec's; ongoing federal consultation with the provinces; and a more balanced federation that permitted provincial involvement in areas of federal jurisdiction affecting provincial jurisdiction.

The 2007 federal budget added further detail to the concept as:[8]

- enhancing the accountability of governments through the clarification of their respective roles and responsibilities;
- using excess federal revenues primarily to reduce taxes rather than to launch new federal programs in areas that are primarily of provincial and territorial responsibility;
- focusing new spending on areas of federal responsibility and, to the extent that new initiatives are introduced in areas of primary provincial and territorial responsibility, doing it in a respectful manner, at the request of provinces and territories;
- limiting the use of the "federal spending power" by ensuring (1) that new cost-shared programs in areas of provincial responsibility have the consent of the majority of provinces to proceed and (2) that provinces and territories have the right to opt out of cost-shared federal programs with compensation if they offer similar programs with comparable accountability structures; and
- aiding transparency by reporting in all future budgets, on new investments (1) in areas of core federal and shared responsibility and (2) in transfers to support provinces and territories.

The Significance of Open Federalism

For a concept so young and so undeveloped, there is a significant diversity of views on the meaning and significance of Open Federalism.

Open Federalism as a Business Agenda

Adam Harmes takes a political economy approach to Open Federalism, seeing it as consistent with the broader neoliberal approach to federalism, which emphasizes institutional reforms to "lock in" market-oriented policies, in this case "market-preserving federalism." He challenges the views of other political economists who maintain that neoliberals do not have a fully developed theory of federalism and are generally agnostic on the question of assigning powers permanently to one or another level of government. These political economists will at most venture only that there is a tendency on the right to weaken the central government's powers while simultaneously strengthening its power to defeat provincial economic interventionism.

Drawing on Friedrich Hayek, Milton Friedman, Barry R. Weingast and James M. Buchanan, Harmes contends that there is a coherent neoliberal theory of federalism rooted in "market-enabling government intervention" and "market-enabling federalism." In his view:

> Market-enabling government intervention is taken to include those policy capabilities whose primary aim is to liberalize and stabilize markets as well as to protect property rights. In contrast, market-inhibiting government intervention includes those policy capabilities whose primary aim is to regulate markets such as environmental, labour and social policy as well as to redistribute income and wealth through various forms of fiscal policy.[9]

Weingast envisaged "market-enabling federalism" as including a hierarchy of governments, institutionalized autonomy for each level of government, primary economic regulation being exercised by subnational governments, a common market to prevent them from establishing trade barriers, and hard budget constraints for lower governments. Thriving markets, not confiscation of wealth, is the aim of such an institutional arrangement. Buchanan sees federalism as a self-enforcing backup to constitutional protections of property rights, balanced budgets, and free markets; whereas constitutional protections provide a valuable alternative exit option to politics, federalism provides, through the workings of competition, another option. So the common theme is a locking in of protections for the market, and a disciplining of governments rather than enabling them.

Harmes sees such discipline reflected in the 2006 federal budget's five principles of Open Federalism (clarity of roles and responsibilities, fiscal responsibility and budget transparency, predictable long-term fiscal arrangements, a competitive and efficient economic union, and effective collaborative management of the federation). Nonetheless, he concludes somewhat contradictorily that "taken as a whole, it is apparent that, while democratic reform, national unity and partisan interests may be the main drivers of the federal Conservative Party's Open Federalism, it clearly also includes a strong political-economic dimension."[10]

Open Federalism as Provincial Accommodation

Kathy Brock sees Open Federalism as an alternative to the tortured logic of some analysts who interpret section 94 of the Constitution Act of 1867 as an unexpected constitutional route to introducing asymmetrical federalism and/or special status for Quebec in the Constitution.[11] Ignored for most of

Canadian history, this rather innocuous section affirms that the Parliament of Canada, with provincial legislative consent, may make provision for the uniformity of any and all laws relating to "Property and Civil Rights" in the three common law provinces (Ontario, Nova Scotia, and New Brunswick—a provision now generally conceded to apply to all of the common law provinces) and uniformity of procedure in any or all of the courts of those provinces. Some analysts regarded the exclusion of one of the four founding provinces—a civil law province, Quebec—as indicative either of a constitutional rule permitting asymmetrical federalism in Canada and especially differential status for Quebec, or of a constitutional basis for intergovernmental relations in Canada. The latter would imply, among other things, provincial rights to opt out of federal interventions, in matters affecting property and civil rights, with compensation.

Deeming these views counterproductive, Brock prefers the Open Federalism alternative:

> Asymmetry applied to justify special arrangements for one unit in a federation may be fair if also open to all, or if denied to the other units, it may be tantamount to dictating the sameness of all but that one. This is a recipe for jealousies and competitions that are unhealthy to the functioning of a federation.[12]

In her assessment, the federal government should strive to accommodate provincial differences in the mode of Open Federalism rather that engage in one-off deals or "checkerboard" federalism.[13] Examples she approves of are negotiated-compromises like the deal on the fiscal imbalance included in the 2007 federal budget, moves that allow provinces to opt in or out of federal legislative proposals while keeping in mind the national interest and other provinces' interests, and the federal government stressing its own jurisdictional competences.

Open Federalism as Fiscally Short-Changing Quebec

Quebec intellectuals have so far focused on the fiscal aspects of the Open Federalism (called *le fédéralisme d'ouverture* in French). Éric Montpetit considers the three fiscal modalities that may be used to fulfill the promise of Harper's federal plan—an increase in transfer payments from the federal government, improved equalization, and a tax point transfer—and comes to the conclusion that the transfer of tax points is the preferable option. (Tax point transfers essentially involve one level of government, usually the central government, retreating from a tax field and the other level entering it, therefore achieving an increase in its own revenue.) It is preferable because of its durability: "une fois le transfert realisé, il ne serait pas facile pour le gouvernement fédérale de recreér une déséquilibre fiscal."[14] The other options would involve increased revenues as well, but the federal government could reintroduce fiscal imbalance simply by increasing its own taxes unilaterally. According to Montpetit, a government practicing Open Federalism would have to accept an asymmetrical solution if some provinces preferred federal involvement in their jurisdiction over tax points. In contrast, Luc Godbout contends that sound principles need to be established before decisions on fiscal relations are taken. He requires these to include non-subordination of one government to another, adequate fiscal capacity, accountability, fiscal forecasting, and interdependence/cooperation.[15]

Open Federalism as a Continuation of the Past

Some analysts see Harper's Open Federalism as a mere continuation of past federal–provincial relations. Graham Fox contends that it neither ends interdependence nor break with recent developments toward collaborative governance. Indeed, Harper has been clear that he sees a continuing substantial role on three areas of provincial jurisdiction—health care, infrastructure, and postsecondary education (PSE).[16] Keith Banting also saw signs of continuation in some of his early policies.[17] Shared cost programs are still included in Conservative government's plans (for example, the 2004 Health Accord, federal–provincial patient wait times program, a five year Canadian Strategy for Cancer Control). The Conservative platform called for a new separate PSE transfer, but there were no consultations on this matter. Other signs included plans for a new shared-cost program to add 2500 more municipal police; the May 2006 budget pledge to continue infrastructure programs; and the lack of consultation on federal–provincial program changes (such as daycare). "The Conservatives simultaneously embraced core features of federalism as currently practiced, leaving no hostages to fortune in English Canada, and created a distinctive appeal in Quebec, conveying sensitivity to cultural difference and fiscal pressures," Banting declared, ".... The fact that this twin agenda was accomplished on the basis of remarkably little real change, at least in the case of the social and economic union, is a testament to the importance of creative ambiguity in Canadian politics and the Canadian Federation."[18]

All of these views of Open Federalism are intriguing and welcome additions to the literature on this nascent concept, but they fall short. Harmes' thesis is indistinct, arguing mostly for a business interest agenda, but then adding qualifications relating to national unity and partisan interests almost as an afterthought. In addition, the policies that he cites as evidence of a business agenda from the 2006 budget (which are like those in the 2007 budget) are not identifiably similar to those cited from market-enabling federalist authorities. The economic union initiatives of the Conservative government, the basis for much of his thesis, are not the primary focus of Open Federalism policy documents. In fact, Bay Street has not been a concern for this government, focused as it is on cultivating its base in the working- and middle classes. The 2007 Budget included relatively little for big business (a $735-million accelerated equipment write-off) and much more for working-class parents (a permanent tax break for parents with children under 18, costing Ottawa $3.3 billion over the first three years).[19] Business was also alienated by Finance Minister Jim Flaherty's income trust decision of 2006. "On the face of it," said one financial observer, "Finance Minister Jim Flaherty's decision to tax income trust distributions comes as a body blow to the government's biggest fans—Bay Street, the oil patch and seniors."[20]

Brock's alternative to centralist federalism—opting out—has not been a feature of the Open Federalism to date, and section 94 is a focus only for policy wonks. Nor is the continuity argument persuasive. Mention of the fiscal imbalance and opting out of new shared cost programs with compensation are radical departures from the practice of past Liberal governments. A simpler and more valid explanation for the origins and current configuration of the Open Federalism has to do with political lessons learned over the course of Canadian history by the perennially second-place Conservative Party.

The Origins of Harper's Open Federalism

The rationale for Harper's Open Federalism is simple: it is one part of a strategy to reconstruct permanently the type of "Grand Conservative Coalition" that has occasionally propelled the Conservatives to power in the twentieth century. It is composed of former Reform Party populists, old-fashioned Central and Eastern Canadian Tories, and Quebec Nationalists, now buttressed by new appeals to middle-class voters and big city dwellers concerned with environmental and infrastructure issues.

Such a strategy has been in place for some time. As academic and former Reform Party research boss Tom Flanagan attested, the strategy unveiled in Harper's speech at the Calgary "Winds of Change" conference in 1996 resulted in the election of a resurrected coalition within a decade. It led the Western populist Reform Party (formed in 1987) and some dissident Conservatives to form the Canadian Alliance Party in 2000. Later, there was a formal union of the Canadian Alliance, now under Harper, and the Progressive Conservatives in 2003 to form the Conservative Party, which Harper also came to lead. Flanagan, probably the single-most important contributor to Harper's success, helped the future Prime Minister write the 1996 speech, nicknaming it the "Three Sisters Theory." In it, says Flanagan, Harper "marshalled historical evidence to show that all winning Conservative coalitions in 20th-century Canadian history had been built around three main elements: populist reformers, strongest in the West but also present in rural Ontario; traditional Tories, strong in Ontario and Atlantic Canada; and francophone nationalists in Quebec."[21] The 1993 election saw Brian Mulroney's grand coalition shatter along these ancient fault lines to form an opposition composed of the Reform Party, the separatist Parti Quebecois (PQ), and a small (two elected members) Progressive Conservative element. Conservatives, to regain national power, had to reconstruct such a coalition.

Harper's strategy was partly realized by the 2003 union of Reform and the Progressive Conservatives, which produced better aggregate results than the old parties. But Quebec, which gave minimal support for the Conservatives in the 2004 federal election, was still a problem. From 2004 on, Harper courted the third sister, culminating in his 2005 Open Federalism speech in Quebec City.[22] His project, according to Flanagan, is to construct a "natural governing party," a status the Liberals had a lock on for most of the twentieth century. The term denotes a party generally able to win majorities, because its representation of the enduring interests of large segments of society makes it the usual option of a strong plurality of voters.[23]

Political consultant Jaime Watt says in effect that the coalition is forming as Harper and others have wished. His focus-groups show it composed of supporters of the old Western Reform/Alliance as (the "core"), together with "angry, right-of-centre Liberals" in BC, Ontario, and Atlantic Canada ("Blue Grits"), Red Tories (left-leaning Conservatives, usually in respect to social policy), and bleu Quebecois.[24] Quebec may be responding because of the novelty of being paid attention to. The same is true of middle-class voters who now have Goods and Services Tax (GST) cuts, child-care grants to families, and wait time and health care guarantees.[25] One qualification has to be added to Flanagan's assessment, however. Some aspects have been added on to the basic strategy incrementally. The Harper Conservatives have adopted most of the Chretien-Martin New Deal for Communities and Infrastructure, the electoral potential of which is too great to ignore.

The Federalism Preferences of Coalition Members

Open Federalism is, in part, a case of the Marxian dictum "from each according to his means, to each according to his needs." Coalition members get part—though not all—of the core historical demands they have long pursued as outsiders to the power structure, but this is enough to satisfy them for the present.

Quebec

Quebec gets federal spending power put on the policy agenda, and gets some action taken. As Prime Minister Pierre Trudeau noted in 1969, this has come to have a special constitutional meaning in Canada. It signifies "the power of Parliament to make payments to people or institutions or governments for purposes on which it (Parliament) does not necessarily have the power to legislate."[26] In 1998, Quebec's intergovernmental affairs secretariat summarized the commonalities in the positions taken by successive Quebec premiers against the use of the federal spending power. They wanted federal government withdrawal from Quebec's provincial jurisdictions, with Québec given a tax base commensurate with its expanded legislative responsibilities. They contended that federal spending power was contrary to the spirit of federalism. They insisted that the people of Quebec should retain full control of the fields affected. Finally, they deemed that the Québec Government should be the sole implementation agent.[27]

At the August 1998 Premiers' Conference, Quebec joined a provincial coalition in support of the "Saskatoon Consensus" on federal–provincial relations in a new Canadian "social union."[28]: This caused surprise given that a separatist government was in power in Quebec and Lucien Bouchard, leader of the Parti Quebecois and Premier of Quebec (1996–2001), was hostile to the social union. The Saskatoon Consensus decreed that:

- the federal government should be prohibited from spending money to create or change national social programs without majority provincial consent
- provinces should be able to opt out of any new or modified national social program with full financial compensation, providing that dissenting provinces provide a program that Aaddresses the priority areas@ dealt with in the national program
- there should be a joint role in setting, interpreting, and enforcing national standards for medicare and other national programs
- a mechanism should be instituted that would give provinces a role in resolving disputes over standards and disagreements over whether opting-out provinces have met the conditions for receiving compensation.

Over and above its agreement to sign on to the social union discussions, Quebec made the additional concession of abandoning its traditional insistence that opting-out provinces receive *unconditional* compensation from the federal government. Although the federal government succeeded in watering down these demands in 1999, they were indicative of Quebec's minimal requirements if it is to feel secure in the Canadian Union.

Open Federalism answered the needs of Quebec nationalists on a number of fronts. Foremost was its call for limiting the federal spending power. Also attractive was its proposed Charter of Open Federalism in response to Quebec's oft-expressed sentiment for the codification of intergovernmental relations. The mention of tax room for provinces as one method of fixing the fiscal imbalance was also pitched at Quebec. Most significant overall was the frequent mention of Quebec in Open Federalism's landmark declarations.

Western Populists

The modern Conservative Party's concern with Quebec and nods to asymmetry signify that the Conservatives are at odds with its Reform Party antecedents. A generation ago, Reform Party founder Preston Manning claimed that a "New Canada" rather than French–English dualism was implicit in the Confederation of 1867.[29] He advocated symmetrical federalism, equal individual rights, and no special status for Quebec. During the Meech Lake Accord debate, he expressed alarm at the implication that the Accord's "distinct society" clause implied rights and privileges for Quebec not enjoyed by other provinces.[30] Manning and Stephen Harper, Reform's former policy adviser, considered that provincial equality meant identical provincial legislative authority.[31]

However, some aspects of official Reform Party policy are remarkably similar to Harper's Open Federalism. Its "Blue Book," the 1996–1997 statement of Principles and Policies, foreshadowed familiar Conservative themes.[32] These included contentions that: the Federal Government should protect the economic union, eliminate internal trade barriers, and represent Canada in international trade negotiations; jurisdictional decisions should lean in favor of decentralization; provinces should have exclusive jurisdiction over apprenticeship programs, culture, education, health, housing, language, manpower training, natural resources, sport fishing, sports and recreation, social assistance, and tourism; legally entrenched measures should prohibit the Federal Government from using its "spending power" in areas of provincial jurisdiction; the role of the Federal Government in social programs should be merely to develop national standards through cooperative agreements rather than to impose standards unilaterally and withhold transfer payments when those standards are not met; and Federal cash grants to the provinces should be replaced with unconditional transfers.

The genesis of Open Federalism ideas—a federal government operating increasingly in its own sphere o f jurisdiction, bolstering the jurisdictional and fiscal strength of the provinces, restricting the spending power, promoting collaboration over command and control—thus seem to have originated in the populist era of the party. The overlap between Reform ideas and Quebec nationalism on decentralization and the spending power also indicates that Harper built on existing ideas.

Mainline Tories

In Canadian politics, "Tories" is a label for the old Conservative (after 1942 renamed the Progressive Conservative [PC]) Party. The historic founding party of Confederation, it ceased to exist only in 2003. The Tories were assiduous in their desire to distinguish themselves from the Trudeau constitutional legacy. Trudeau's concern to protect the levers of central power manifested itself in constitutional packages that emphasized rights and institutional reform but did not markedly affect the division of powers. The PCs were more prone to decentralize power in their own constitutional proposals: the *Meech Lake Accord* (1987); *Shaping Canada's Future Together* (1991): the Beaudoin-Dobbie Report, *Report of the Special Joint Committee on a Renewed Canada* (1992); and the *Charlottetown Accord* (1992).

The Conservatives and the provinces were in accord, as follows, about the tests they wanted applied to federal–provincial relations. The future use of the federal spending power should avoid federal unilateralism in the initiation and termination of fully funded federal programs or shared-cost programs in areas of provincial jurisdiction. It should be implemented only in policy areas of overriding national importance. A cooperative approach to determining national objectives was preferable to unilateral federal definition.

The federal principle—non-subordination—would predominate: one level of government would not be subordinated to another in areas of its own jurisdiction. Provinces had a right to reject the introduction of new shared-cost programs and to reasonable fiscal compensation if they operated a program consistent with national objectives.

In relation to the Quebec and Western proposals, the Progressive Conservative Government's proposals appear pretty tame, but they should be seen in historical context. The diminution of the federal spending power had been a hot-button issue since the Meech Lake Accord. The PCs were the first federal government to draft and promote proposals placing constitutional limits on the spending power, while implicitly allowing its continued use in areas of provincial jurisdiction. They were also more collaborative than the Liberals in allowing for federal–provincial involvement in generating "national objectives" and the toleration of prolonged negotiations of these accords. Various PC Government documents also called for the decentralization of certain "grey areas" of exclusive provincial jurisdiction. In some ways, then, there is a definite Tory element in the Open Federalism.

It is not unreasonable to speculate that the Tory rump in the Conservative Party is still battling the Trudeau legacy. Unlike the Chretien/Martin Liberals, who disavowed any constitutional change packages, Harper has not ruled it out, mainly in reference to ensuring Quebec specificity.

Cultivating a Broader Voter Base through the Open Federalism

Open Federalism is about not only coalitions, regions, and parties, but also reaching out to new supporters, namely the middle- and working class and big-city voters concerned with environmental and infrastructure issues. The concern with this demographic resulted in the distinct financial configuration of Open Federalism in the federal Budget Plan.

Harper's strategic policy and communications advisor Patrick Muttart, described as "the Canadian version of Karl Rove," was instrumental in this development. Instead of bureaucratic-sounding promises like regional transfers, he wanted a populist emphasis on putting money in pockets through tax cuts or allowances for families and individuals. This has found expression in Conservative budgets tied to the Open Federalism.

Big-city voters are also especially alert to infrastructural and environmental issues. The Liberals had reaped handsome electoral dividends from targeting this agenda in a way that bypassed the provinces.[33] It solidified their support in the major cities to such an extent that these were the bulwark of their remaining strength. Yet the bypassing of the provinces to build up a Liberal base was risky. Voters have too much trouble identifying government programs at the best of time, let alone esoteric ones with an urban institutional focus. The Harper Conservatives approached the institutional federal ramifications with greater caution. They continued the infrastructural and environmental programs while avoiding such bypassing of the provinces.

Open Federalism offers a channel to ensure that programs are high-profile enough to woo the voters of large urban centers but respectful of the provinces' constitutional jurisdiction over municipalities.

The Current Meaning of Open Federalism: Open Federalism, or Restoring Fiscal Balance?

The Harper program has begun what appears to be a conscious effort to blend questions of federalism and public spending. The expression "Open Federalism" is used only once in the 2007 Budget documents, and even then it becomes identified with "restoring fiscal balance." It is not clear from the Budget whether it means the same thing as respectful relations (with taxpayers and governments) and greater collaboration, or is apart from them.[34] It appears that *Open Federalism* is being conflated with *restoring fiscal balance*, which, in the Budget's language, means: putting transfers on a long-term principles-based footing; major tax reductions and the Tax Back Guarantee; clarifying roles and responsibilities of the various levels of government; and strengthening the economic union based on the plan set out in *Advantage Canada. Bluntly put,* federalism questions in Canada have become inseparable from money issues.

- *Putting transfers on a long-term principles-based footing* means more money for governments and for taxpayers. Cash funding to provinces and territories was $43 billion when the Harper Government took office in 2006, and will rise to at least $18 billion higher in 2013–2014. In the Budget of 2007, restoring fiscal balance is associated with more money under: Equalization ($1.9 billion more over the years 2007–2008 and 2008–2009 than the previous system would have provided); health care ($1.2 billion more to provinces and territories in 2007–2008 and a *"10-Year Plan to Strengthen Health Care"*); a modified CST (over $16 billion in new funding over seven years, beginning in 2008–2009, for postsecondary education, children, and social programs); labour market training (a total of $3 billion more for training by 2013–2014); and infrastructure (more than $16 billion in new funding over the next seven years).
- *Tax reductions* means more money for taxpayers and others: (a reduction in personal income tax by $2.4 billion in the next two years by way of the "Tax Back Guarantee," roughly 25 percent of the $9.7 billion in the budget's tax relief), and less money for federal program expenditures through a reformed Expenditure Management System (the federal budgeting framework).
- *Clarifying roles and responsibilities* means focusing more ("new") spending on areas of federal responsibility, and reporting it more clearly, but it also means finessing the whole jurisdiction thing by establishing an "ecoTrust for Clean Air and Climate Change" (a third-party trust to provide more than $1.5 billion to provinces and territories over three years for environmental projects).

- *Strengthening the economic union* includes more abstract matters like working toward a "common securities regulator" (to generate principles-based regulations for the benefit of investors, business, and the economy); but there are also benefits for the working class and low-income groups (a Working Income Tax Benefit) and immigrants (a more efficient foreign credentials process).
- Cash funding to provinces and territories, which stood at $43 billion when this Government took office in 2006, will be at least $18 billion higher in 2013–2014.

Apparently, the message of "more money" bore repeating and amplifying. On October 30, 2007, Finance Minister Flaherty introduced an Economic Statement in the Commons that added to the largesse of the March 2007 Budget. The Economic Statement announced $60 billion over five years in broad-based tax reductions. Most of that amount seemed destined for business, but the amounts for business were not specified while those for individual taxpayers were. In the area of individual tax reductions, there was a further tax reduction from 6 percent to 5 percent, a lowering of the lowest personal income tax rate on taxable income up to $37,178, from 15.5 percent to 15 percent (for which Opposition Liberals had clamored); and an increase in the "basic personal amount" (the total amount Canadian taxpayers can earn without paying federal income tax) retroactive to $9600 in 2007 and $10,100 in 2009. "Open Federalism," however, was not mentioned even once.

Why this terminological retreat from Open Federalism? There are a number of explanations. It is likely too abstract for voters, who usually think in terms of pocketbook issues. It may resonate in Quebec but not as much in the rest of Canada. In reserving it for use in Quebec, attention is diverted nationally from policies favorable to Quebec that generate political resentment elsewhere.

The Current Meaning of Open Federalism: The French/English Dimension

The current Open Federalism also has a French/English dimension that is important. In Quebec, financial matters matter, but they are not enough. So the Conservatives, in addition to offering all the programs and broad theoretical nuances previously discussed, have to offer special considerations for Quebec in the form of economic and nationalist policies of interest to it. Fulfilling a Campaign 2006 promise, it has been offered a formal role as a participating government in UNESCO.[35] In 2007, Harper also made sure that Quebec became the first recipient provincial government of aid ($349.9 million) under the new "Canada ecoTrust for Clean Air and Climate Change."[36] Politically the program was made more palatable to Quebec by use of a third-party funding agency and clearly deferred to Quebec's priorities as identified in its 2006–2012 action plan for climate change. This was a new federal program designed to provide simultaneously for reductions in greenhouse gas emissions and air pollutants and for aid to provinces for research and infrastructure. In late November 2006, the Prime Minister introduced a motion in the House of Commons stating that "this House recognizes that Québécois form a nation within a united Canada."[37] It passed within a week. This was a significant use of terminology in Canada because it implied a special status for Quebec, and because such terminology had been steadfastly avoided by the Liberal Party for over fifty years, even though three Liberal prime ministers came from Quebec. There were, in short, far more announcements relating to the Open Federalism in Quebec than to elsewhere in Canada where the concept was less familiar and was usually associated with financial grants along the lines of the ecoTrust program. Respect for Council of the Federation concept has been a distinguishing characteristic of official Conservative announcements in speeches and budget documents.[38] Hostility toward the spending power in official documents is as commonplace in Conservative Party and federal government policy documents as it is in those issued by Quebec.

The Future of Open Federalism

Open Federalism faces problems, however, in regard to its meaning in Quebec and in other provinces in light of the Conservative record. The Harper government also shows little intention of completing the work still undone in the Open Federalism dossier. In August 2007, the Quebec intergovernmental affairs minister, Benoit Pelletier, made some Quebec-related comments critical of the record of the Open Federalism that showed how far federal policy had fallen short of rhetoric for all provinces as well as his.[39] He charged that the federal government's recognition of Quebec's national characteristics and its commitment to limiting the federal spending power lacked specifics. His checklist of what still needed to be done went as follows:

- The Charter of Open Federalism should be a specific, not vague blueprint for future federal–provincial relations and the operation of the federation
- Quebec's distinctiveness should be recognized constitutionally in a charter of Open Federalism.
- The federal government should address the federal–provincial division of jurisdictions.
- The federal government should specify how Ottawa plans to limit its spending in areas of provincial jurisdiction ...
- Quebec should have protections, such as the right to opt out with financial compensation, should the federal government intrude into such Quebec jurisdictions as health and education.

This commentary has some validity. The 2007 federal budget, purportedly an exhaustive list of federal actions on the federal–provincial front, mentioned neither a Charter of Open Federalism nor Quebec's distinct status, particular status, special status, or any other form of distinctiveness that pays it special attention. In fact, it was only mentioned once in the budget paper to list federal expenditures in the province in common with all the others. There was no reference to any impending plan to review the division of powers in the constitution (but, in fairness, the Harper government had only promised to respect the division of powers, not to reform it). Arguably, the budget's promise to allow provinces and territories "to opt out of cost-shared federal programs with compensation if they offer similar programs with comparable accountability structures" is a response to Quebec's demand for opting out, but Quebec, notably, does not make mention of the proviso of similar programs or comparable accountability structures. There has been no further mention of a federal tax point transfer to Quebec or to any other province. Limiting the use of the federal spending power is in fact mentioned in the budget paper (majority provincial agreement, similar programs requirement), but when one compares these slight references to the more detailed Social Union Framework Agreement (SUFA), the Conservative protocol pales in comparison.

To some extent, Open Federalism must be judged by its effect on a target that it is designed to combat—Quebec separatism—and here the record is mixed. On one hand, Quebec separatism, a year and a half after the election of the minority Conservative government, is on the rise. A survey by the polling company CROP for the Montreal newspaper *La Presse* found in August 2007 that support for the separatist Parti Quebecois stood at 33 percent, up from 28 percent received in the March 2007 election.[40]

Friends of Open Federalism do not fare well. Quebec Premier Jean Charest, the federalist Liberal premier who forged a strong alliance with Harper and benefited from several Open Federalism policies, saw his party lose many seats (from 75 to 48) and decline in the popular vote (from 46 percent to 33 percent) in 2007. This has to be qualified by the fact that the PQ had an ineffectual leader, and the Action Democratique du Quebec (ADQ) had connected with a right-wing sentiment prevalent in the Quebec electorate, rising 13 percent in the popular vote to nearly 31 percent and from 37 seats to 41. On the other hand, electoral support for the separatists at the polls had gone down. The PQ had won 45 seats in the 2003 general election and about 33 percent of the popular vote. Now it had slipped nine seats and nearly 5 percent in the popular vote to a little over 28 percent.

There were also indications that the Harper approach was gaining traction in Quebec. The Liberals and Conservatives were tied at 33 percent support nationally in a Globe and Mail/CTV Strategic Counsel poll in August 2007. In Quebec, however, the Conservatives held second place to the Bloc Québécois outside Montreal, a position usually enjoyed by the federal Liberals, in an area of traditional support for the BQ. The percentage of Quebeckers who believe "the country is on the right track" nearly doubled in two years, from 34 per cent at the start of the last federal election in late 2005, to 59 per cent in early August 2007 (versus 57 percent nationally).[41]

Leading up to three September 2007 federal by-elections in Quebec, the Liberal Party found itself battling with the New Democratic Party (NDP), a bit player in Quebec, for third place in two of the ridings. In the normally "sovereignist" Roberval-Lac-Saint-Jean, a two-way race saw the Conservative candidate victorious with nearly 60 percent support over the BQ candidate's 27 percent. The BQ held on to Saint-Hyacinthe-Bagot, but in Outremont, a francophone Liberal bastion, it was bested by the NDP.[42]

In the rest of Canada, Open Federalism is not often mentioned. There has not been a prime minister's news release using the term in its title since April 20, 2006.[43] One can surmise that using the term would be too much of a reminder that much of the promised agenda remains unfinished. It might also engender cognitive dissonance: respect for provincial governments does not seem to jibe well with the fact that three provinces—Newfoundland, Nova Scotia, and Saskatchewan—have criticized the Harper Government's 2007 budget because it resulted in less equalization than they had expected from the new Conservative government and unilaterally changed federal–provincial agreements on equalization offset payment arrangements. Still another reason is that overt attacks on the federal spending power can backfire in English Canada, where it is still associated with social progress.

Conclusion

Thus it appears that the future of the Open Federalism is more modest than its original promise. It seems to have been relegated to use as a regional slogan in Quebec and replaced elsewhere by the economic imagery of fiscal balance and pocketbook federalism. It did its job, however. It got the Conservatives a beachhead in Quebec federal politics and calmed the waters of federal–provincial relations. Whether Open Federalism will be brought out of its early retirement to renew battle on the hustings remains to be seen.

Notes

1. Christopher Dunn, "The Federal Spending Power," in Christopher Dunn, ed., *The Handbook of Canadian Public Administration* (Don Mills, Ontario: Oxford University Press, 2002), 225–248.
2. David Milne, "Equality or Asymmetry: Why Choose?" in Ronald L. Watts and Douglas M. Brown, eds., *Options for a New Canada* (Toronto: University of Toronto Press, 1991), 285.
3. Peter H. Russell, *Constitutional Odyssey: Can Canadians Become a Sovereign People?* 2nd ed. (Toronto: University of Toronto Press, 1993), 178.
4. Steven Harper, "My Plan for Open Federalism," *National Post*, October 27, 2004.
5. Conservative Party of Canada, Policy Declaration 2005. http://www.conservative.ca.
6. Robert Young, "Open Federalism and Canadian Municipalities," in Keith G. Banting, Roger Gibbons, Peter Leslie, Alain Noel, Richard Simeon and

Robert Young et al., *Open Federalism: Interpretations, Significance* (Kingston, Ontario: Queen's University Institute of Intergovernmental Relations, 2006), 17. See also Adam Harmes, "The Political Economy of Open Federalism," *Canadian Journal of Political Science* 40, 2 (June 2007): 417–437 at 419.

7. Conservative Party of Canada, "For Real Change: The Conservative Party of Canada's Commitment to Quebecers," (Ottawa, 2005). http://www.conservative. ca/media/2005129-Quebec-Platform.pdf .

8. Government of Canada, *Budget 2007.* http://www.budget.gc.ca/2007/bp/bpc4e.html.

9. Harmes, "The Political Economy of Open Federalism," 434.

10. Ibid., 434

11. Kathy L. Brock, "Open Federalism, Section 94, and Principled Federalism: Contradictions in Vision," Paper prepared for the annual meetings of the Canadian Political Science Association, University of Saskatchewan, Saskatoon, Saskatchewan, May 29–June 1, 2007.

12. Ibid., 18.

13. Ibid., 19.

14. Éric Montpetit, "Le Déséquilibre fiscal a l'heure du *fédéralisme d'ouverture*," *Policy Options* 28, 3 (March 2007): 42.

15. Luc Godbout, "Rétablir l'équilibre fiscal: au-delà de l'argent, des priénci-pes," *Policy Options* 28, 3 (March 2007): 48–53.

16. Graham Fox, "Harper's 'Open Federalism': From the Fiscal Imbalance to 'Effective Collaborative Management' of the Federation," *Policy Options* 28, 3 (March 2007): 44–47 at 47.

17. Keith G. Banting, "Open Federalism and Canada's Social and Economic Union: Back to the Future?" In Keith G. Banting et al., *Open Federalism*, 77–86.

18. Banting, "Open Federalism," 85.

19. John Geddes and Paul Wells, "The Conservative Budget Leaves Business Feeling Neglected," *Maclean's*, April 2, 2007.

20. Jason Kirby, "Breach of Trust?" *Maclean's*, November 20, 2007.

21. *Tom Flanagan, "Harper's Road Map to Power," Globe and Mail, May 23, 2006.*

22. Ibid.

23. Ibid.

24. Jaime Watt, "Rebuilding the Mulroney Coalition—Welcome the 'New' Harper Conservatives," *Policy Options* (March 2006): 41–46.

25. Ibid., 46.

26. Pierre Elliott Trudeau, *Federal–Provincial Grants and the Spending Power of Parliament* (Ottawa: Queen's Printer, 1969).

27. Source: Summarized from Secrétariat aux Affaires Integouvernmentales can-adiennes, Ministère du Conseil exécutif, Gouvernement du Québec, July 1998, *Québec=s Historical Position on the Federal Spending Power, 1994–1998.* Web location: http://www.cex.gouv.qc.ca/saic/english.htm.

28. Sections quoted from Elizabeth Thompson and Joan Bryden, "Premiers United on Demands on Ottawa," *Montreal Gazette*, August 7, 1998. Some minor alteration in wording has been done to make the text read more smoothly.

29. Preston Manning, "The Road to New Canada," an address to the 1991 assembly of the Reform Party of Canada, Saskatoon, April 6, 1991, 10.
30. Preston Manning, "Reform Party Position on the Meech Lake Accord," news release, May 18, 1990.
31. Stephen Harper, "The *Reform* Vision of Canada," speech to the Party Assembly, Saskatoon, April 5, 1991; Preston Manning and Stephen Harper, "The Road to Conflict in Canada," *Globe and Mail*, June 28, 1990.
32. Reform Party of Canada, Blue Book: 1996–1997 Principles and Policies of the Reform Party of Canada—A Fresh Start for Canadians (Calgary, Alberta: Reform Fund Canada, 1996), 10, 19–22.
33. Christopher Dunn, "Urban Asymmetry and Provincial Mediation of Federal–Municipal Relations in Newfoundland and Labrador," forthcoming, in The State of the Federation Series, published by the Queen's University Institute for Intergovernmental Relations, and edited by Robert A. Young.
34. The expression appears in a budget paper, and in Chapter 4 of the Budget Plan, both entitled "Restoring Fiscal Balance for a Stronger Federation." The Budget Paper begins:

    Canada's New Government is building a stronger federation in which all governments come together to help Canadians realize their potential. This stronger federation is built on a vision of open federalism, with more respectful relations with taxpayers and governments, and with greater collaboration to deliver results for Canadians.

    and Chapter 4 begins:

    Canada's New Government is building a stronger federation in which all governments come together to help Canadians realize their potential. This stronger federation is built on a vision of open federalism and respectful relations, where governments collaborate effectively to deliver results for Canadians.

35. CTV News (online), "Harper Announces UNESCO Deal with Quebec," May 5, 2006. http://www.ctv.ca/servlet/ArticleNews/story/CTVNews/20060505/quebec_unesco_060505/20060505/.
36. Canada, Prime Minister's Office, "Prime Minister unveils new Canada ecoTrust: Quebec investment the first of new funding to deliver real results for Canadians," Ottawa, Ontario, February 12, 2007.
37. As reported in CBC News online, "Quebecers form a nation within Canada: PM," November 22, 2006. http://www.cbc.ca/canada/story/2006/11/22/harper-quebec.html, accessed August 15, 2007.
38. Budget 2007, for example, references it as an authoritative voice of the provinces: it says "As elaborated in Chapter 5 of *The Budget Plan* in the 'Knowledge Advantage' section, the increase [of post-secondary money for the provinces by way of the Canada Social Transfer (CST) of $800 Million annually beginning in 2008] will take effect in 2008–2009, following discussions with provinces and territories on how best to make use of those new investments and ensure appropriate reporting and accountability to Canadians."
39. Canadian Press, "Quebec Wants Distinctiveness in the Constitution," http://www.ctv.ca/servlet/ArticleNews/story/CTVNews/20070806/que_constitution_070806?s_name=&no_ads=.

40. David Ljunggren, Reuters, "Support for Quebec Separatists on the Rise: Poll," August 29, 2007. http://www.canada.com/ottawacitizen/news/story.html?id=efb4c7ec-f77f-429d-b311-c447f54b5ff0&k=8502.
41. *Gloria Galloway, "The Harper Paradox,"* Globe and Mail, *August 27, 2007.*
42. *Chantal Hébert, "Liberals Under the Gun in Quebec," Toronto Star, September 3, 2007.* http://www.thestar.com/comment/article/252619.
43. Canada, Prime Minister's Office, "Prime Minister Harper Outlines His Government's Priorities and Open Federalism Approach," April 20, 2007. http://www.pm.gc.ca/eng/media.asp?category=1&id=1118.

Part II

Intergovernmental Strategies in Contemporary Federalism

Chapter 4

Three Faces of Contemporary American Federalism

John Kincaid

American federalism today can be described as coercive federalism in contrast to previous eras of dual federalism and cooperative federalism. The current system is "coercive" because the predominant political, fiscal, statutory, regulatory, and judicial trends entail impositions of federal dictates on state and local governments. This new phase of American federalism began in the late 1960s in succession to the previous stage of cooperative federalism that had commenced in the early 1930s.

Coercive federalism has been characterized by a shift of focus in federal policymaking from the interests of places (namely, state and local governments) to the interests of persons (namely, voters and interest groups). Not only elected federal officials but also unelected federal judges have grown highly responsive to electoral coalitions, interest groups, and campaign contributors, and correspondingly less responsive to elected state and local government officials. Lacking a privileged voice in Washington DC's corridors of power, the latter have been reduced under coercive federalism to the status of interest-group lobbyists. They have to compete in the federal policymaking arena with other interests, many of whom possess greater resources—financial, ideological, or electoral—to influence federal officials. Consequently, as U.S. Senator Carl Levin (D-MI) commented to this author in 1988, "There is no political capital [for members of Congress] in intergovernmental relations." In other words, federal legislators and other officials have little to gain from catering to the concerns of governors, state legislators, county commissioners, mayors, township supervisors, and the like.

Nevertheless, an element of cooperative federalism endures within the administrative interstices of contemporary federalism. Federal, state, and local bureaucrats generally cooperate and coordinate when implementing intergovernmental policies. Federal officials—judicial ones excepted—rarely coerce state and local policy administration, and state and local bureaucrats rarely obstruct federal objectives. Even elected state and local officials are usually cooperative with respect to implementation. There are, of course, conflicts in intergovernmental administrative relations, but bargaining and negotiation are the principal tools of conflict resolution. Even under coercive federalism, therefore, recourse to the courts is very much a last resort in cases of irreconcilable differences between different levels of government.

Meanwhile, a third face of American federalism reflects the continuing vitality of dual federalism's reserved powers for the states, which allow state and local governments to legislate across a broad range of policy fields, and the federal government's willingness to leave some room for independent state and local action in some fields otherwise occupied by federal law. This third face supports another long-standing characteristic of the system. As James Bryce observed at the end of the nineteenth century, American federalism enabled "a people to try experiments in legislation and administration which could not be safely tried in a large centralized country."[1] In 1932, U.S. Supreme Court Justice Louis D. Brandeis conceptualized this facet of federalism as that of the states serving as laboratories of democracy.[2] Federal–state minimum-wage differentials offer an example of its ongoing significance. The federal government did not raise the nationally mandated minimum level of $5.15 per hour between 1997 and 2007, but twenty-nine states mandated a higher minimum during the same period. Gay marriage offers a more controversial example of state experimentation under federalism. Congress has so far failed to propose an amendment to the U.S. Constitution prohibiting this. However, twenty-six states have a state constitutional amendment prohibiting same-sex marriage, and forty-three states have a statute restricting marriage to a union between a woman and a man. Conversely, Massachusetts legalized same-sex marriage in 2004, California, Connecticut, New Jersey, and Vermont have established civil unions that offer gay couples nearly all the legal rights and responsibilities of marriage, and Hawaii, Maine, and the District of Columbia permit same-sex civil unions that provide various rights and responsibilities associated with marriage under their laws.

From Dual to Coercive Federalism

The first stage of U.S. federalism, born with the U.S. Constitution and usually labeled dual federalism, was rooted in the dual federal–state constitutionalism, dual sovereignty, and dual citizenship attributes of the federal arrangement. Constitutional scholar Edward S. Corwin, an advocate of national supremacy,[3] argued that dual federalism had four characteristics:

> (1) The national government is one of enumerated powers only; (2) Also, the purposes which it may constitutionally promote are few; (3) Within their respective spheres the two centers of government are "sovereign" and hence "equal"; [and] (4) The relation of the two centers with each other is one of tension rather than collaboration.[4]

Although this model was criticized as a simplistic caricature of what was actually a cooperative system,[5] the dual-federalism model endured as a rhetorical foil for champions of national power over states' rights. Morton Grodzins, a critic of the dual-federalism view, inadvertently immortalized it when he christened it "layer-cake" federalism, in contrast to what he saw as a more accurate "marble-cake" (or rainbow-cake) metaphor for a system characterized by both chaos and cooperation in which "no important activity of government … is the exclusive province" of any sphere of government.[6] The layer-cake metaphor is itself flawed, however, because it portrays a hierarchy with the federal government on top. Dual federalism envisioned separate, equally sovereign, coordinate spheres of government.

One kernel of truth in the dual-federalism model was that the federal government exercised little direct power over the states (apart from the post–Civil War Reconstruction of the South) and citizens in the states had relatively little direct contact with the federal government beyond their local U.S. post office and mailman. Different dates have been given for the end of dual federalism, but–to the extent it existed–there is wide agreement that it fully expired by the close of the New-Deal era in 1940.

The starting point of cooperative federalism is also variously dated, but 1932 is widely regarded as decisive. Cooperative federalism was championed during the 1930s as a way to expand federal powers without subordinating state powers.[7] Federal policies were to support, backstop, and even amplify state capacities. Key tenets of cooperative federalism are that (1) virtually all public functions are shared, not divided, federal–state–local responsibilities; (2) power is distributed throughout the system in a noncentralized (rather than decentralized) manner, thereby making it nearly impossible to identify a single locus of decision-making power;[8] (3) federalism is not a zero-sum game in which increased federal power necessarily decreases state powers; (4) chaotic noncentralized political parties mediate conflict and facilitate consent throughout the system; (5) intergovernmental bargaining and negotiation produce systemic cooperation and collaboration that minimizes "the amount of coercion exercised" intergovernmentally;[9] (6) federal, state, and local officials are colleagues, not adversaries; and (7) "the American system is best conceived as one government serving one people."[10] Cooperative federalism's leading operational attribute is the federal grant-in-aid system, which showers money on state and local governments (about $449 billion in 2007).

Although the New Deal (1933–1940) and World War II are commonly seen as great centralizing periods, federal programs in those eras hardly disturbed state and local powers, primarily because President Franklin D. Roosevelt (1933–1945) refused to attack the powerful state- and local political-party bosses who provided essential electoral support for his Democratic coalition.[11] The New Deal's major domestic legacy, the Social Security Act of 1935, was a paradigm of cooperative federalism. Also, despite hugely expanded federal regulation of the economy, Congress maintained dual state–federal regulation and taxation of banking, telecommunications, securities, and other industries, countermanded the U.S. Supreme Court by preserving exclusive state regulation of insurance, and interfered little with state and local regulation of small businesses, occupational licensing and such traditional state functions as transportation, education, and criminal justice. The U.S. Treasury transferred money to state and local governments with few conditions, rules and regulations and no effective apparatus to audit expenditures. Moreover, the New Deal did not champion nationalization of the U.S. Bill of Rights under the Fourteenth Amendment and nor did it challenge racial segregation in the then solidly Democratic South.

The New Deal's signature federalism case—*United States v. Darby Lumber Co.* (1941)—sounded the death knell for the Tenth Amendment to the U.S. Constitution by declaring it "a truism," but the ruling had little practical impact on federalism. The federal Fair Labor Standards Act of 1938 (FLSA), upheld in *Darby*, applied to employees of only private firms, not to state and local government employees. Hence, many state and local bosses supported the FLSA because they never imagined that Congress would apply its terms to employees of "sovereign" state and local governments three decades later.[12]

Cooperative federalism did, however, lay foundations for coercive federalism in four fundamental ways. First, local governments, especially those of big cities that were mostly controlled by Democrats, gained a seat at the intergovernmental table as the "third partner" in the federal system. This undercut the legitimacy of the states as the Constitution's authorized partner in cooperative federalism. Cities also received direct federal aid that bypassed their state capitals.

Second, the federal government became the dominant fiscal partner. In 1927, federal spending amounted to only 31 percent of all own-source government expenditures, compared to 52 percent for local governments and 17 percent for the states. The federal share increased to 50 percent by 1940 and to 77 percent in 1958, fluctuating thereafter in the 62–69 percent range (64 percent in 2006).

Third, the New Deal and the Great Society of Democratic President Lyndon B. Johnson (1963–1969) highlighted weaknesses in the ability of state and local governments to solve the problems of an urban-industrial society, cope with national crises, and serve justice. Americans began to view the federal government as the most progressive partner in the system—an engine for social change and personal benefits (notably with the enactment of both Medicare and Medicaid in 1965). The corrupt behavior of many Northern urban bosses and the odious practices of Southern white supremacists discredited states' rights. Voicing the widely held view of the national government and the southern states as, respectively, the champion and enemy of civil rights, scholar William H. Riker commented: "if in the United States one disapproves of racism, one should disapprove of federalism."[13]

Finally, the rise of the New-Deal idea that the federal Constitution is a "living document" that judges and legislators must adapt to modernity, coupled with the view of the federal system as being a single government serving one people under conditions of shared responsibilities, fostered a pragmatic federalism that motivated interest groups and public officials to forum-shop and place policy objectives above constitutional niceties. Constitutional questions, such as which government is authorized to do what, were replaced with political questions, such as which government can do what—a shift that almost always favored national power.

The development of coercive federalism was, in essence, a massive effort to liberate persons from the tyranny of places in the form of state and local jurisdictions, whose discriminatory social and legal practices had long oppressed African Americas, Hispanics, women, gays, and other groups termed "minorities." Despite the federal government's dismal record on race for most of its existence—exemplified by its genocidal policies toward Native Americas and its judicial bias against equality for African Americans—it assumed the mantle of civil-rights champion against reactionary, uncooperative states from the 1950s onward.

If any single event marked the collapse of cooperative federalism, it was the tumultuous Democratic presidential nominating convention in Chicago in August 1968. This prompted a new campaign for reform that drove the traditional state and local bosses out of the nominating system and reoriented the party's representative base from places to persons by mandating rules for proportional representation of blacks, women, young adults, and other minorities, and by emphasizing primary elections to choose party candidates. Republicans were initially more resistant to undertaking comparable party reforms. Consequently, while federalism declined as an issue for Democrats, Republicans still defended states' rights, a position that fitted Richard M. Nixon's strategy of building up the GOP in the South.

The Chicago convention dramatically reflected the confluence of political, social, and cultural forces unleashed in pursuit of personal and political liberation during the late 1950s and early 1960s. The preeminent struggle for the liberation of persons from the tyranny of places was the black civil-rights movement. The federal government had to invade the historic realms of state and local authority to address its demands. The drive for equality by African American groups and other social movements assaulted the legitimacy of the place diversity principle that sustained state and local powers under dual and cooperative federalism. It questioned why such fundamental rights as suffrage or abortion could be denied by some states in violation of national principles of civil and human rights. Interest groups spawned by rights-based social movements also fostered public awareness of many other issues, such as environmental degradation, that crosscut state and local boundaries. More and more public matters were perceived to have negative interstate externalities requiring remedial action by the federal government.

Changes engendered by the rise of new media reinforced the challenge to local diversity. By 1962, there was television in 90 percent of U.S. households—a potent medium for social movements to focus public attention on the federal government. Television also changed political campaigns, reducing the role of local political-party foot soldiers in mobilizing voters and vastly increasing the role of national interest groups able to fund costly television advertising.

The U.S. Supreme Court also played a pivotal role in transforming federalism. It nationalized much of the U.S. Bill of Rights so as to protect individuals' rights against state–local as well as federal infringements. The *Brown v. Board of Education, Topeka* judgments in 1954–1955, which struck down the "separate but equal" doctrine that justified segregation of public schools in many states, marked a new era of judicial activism. Thereafter, the Supreme Court massively expanded federal power not only to protect individuals' rights but also to reform state and local governments. Although judicial activism substantially abated after the *Roe v. Wade* judgment of 1973 overturned state antiabortion laws, the federal courts had achieved unprecedented levels of rights protection and intervention into state and local affairs, from which there has been little retreat, except in criminal rights.

Reinforcing this change, the Supreme Court's "one person, one vote" rulings in 1964[14] shifted representation in both the U.S. House of Representatives and the state legislatures from places to persons. Before 1964, most election districts conformed to county and municipal boundaries, thereby emphasizing the representation of local government jurisdictions rather than of individuals and social groups in legislative bodies. Counties, moreover, were the key power centers of the party system. The full impact of the new apportionment system was felt when Congress became more individualistic and "atomistic" in the early 1970s.[15] Thereafter, members of the House and Senate became more attentive to interest groups representing nationally organized groups of persons and less attentive to hometown, state, and local government officials to whom they were previously bound by the once strong ties of community and party.

The last powerful political machines had collapsed by the mid-1970s. Nothing symbolized this more than the death in 1976 of Richard J. Daley, who had been Chicago mayor since 1955. Northern urban machines caved in as white voters moved to the suburbs, the federal government imposed accountability rules on urban aid, and the courts cleaned up municipal government. In turn, Southern white political machines were decimated by the civil-rights movement, federal legislation and judicial action, and Northern migration into the newly air-conditioned Sunbelt. As a result, Southern defenders of states' rights no longer controlled key committee chairs in Congress, thus opening the procedural floodgates for federal legislation overriding state and local powers.

The machines' demise facilitated the rise of professional state and local bureaucracies and public-employee unions. Control over patronage employees ensured that political bosses faced little opposition to their prerogatives from within the state–local public sector. However, civil-service employees and unions tended to welcome federal intervention, notably regarding extensions of the FLSA to state and local governments in 1968, 1974, and 1985, as a way of challenging boss power. Civil-service employees sometimes solicit federal intervention to compel their state and local employers to provide better job benefits, more funds for their agencies, and more personnel for programs. In some cases, state and local bureaucrats also used the federal courts to extract funds or policy concessions from elected state and local officials.

Reinforcing these decisive factors in the demise of cooperative federalism were the giant federal budget deficits that placed spending retrenchment at the heart of national politics in the 1980s and much of the 1990s. As a consequence, grants-in-aid to states and localities felt the unaccustomed effect of cost-cutting pressures that had not afflicted them in the mid-twentieth-century heyday of cooperative federalism.

Elements of Coercive Federalism

Grants-in-Aid

Federal grants-in-aid have acquired three new characteristics under coercive federalism. First, federal grants have shifted substantially from place functions to person functions. Almost two-thirds (63.5 percent) of federal aid was dedicated for payments to individuals (i.e., social welfare) in 2007. Medicaid (health care for the poor), which accounts for almost 45 percent of all aid, is the leading example and cause of this transformation. By contrast, in 1978—the year that marked the second highest point of federal aid in the nation's history (whether measured as a percentage of state–local spending, federal outlays, or GDP)—68.2 percent of all federal aid was dedicated to state–local place functions, such as economic development, highways, education, criminal justice, environmental protection, and government administration.[16] As a consequence of this shift, place-based aid for infrastructure, economic development, education, and the like has declined sharply, increased aid for social welfare has locked state budgets into programs ripe for escalating federal regulation and matching state costs, and local governments have experienced a steep decline in federal aid.

President Bill Clinton bucked this latter trend in some grant areas, such as the Community Oriented Policing Services program. However, federal funding for policing has dropped precipitously since 2000 and only comprised about 1 percent of local police spending in 2007. Another example of diminished federal aid is the Community Development Block Grant (CDBG), which experienced a 14 percent drop in formula funding in 2005–2006. Although the number of communities receiving CDBG funds directly from the federal government increased from 606 in 1975 to 1,128 in 2006, real per-capita CDBG funding plunged from $48 in 1978 to $13 in 2006.

A second coercive aid-characteristic is the increased use of conditions of aid to achieve federal objectives that lie outside Congress's constitutionally enumerated powers and to extract more state–local spending on federal objectives. For example, Congress attached conditions to federal highway-aid, requiring all states to increase the alcoholic-beverage purchase age to twenty-one and, later, to lower the blood-alcohol level needed for a drunk-driving conviction. Such conditions, often mistakenly called unfunded or underfunded "mandates," are a powerful federal policy tool. The No Child Left Behind Act (NCLB) of 2001 is the states' current *bete noir* because of its costly testing, performance, and accountability requirements.

The third and more recent notable federal-aid change has been the growth in congressional earmarking (i.e., specific state or local pork-barrel projects inserted in bills by members of Congress). According to Citizens Against Government Waste, earmarks in appropriations bills increased from 1,439 in 1995 to 13,997 in 2005 and then dropped to 9,963 in 2006. Their total cost increased from $27.3 billion in 2005 to $29 billion in 2006. In 1987, President Ronald Reagan vetoed a transportation bill because it had 152 earmarks. However, the Surface-Transportation Reauthorization Act of 2005 made it onto the statute books despite containing more than 6,000 earmarks. More than fifty bills, such as the Pork-Barrel Reduction Act, were introduced in Congress from 2005 through 2007 to reform-earmarking, but the only outcome was a widely derided and toothless reform in 2007.

Some members of Congress defend earmarks because they keep spending decisions in the hands of Congress, which possesses the constitutional power of the purse, rather than awarding discretion to the president and federal agencies. Also, earmarks send money directly to state and local governments rather than funneling it through federal agencies. Indeed, state and local officials underwrite the proliferation of earmarks by lobbying for them, perhaps out of necessity. With federal aid for places declining, earmarks are alternate sources of money for bridges, bicycle paths, sewers, parks, museums, and so on.

However, many state officials oppose earmarks. As a Colorado transportation official remarked: "Why do we spend 18 months at public hearings, meetings and planning sessions to put together our statewide plan if Congress is going to earmark projects that displace our priorities?"[17] Occasionally, a state or locality rejects an earmark,[18] but in doing so it risks losing the money rather than being able to reallocate it to its own priorities.

Mandates

Another defining characteristic of coercive federalism is the increased use of mandates, which are legal requirements necessitating state or local officials to perform functions under pain of civil or criminal penalties. Congress enacted one major mandate in 1931, one in 1940, and none at all from 1941 to 1963, but the number rose to nine during the 1964–1969 period, twenty-five in the 1970s, and twenty-seven in the 1980s. The combination of state and local objections and the Contract with America Republican desire to limit federal government resulted in enactment of the Unfunded Mandates Reform Act (UMRA) of 1995. This measure constitutes one of the few restraints on coercive federalism. UMRA cut mandate enactments but did not eliminate existing mandates. Only seven intergovernmental mandates bearing costs above UMRA's threshold have been enacted since 1995.

The most recent of these was a 2006 tax law requiring any state or local government that spends more than $100 million annually on employees, goods, and services to withhold for federal taxes 3 percent of any payments to a private for-profit vendor that provides it with goods or services and to pass that money onto the federal government. The law, which takes effect in 2011, was opposed by state and local officials. Pursuant to the U.S. Supreme Court's ruling in *Printz v. United States* (1997), however, the measure might be vulnerable to challenge as an unconstitutional commandeering of state and local governments.

In the wake of UMRA, Congress appears to be shifting from de jure to de facto mandates. A prime example is the REAL ID Act of 2005, which states complain is underfunded and could cost them $13 billion to produce compliant driver's licenses. States were to comply with the measure by May 2008. Although they can opt out of its rules, their residents' licenses will then not be accepted for any federal-government purpose, including boarding an airplane, riding Amtrak trains, purchasing a firearm, opening a bank account, applying for federal benefits, and entering a federal building. In May 2006, the National Governors' Association (NGA), National Conference of State Legislatures (NCSL), and American Association of Motor Vehicle Administrators declared that the states need more federal money and another eight years to implement REAL ID.

Many state and local officials lobbied Congress in 2006 to include conditions of aid in UMRA's definition of unfunded mandates. By one estimate, federal programs cost state and local governments some $51 billion in 2004 and 2005.[19] However, Congress is unlikely to add aid conditions to UMRA in the foreseeable future. State and local governments have greater hopes of convincing it to increase funding, though not fully, for such costly programs as NCLB and REAL ID.

Preemption

Federal preemption of state laws under the U.S. Constitution's supremacy clause is another salient characteristic of coercive federalism. From 1970 to 2004, Congress enacted some 320 explicit preemptions compared to about 200 preemptions enacted from 1789 to 1969.[20] In other words, 62 percent of all explicit preemptions in U.S. history have been enacted since 1970.

U.S. Representative Henry Waxman (D-CA) reported in June 2006 that Congress had voted at least fifty-seven times to preempt state laws over the previous five years. These votes yielded twenty-seven preemption bills, all of them signed by President George W. Bush.

For state officials, an egregious 2006 preemption was the John Warner National Defense Authorization Act, which allows the president to federalize any state's National Guard without the consent of the governor

> when, as a result of a natural disaster, epidemic, or other serious public health emergency, terrorist attack or incident, or other condition in any State or

possession of the United States, the President determines that—(i) domestic violence has occurred to such an extent that the constituted authorities of the State or possession are incapable of maintaining public order; and (ii) such violence results in a condition that—(A) so hinders the execution of the laws of a State or possession…and of the United States within that State or possession, that any part or class of its people is deprived of a right, privilege, immunity, or protection named in the Constitution and secured by law.[21]

The president also can act when, in his view, state authorities are "unable, fail, or refuse to protect" federal constitutional rights. This measure, opposed by all fifty governors, was hastened along by the relief disaster that followed Hurricane Katrina in 2005. The legislation constitutes an unprecedented expansion of presidential power over state militia powers.

It also became evident in 2006 that President Bush will use executive rule-making to advance preemption when Congress drags its feet. For example, the Food and Drug Administration (FDA) issued a prescription-drug labeling regulation saying that FDA approval of manufacturers' labels "preempts conflicting or contrary state law." The rule's preamble preempts state liability laws. Manufacturers who comply with the federal standard cannot be sued in state courts by persons injured by their products. Many Democrats accused the FDA of abusing its power. The NCSL accused the FDA of inadequate consultation in formulating the rule. Other critics noted that the lawsuit-immunization provision was cleverly placed in the preamble, which is not usually subject to public comment. The federal courts will have to sort out this preemption issue. In the meantime, however, some state courts might hold that they are not bound by the FDA's rule unless Congress explicitly affirms the preemption.

Many state attorneys general and other critics argue that such preemptions disadvantage consumers to the benefit of corporations. A spokesman for the president's Office of Management and Budget replied: "State courts and juries often lack the information, expertise and staff that the federal agencies rely upon in performing their scientific, risk-based calculations .... having a single federal standard can be the best way to guarantee safety and protect consumers."[22]

The Supreme Court frequently upholds preemptions. Indeed, the so-called "Federalism Five" group of justices on the Rehnquist Court (Anthony Kennedy, Sandra Day O'Connor, William H. Rehnquist, Antonin Scalia, and Clarence Thomas) voted for federal preemptions of state laws much more often than did their liberal colleagues.

Intergovernmental Tax Immunities

Another characteristic of coercive federalism has been federal constraints on state and local taxation and borrowing, beginning especially with federal limits placed on tax-exempt private-activity bonds in 1984 and elimination of the deduction for state–local sales taxes from federal personal income-tax liabilities in 1986. Federal statutory and judicial prohibitions of state taxation of Internet services and mail-order sales are among the most prominent current constraints. In November 2004, Congress extended its Internet-access tax ban (i.e., the Internet Tax Non-Discrimination Act) to November 2007.

In response to the federal prohibition of state taxation of interstate mail-order sales, a Streamlined Sales and Use Tax Agreement to try to collect sales taxes on interstate mail-order sales has been implemented voluntarily by twenty-three states to date. Although several large retailers comply with the agreement, Congress has not approved it and has not authorized states to require sales-tax collections by out-of-state vendors. Obtaining congressional recognition of the agreement, even with a Democratic majority, will be difficult.

In 2005, the President's Advisory Panel on Federal Tax Reform recommended eliminating deductions for all state and local taxes. Most state and local officials support these deductions. This issue has a partisan dimension because the average state–local tax payment in blue (Democratic) states was $7,487 in 2005 compared to $4,834 in red (Republican) states. State–local tax deductions equaled 5.9 percent of average income in the blue states and 3.7 percent in the red states.[23] Because income taxes in most states are coupled to the federal tax code, changes in federal tax laws, especially tax cuts and retroactive changes, can reduce state tax-revenues.

Federalization of Criminal Law

Another feature of coercive federalism is the federalization of criminal law. There are currently some 3,500 federal criminal offenses, more than half of them enacted since the mid-1960s. These laws cover a wide range of behavior from terrorism to carjacking, disrupting a rodeo, impersonating a 4-H Club member, and carrying unlicensed dentures across state lines. Generally, federal criminal laws are tougher than comparable state laws, including some fifty federal laws entailing capital punishment. This trend raises troublesome civil-rights issues, in part because defendants can be whipsawed between state and federal prosecutors. A person arrested for violating a state drug-law that carries a short prison sentence might be turned over to a U.S. attorney to be tried under the comparable federal drug-law that requires a longer prison sentence.

Another aspect of this federalization of criminal law has been an effort by the Bush administration to enforce federal death-penalty statutes more vigorously, even in states that prohibit capital punishment. In 2006, for example, a federally empanelled jury in North Dakota imposed execution on a murderer. This was the first death sentence since 1914 in a state that does not have the death penalty.

Demise of Intergovernmental Institutions

Coercive federalism has also been marked by the demise of executive and congressional intergovernmental institutions established during the era of cooperative federalism. Most notable was the termination of the U.S. Advisory Commission on Intergovernmental Relations (ACIR) in 1996 after thirty-seven years of operation. Congress no longer has important committees devoted to federalism and intergovernmental relations, and federal departments either have no intergovernmental office or have a highly political one.

Decline of Political Cooperation

Federal–state cooperation also has declined in major intergovernmental programs such as Medicaid and surface transportation. Congress earmarks monies and alters programs more in response to national and regional interest groups than to elected state and local officials. A coalition led by Americans for Tax Reform (ATR) has even petitioned Congress to terminate the exemption from federal lobbying rules currently accorded state and local government lobbyists. The ATR also wants to defund the state-funded National Governors Association, which it labels "another liberal lobbying group."[24]

Presidential depletion of National Guard personnel and equipment for the Iraq war also reflects diminished cooperation. All fifty governors petitioned the president and the Pentagon for enhanced resources for the National Guard and for replacements of equipment left in Iraq. About one-third of the ground troops in Iraq belong to the Army National Guard.

Federal Court Orders

Under coercive federalism, there has been unprecedented numbers of federal court orders requiring state and local governments to undertake, at their own expense, often extraordinarily costly and long-term policy actions. Court orders to desegregate public schools were the paradigmatic models for later orders governing a wide range of state and local functions. With the appointment of so many Republican judges to the federal courts under Presidents Reagan, George H. W. Bush, and George W. Bush, the pace and scope of orders abated considerably. However, a multitude of consent decrees, some issued decades ago, continue to govern state and local officials and budget resources in many policy fields. Citizen litigation against state and local governments in federal courts under federal laws marks another unprecedented characteristic of coercive federalism.

The U.S. Supreme Court's Federalism-Lite

From 1991 until 2002, the Supreme Court seemed to foster a federalism revolution by restricting the reach of Congress under the U.S. Constitution's commerce clause, reviving state sovereign immunity under the Eleventh Amendment, and protecting state powers in a number of other ways. These state-friendly rulings, which generated a storm of controversy, were invariably very close 5–4 decisions that reflected the Court's own divisions on the issue. Since 2002, however, the Court has reversed course to make federalism, in the words of Justice Ruth Bader Ginsburg, "the dog that [doesn't] bark."[25] This was reflected in two Eleventh-Amendment sovereign-immunity cases in 2006, which held that states are not immune from suits brought under the Americans With Disabilities Act by disabled prisoners and from private lawsuits brought under federal bankruptcy law. The Court also ruled unanimously that the Eleventh Amendment does not protect local governments.[26] Consequently, the Supreme Court, which had nurtured the rise of coercive federalism during a liberal phase of its history, has not reversed course in any significant way since entering a more conservative phase.

Intergovernmental Administrative Cooperation

Leaving behind political and judicial policymaking to enter the realm of administration, one finds fairly consistent patterns of intergovernmental cooperation, notwithstanding the catastrophe of Hurricane Katrina in 2005. Indeed, the failure of intergovernmental coordination in response to this disaster sparked almost universal condemnation because it represented a shocking violation of long-standing federalism norms.

Even so, a majority of Americans responded positively to the following question asked about President Bush in a February 2007 national poll: "Considering President George W. Bush's response to New York City after 9/11 in 2001, his response to New Orleans after Hurricane Katrina in 2005, and his support for the No Child Left Behind education law, overall, would you say that President Bush's policies for our state and local governments have been very helpful, somewhat helpful, not very helpful, or not at all helpful?"[27] Of those polled, 51.7 percent termed Bush's actions very helpful or somewhat helpful to state and local governments and 48.3 percent labeled his policies not very helpful or not at all helpful. The sharp divide among respondents along lines of party identification testified to Bush's polarization of partisan opinion: 70.5 percent of Democrats adjudged his intergovernmental actions not very helpful or not helpful at all, but 81.2 percent of Republicans deemed them very helpful or somewhat helpful.

Administrative cooperation has deep roots, dating back especially to ideas of intergovernmental cooperation articulated by Albert Gallatin in the early nineteenth century.[28] Such cooperation was, as Daniel J. Elazar contended, prevalent during the nineteenth-century era of so-called dual federalism.[29] Cooperation accelerated tremendously during the twentieth-century era of cooperative federalism. Its strongly institutionalized roots ensured that coercive federalism could not kill it off. Indeed, implementation of many of the policies imposed on state and local governments requires intergovernmental cooperation for success. This state–local cooperation with federal coercion may seem paradoxical, but it endures because other forces sustain it.

For one, the carrots-and-sticks of federal aid play important roles in ensuring cooperation. Federal aid accounts for about one-quarter of state–local budgets. All fifty states, for example, complied with the federal drinking-age condition attached to surface-transportation aid because no state could afford to lose the funds and there is no apparent mechanism for the states to withhold the federal gas tax collected within their borders. Second, many federal statutes associated with coercive federalism contain penalties, including civil or criminal ones in some cases, aimed at uncooperative state and local officials.

The courts also have an important role in intergovernmental relations. Following the period of massive resistance by Southern state and local governments to the federal courts in the 1950s and 1960s, state and local officials became generally more cooperative with judicial decisions, which were seen as central to the rule of law. Since the federal courts have proved their capacity to compel compliance, state and local officials have incentives to cooperate with federal officials. In turn, federal officials, in seeking to foster compliance, ordinarily negotiate and bargain with state and local officials before seeking judicial intervention.

Additionally, the U.S. federal system is not one of executive federalism (as exists, for example, in Germany) whereby states are constitutionally obligated to execute federal framework-legislation. The federal government is expected, for the most part, to carry out its own policies or pay the states to do so. Given its very limited administrative capabilities, the federal government must seek the assistance of state and local officials. Federal administrators, therefore, usually have incentives to work cooperatively with their state and local counterparts. Furthermore, the federal government does not, per se, share revenue with the states or engage in fiscal equalization, so it does not need the administrative control and co-decision mechanisms usually required for such policies. Instead, it operates a sprawling grant-in-aid system consisting of about 608 categorical grant programs and seventeen block grants. Given that most federal-aid money flows through categorical grants, the federal government exercises control through the purposes for which the grants are established, but otherwise works cooperatively on the administration of those grants and usually allows state and local officials discretion in their implementation as long as each grant's purposes are realized, at least approximately. Block grants afford state and local officials even more discretion, although these have never accounted for more than about 18 percent of all federal aid.

Since the fall of massive resistance to desegregation in the South, no cultural, ethnic, religious, or linguistic group anywhere in the United States has had a strong incentive to thwart or distort intergovernmental administrative relations. Similarly, partisanship does not play a major role in intergovernmental administration. A predominantly Democratic state, for example, is not necessarily uncooperative, or less cooperative than a predominantly Republican state, with policies emanating from a Republican Congress and/or White House. In the political arena, there may be vigorous partisan conflict over such huge intergovernmental grant programs as Medicaid and surface transportation and over costly mandates such as environmental regulations, but once federal policies on these matters are enacted into law, there are strong incentives for the bureaucrats to cooperate across party lines so as to administer the programs as effectively and efficiently as possible.

Due to similar civil-service rules and shared professional norms, most federal, state, and local administrators dull the sharp edges of partisanship so as to focus on cooperative task execution under existing rules and budgets. In addition, federal, state, and local administrators within policy fields often share the same education and training pedigrees and interact with each other in the same national and regional professional associations, which are usually more important to them than party affiliations. Federal, state, and local law-enforcement officials, for example, share common training and professional backgrounds as well as a general professional camaraderie that facilitate interagency cooperation.

Additionally, state and local administrators are often advocates of tougher policy and higher spending in their policy field and, thus, often welcome federal intervention. State and local environmental officials, for example, are likely to welcome federal rules that set stricter environmental standards and require more state and local spending on environmental protection. Indeed, it is not uncommon for state and local bureaucrats to lobby for federal policies that are opposed by state and local elected officials who can be punished at the ballot box for implementing unpopular federal policies or raising taxes in order to pay for state or local implementation of those policies.

Interest groups also have a part to play in fostering intergovernmental cooperation in the era of coercive federalism. After achieving a federal policy objective, they pressure state and local governments to cooperate in implementing that objective. This has been a major factor in the growth of interest-group activity within the states since the late 1960s.

Finally, a process of socialization has underpinned administrative cooperation across different levels of government. The dominance of the federal government in so many policy fields in the era of coercive federalism has become an unquestioned fact of administrative life. Furthermore, many of today's senior federal, state, and local administrators entered public service in the late 1960s and early 1970s with a common passion for reform. For rank-and-file administrators, the origins of what their work dictates are less important to them than their preoccupation with how to implement those dictates and satisfy the citizens who will ultimately vote for or against the elected officials who preside only in a general and distant way over policy implementation.

State Policy Activism

A seemingly contrary development under coercive federalism has been state policy activism, especially since the early 1980s. However, this activism has been both a response to coercive federalism, as states have bucked some federal policies and filled federal policy voids, and a stimulant of coercive federalism, as interest groups have sought federal tranquilization of hyperactive state policymaking. This activism is the third face of contemporary American federalism—a face that reflects the persistence of dual federalism wherein states still have many constitutionally reserved powers that can be exercised independently of the federal government.

This activism is often attributed to the reform and resurgence of state governments during the 1950s and 1960s. Although reforms strengthened state capabilities, state activism switched into high gear in reaction to the rise of coercive federalism under which both conservatives and liberals have found many reasons to seek refuge in state policymaking when they cannot achieve their objectives through federal policymaking.

This face of federalism is featured prominently in the so-called culture wars, frequently producing strange political bedfellows and partisan flip-flops. Given Republican control of the presidency for all but twelve years between 1969 and 2009, liberal Democrats—the traditional champions of federal power—have increasingly become guardians of states' rights. Among other causes, they have protected assisted suicide, gay marriage, medicinal marijuana, and a range of state consumer-protection, environmental, labor, and tort laws against federal preemption. In an essay that appeared in *The Nation*, a venerable left-wing magazine, one analyst argued that liberals would do better to pursue their policy goals through the states, which had produced a significant output of progressive legislation in the recent era of conservative domination of national politics.[30] In turn, many conservatives who were traditionally hostile to federal power now champion it. In particular, social conservatives have sought to overturn liberal state policies friendly to abortion, assisted suicide, gay rights, marijuana, stem-cell research, and the like. Economic conservatives correspondingly seek federal preemption of state economic regulation, with big business preferring to be regulated by a single 500-pound gorilla in Washington, DC, than by fifty monkeys on steroids.

Yet social conservatives also turn to the states when thwarted in the federal arena. Appalled by U.S. Supreme Court rulings on abortion and sodomy, moral conservatives have sought to reverse such judicial policymaking through state regulation. Pro-life activists, for example, press for state laws to add requirements to abortions (for example, a 24-hour waiting period and parental notification), to prohibit state funding of abortions, and to criminalize injury to a fetus. According to the American Life League, "You can do a lot more in the [state] legislatures than on the federal level right now."[31]

Meanwhile, liberal activists responding to conservative Supreme Court rulings and to deregulation since the Reagan years also have stimulated state-policy activism. For example, several multistate lawsuits have been initiated against the U.S. Environmental Protection Agency for its lax enforcement or lack of enforcement of federal environmental standards. State officials have pursued litigation and regulation in many policy areas, especially environmental and consumer protection. Connecticut's attorney general, Richard Blumenthal, offered a straightforward justification for such activism: "Our action is the result of federal inaction."[32] Also, in an effort to compete with the conservative American Legislative Exchange Council (ALEC), several hundred state legislators launched the Progressive Legislative Action Network (PLAN) in 2005. According to the policy director of the liberal Center for Policy Alternatives, "states are now the vanguard of the progressive movement."[33]

State action on environmental protection garnered considerable attention in 2006, especially when California's governor, Arnold Schwarzenegger, joined Prime Minister Tony Blair of the United Kingdom to sign an accord on global warming in August 2006. In September, Schwarzenegger signed a bill to reduce California's greenhouse gas emissions by 25 percent by 2020. In 2004, California implemented rules on vehicular greenhouse gases that are stricter than the federal standards. Ten other states have adopted California's rules, which limit the amounts of carbon dioxide and other gases expelled by automobiles. In addition, California, New York, and eight other states sued the U.S. Environmental Protection Agency for failing to regulate carbon dioxide emissions from power plants. Some twenty-three states have set standards requiring utilities to generate up to 33 percent of their energy from renewable sources by 2020.

Conclusion

Near-term changes in policy will be instituted by new congressional and presidential regimes in Washington, DC, but the long-term trends in federalism will remain largely on course regardless of partisan and personnel changes in control of national government. Coercive federalism has been a bipartisan phenomenon and there is no sign of significant realignment in the forces that have propelled its development. Cooperation is likely to endure in intergovernmental administration unless a new generation of administrators infects it with the same partisan and ideological polarization found in the national political arena. State activism will ebb and flow, receding when liberal Democrats control the federal government and surging when conservative Republicans control the federal government. Dual federalism is the constitutional basis for this activism, but socioeconomic realities are its lifeblood because most U.S. states have more wealth, more people, and bigger governments than most of the world's nation-states. California, for example, has the world's seventh largest GDP and a population larger than that of 84 percent of the world's nation-states (including Canada). It will cooperate with federal coercion because the United States is much bigger than California, but it will not fade into quiescence.

Notes

1. James Bryce, *The American Commonwealth* (New York: Macmillan, 1907), 353.
2. *New State Ice Company v. Liebmann*, 285 U.S. 262 (1932).

  3. Edward S. Corwin, *National Supremacy* (New York: Henry Holt and Co., 1913).
  4. Edward S. Corwin, "A Constitution of Powers and Modern Federalism," in *Essays in Constitutional Law*, ed. Robert G. McCloskey (New York: Knopf, 1962), 188–189.
  5. Daniel J. Elazar, *The American Partnership: Intergovernmental Co-operation in the Nineteenth-Century United States* (Chicago: University of Chicago Press, 1962) and Morton Grodzins, *The American System: A New View of Government in the United States*, ed. Daniel J. Elazar (Chicago: Rand McNally, 1966).
  6. Grodzins, *The American System*, 8.
  7. For example, Jane Perry Clark, *The Rise of a New Federalism: Federal-State Cooperation in the United States* (New York: Columbia University Press, 1938).
  8. Grodzins, *The American System*, 11.
  9. Daniel J. Elazar, "Cooperative Federalism," in *Competition among States and Local Governments: Efficiency and Equity in American Federalism*, ed. Daphne A. Kenyon and John Kincaid (Washington, DC: Urban Institute Press, 1991), 73.
 10. Morton Grodzins, "Centralization and Decentralization in the American Federal System," in *A Nation of States*, ed. Robert A. Goldwin, 2nd ed. (Chicago: Rand McNally, 1974), 24.
 11. John Kincaid, "Frank Hague and Franklin Roosevelt: The Hudson Dictator and the Country Democrat," in *Franklin D. Roosevelt: The Man, The Myth, The Era*, ed. Herbert D. Rosenbaum and Elizabeth Bartelme (Westport, CT: Greenwood, 1987), 13–39.
 12. John Kincaid, "Constitutional Federalism: Labor's Role in Displacing Places to Benefit Persons," *PS: Political Science & Politics* 26 (June 1993): 172–177.
 13. William H. Riker, *Federalism: Origin, Operation, Significance* (Boston: Little, Brown, 1964), 155.
 14. *Wesberry v. Sanders*, 376 U.S. 1 (1964) and *Reynolds* v. *Sims*, 377 U.S. 533 (1964).
 15. Allen D. Hertzke and Ronald M. Peters, eds. *The Atomistic Congress: An Interpretation of Congressional Change* (Armonk, NY: M. E. Sharpe, 1992).
 16. John Kincaid, "The State of U.S. Federalism, 2000–2001," *Publius: The Journal of Federalism* 31 (Summer 2001): 1–69.
 17. Quoted in Brody Mullins, "As Earmarked Funding Swells, Some Recipients Don't Want It," *Wall Street Journal*, December 26, 2006, A10.
 18. David Kirkpatrick, "A Congressman's $10 Million Gift for Road is Rebuffed," *New York Times*, August 18, 2007, A7.
 19. William Wyatt, "Washington Watch: 10 Top Issues for States," *State Legislatures* 32 (January 2006): 15.
 20. National Academy of Public Administration, *Beyond Preemption: Intergovernmental Partnerships to Enhance the New Economy* (Washington, DC: National Academy of Public Administration, 2006).
 21. P.L. 109–364, Sec. 1076.
 22. Stephen Labaton, " 'Silent Tort Reform' Is Overriding States' Powers," *New York Times*, March 10, 2006, C5.
 23. John Maggs, "Limping Toward Tax Reform," *National Journal* 37 (October 22, 2005): 3280.

24. Peter J. Ferrara, "The NGA Should Pay Its Own Way," *Policy Brief* (Washington, DC: Americans for Tax Reform, 2005).

25. CNN, "Justice Ginsburg: Supreme Court Faces Stormy Times," June 12, 2003, www.cnn.com/2003/LAW/06/12/ginsburg.aclu.ap/.

26. *Northern Insurance Company New York v. Chatham County*, 126 S.Ct. 1689 (2006).

27. John Kincaid and Richard L. Cole, "Public Opinion on Issues of Federalism in 2007: A Bush Plus?" *Publius: The Journal of Federalism* 38 (2008): forthcoming.

28. Rozann Rothman, "Political Method In The Federal System: Albert Gallatin's Contribution," *Publius: The Journal of Federalism* 1 (Winter 1972): 123–141.

29. Elazar, *The American Partnership*.

30. Katrina vanden Huevel, "Taking It to the States," *The Nation*, January 20, 2005, http://www.thenation.com/blogs/edcut?bid=7&pid=2137 (accessed February 1, 2006).

31. Associated Press, "Activists Push for Limits on Abortion through Legislation at State Level," *Express-Times* (Easton), March 12, 2003, A-5.

32. Brooke A. Masters, 2005. "Who's Watching Out for the Consumer?" *Washington Post National Weekly Edition*, January 17, 2005, 30.

33. Quoted in Dennis Cauchon, "Fed-up states defy Washington," *USA Today*, December 8, 2003, www.usatoday.com/news/washington/2003–12-08-states-usat_x.htm.

Chapter 5

Fragmented Structures and Blurred Boundaries: Strategies for Regional Governance

Carl W. Stenberg

Among the enduring topics of debate among reformers, public officials, and civic groups have been the fragmented structure of local government and blurred boundaries in relationships among local units as well as between localities and their state government. Critics have pointed to the excessive number of small jurisdictions performing a limited range of duties, costly duplication of functional responsibilities, parochial nature of interlocal relationships, and time and expertise limitations of part-time elected officials. Because of small size and antiquated governing and administrative structures, many communities are unable to tackle complex and costly problems that spill across local boundary lines and require timely collective remedial actions. As a result, tensions have grown between special and general-purpose units, and disparities have widened between rich and poor jurisdictions

Supporters have argued the need for local accessibility, autonomy, and control, and for placing democratic values above technocratic efficiency and effectiveness. While local structure may not meet ideal standards, in most places it works satisfactorily in delivering services demanded by the public at "prices" (i.e., taxes and fees) citizens are willing to pay. Part-time elected officials, rather than professional politicians, are appropriate leaders of "grassroots" governments because they are close to both the problems and the public.

The real truth lies somewhere between the extremes. The case has usually been made for incremental improvement and fine-tuning of local structure and relationships rather than replacement or overhaul, especially given the strong political and public support for maintenance of the status quo in many communities. Nevertheless, bolder reforms have been proposed and adopted.

This chapter presents an overview of contemporary local structure and relationships in the United States.[1] It provides intergovernmental perspectives, both horizontal and vertical, on the challenges and opportunities local officials can expect to confront, and gives examples of strategies for regional governance.[2]

Local Structure Under Stress

For those who believe that governments are resistant to change, consider local structure an exception. According to the Census of Government, there was a net decline of 29,231 local units, from 116,756 in 1952 to 87,525 in 2002. This decrease was largely due to a dramatic reduction of school districts that was partially offset by creation of new special districts. The number of school districts declined by 80 percent over this period, as a result of consolidation of rural and some suburban districts driven by rising personnel and administrative costs, transportation improvements, and concerns about disparities in per pupil expenditures. Ninety percent of remaining school districts are still fiscally and administratively independent of general-purpose local units, a state of affairs that contributes to structural and administrative fragmentation. Meanwhile, the number of nonschool special districts—90 percent of which provided a single function in a single jurisdiction or part of it—grew by 156 percent between 1952 and 2002.

The number of local government units varies widely across the United States—from Illinois and Pennsylvania, which in 2002 had the most total units, at 6,903 and 5,031 respectively, to Rhode Island and Alaska, with 118 and 175 respectively, to Hawaii, with only 19 units. Among general-purpose units, the major change since 1952 was the creation of 2,622 new municipalities, reflecting continuing suburbanization of the nation.[3]

The Dynamics of Change

While local structures became more fragmented, the problems local officials confronted and needs that their citizens expected to be addressed increasingly spread across boundary lines. It has become difficult to identify local problems over which counties, cities, or other general-purpose units exercise control without significant policy, financial, or regulatory involvement of neighboring jurisdictions or state or federal authorities. Even traditional local functions—such as police and fire protection, libraries, and streets— have become "intergovernmentalized" since the 1960s. Others, such as schools, while remaining legally separate from municipalities and counties in most places, have been recipients of increased state and federal grants accompanied by standards and requirements attached as conditions of aid.

In many metropolitan areas, responding to two critical concerns, sprawl and disparities, has stressed local structure and generated controversy and conflict.

Sprawl. Since post–World War II, government mortgage interest subsidies, low-cost land, and highway transportation improvements have helped spur suburban development. The outer suburbs of most metropolitan areas in the

United States experienced significant population and job growth as the middle class and many businesses sought the amenities offered by suburban lifestyles. The costs of disorderly development are traffic congestion, poor land use, and environmental problems in the suburbs, and concentrations of the poor, homeless, and racial minorities, infrastructure deterioration, and decline in public service in many central cities. The public's unwillingness to further tolerate these trends has been exhibited by support for "smart growth," planning for orderly and sustainable development, preservation of open space and historic communities, and environmental conservation. From architectural control to zoning, local government structure, powers, and relationships are critical to realization of these goals.

Disparities. Social, economic, and service disparities in metropolitan areas and between metropolitan and nonmetropolitan areas have widened. The scenario is well-known: "inelastic" boundaries produced by state restrictions on municipal annexation circumscribe central cities, preventing them from tapping new tax bases in outlying areas; permissive incorporation provisions foster creation of new suburban units; out-migration erodes the central city tax base; middle-income families and individuals of all ethnic groups move to suburbia leaving behind a disproportionate share of poor and minority residents in the city; and businesses locate and relocate in suburban malls rather* than in the central business district. While controls in urban growth, suburban traffic congestion, and "gentrification" are important counterpressures, the general pattern described above persists in the central cities and older inner-ring suburbs of many metropolitan areas.

The stakes in overcoming sprawl and disparities are high. Research by David Rusk has demonstrated a linkage between jurisdictional boundary "elasticity" and reduction of segregation by race and wealth in metropolitan areas. Other studies have found an economic connection between the health of the central city and that of the region. In terms of employment, for example, worsening job creation and retention in the central city are reflected in a worsening condition in the region. Similar connections have been found with respect to population and income.[4]

The State's Key Role

The capacity of local governments to overcome fragmented structure and deal with problems and needs that ignore their boundaries and stress their structures through interlocal cooperation and regional governance arrangements is determined by state constitutional or statutory provisions. Local officials have advocated removal of state restrictions and empowerment of their jurisdictions as a fundamental first step toward working across boundaries.

The "Dillon's Rule" interpretation that local governments are "creatures" of their states has made empowerment a slow and uncertain process.[5] A 1981 Advisory Commission on Intergovernmental Relations report, authored by Joseph F. Zimmerman, found wide state-to-state variations in the extent to which constitutions and legislatures had granted discretionary authority to various types of general-purpose local governments. In general, states had been willing to give local government greater authority over their functional responsibilities, form of government, and personnel policies, than over their finances. Another general finding was that legislatures had been less willing to grant home rule to counties than to cities, mainly because county governments have traditionally operated as administrative arms of their state.[6]

A 1997 compilation of constitutional actions, statutes, court decisions, and attorney generals' opinions on home rule by T.D. Mead reported that forty-five states had granted one of two forms of discretionary authority: (a) "Imperium in Imperio," practiced in nineteen states, where the constitution grants cities and certain other general-purpose local units exclusive authority to act in areas of "local concern" defined in their home rule charter or in statute, typically structure, property, and local affairs; and (b) constitutional or legislative home rule, practiced in twenty-six states, where both general and specific powers are designated, which may be changed from time to time. In several states, constitutional home rule provisions are self-executing, while in others implementing-statutes are needed.[7]

The Zimmerman index remains the definitive reading of local discretionary authority. In 2001 a major state-by-state examination of home rule by Dale Krane, Platon Rigos, Melvin Hill, and a national network of scholars updated and refined state constitutional and statutory activity on the local government front.[8]

Trends in Discretionary Authority

Three trends are revealed in the literature regarding local discretionary authority. Basically, even where local governments have been granted greater home rule powers, local officials have experienced formidable constraints in exercising them.

Home Rule Charters

Actual practice with local home rule has been quite different from constitutional or statutory provisions. Zimmerman found that even where local governments had received wide grants of discretionary authority, subsequent interpretations by judges, attorneys general, bond counsels, and others often had circumscribed the execution of these powers. The separation of powers or "layer cake" approach embodied in "Imperium in Imperio" home rule had proven frustrating to local officials as, given the increasingly complex and regional nature of functions and blurring of the distinction between matters of local as opposed to state concern, judges had tended to resolve disputes between state and local authorities over their interpretation of "local concern" in favor of the state.[9] Contributors to the Krane, Rigos, and Hill handbook expressed similar views that experience with home rule authority had been disappointing and more myth than reality.

Local Collaborative Mechanisms

Local governments have used collaborative mechanisms to overcome limitations on home rule. They have employed traditional instruments, such as interlocal contracts and joint powers agreements, and created special districts. Privatization also has become popular, through contracting with the for-profit and nonprofit sectors for performance of local functions. A variety of fiscal instruments also have been adopted by local officials (e.g., tax increment financing, tax exemptions, revenue bonds, and leasing) to circumvent state restrictions on home rule.

Other State Constraints

State constitutions and legislatures have imposed other constraints on how local governments may conduct their business or on their finances, separate from provisions relating to exercise of discretionary authority. These include public referenda, open meeting and records, codes of ethics, and financial disclosure requirements. In addition, states have attached conditions to grants-in-aid or imposed unfunded mandates on local governments. Even in program areas where the federal government has decentralized authority or reduced regulatory burdens, states have been reluctant to pass along increased flexibility to local governments. In some cases, these actions have been taken to correct mismanagement or prevent abuses of discretionary authority. In others, state "carrots-and-sticks" have been used to accelerate regional collaboration and decision-making.[10]

From Competition to Collaboration

To deal with these realities, practitioners and scholars have advocated less intergovernmental competition and more collaboration. Traditionally, remedial actions to overcome structural constraints have been called "functional" or "pragmatic" regionalism.[11] They have been guided explicitly or implicitly by at least five key values associated with the public sector—efficiency, effectiveness, equity, accountability, and responsiveness. Not only are these values weighted differently depending on the nature of the activity, they may well compete with one another. Studies have shown that as responsibility for performance of a function moves from the local government to the regional level, prospects for achieving administrative effectiveness and equity are enhanced. Economies of scale also may be achieved for some functions to a threshold level when diseconomies occur. However, as the locus of decision-making moves to a more distant unit, accountability and responsiveness may be diminished.[12]

Structural responses have been influenced by three schools of thought: "consolidationists;" "choice" advocates; and "collaborationists."[13]

- *Consolidationists* argue the virtues of structural simplicity achieved by consolidation of all general-purpose units under a single county or metropolitan government. Voters usually have not been persuaded by their arguments. Only thirty-two proposals to create metropolitan government through city–county consolidation have been approved, with Louisville-Jefferson County, Kentucky, the most recent case in 2000. Even successful mergers have excluded some general-purpose jurisdictions and school districts. In other consolidations, such as Nashville–Davidson County, Tennessee, population growth has overrun the boundaries of the original merged area to make the older "metro" the core of a multicounty metropolitan area.

- *Choice* advocates take the opposite position—that local structure should be unaltered, or if changed, it must be to encourage market competition in order to present multiple jurisdictional choices to citizens who will "vote with their feet" in search of services they desire at tax and fee rates they are willing to pay. For example, experience with interdistrict school choice plans in Minnesota and other states demonstrate the values of giving parents options beyond the neighborhood public school and of putting pressure on schools from which students are being transferred to improve their performance. Choice advocates urge private-sector alternatives as well, like charter schools and voucher programs.

- *Collaborationists* support approaches to service delivery focused on neighborhood, citywide, county-based, and multicounty arrangements. They advocate "new regionalism" and emphasize the virtues of a multifaceted response to interjurisdictional needs drawing on the authority of governmental units as well as resources of the nonprofit and for-profit sectors. Governance arrangements offer practical advantages like cost-savings and greater effectiveness, as opposed to relying exclusively on governmental alternatives, and successful regional collaboration enhances regional economic competitiveness. Like the choice and collaborationist schemes, contracts and service agreements play important roles in implementation, and it is assumed that local governments possess sufficient discretionary authority to carry out their responsibilities.[14]

Institutional Responses

The major institutional responses to boundary-crossing problems have been threefold: the reorganized and empowered county; special districts and public authorities; and area-wide planning and coordinating bodies. These have been implemented with varying degrees of success, and usually in tandem with the traditional "arsenal" of legal or procedural mechanisms that states have granted cities and counties to enable them to address cross-jurisdictional matters. These include formal and informal joint powers, agreements, contracts, negotiated boundary adjustments, extraterritorial powers, annexation, and interlocal functional transfers.[15]

County Governments

County governments are readily available responses to address problems or needs that are of an area-wide nature. The county structure is in place in all but two states (Connecticut and Rhode Island) and can provide the geographic scope requisite to achieving scale economies. The chief limitation is the traditional role counties have played as arms of state government responsible for performing a limited range of functions—law enforcement, tax assessment and collection, road maintenance, and elections—in unincorporated areas. The governing body of many counties—part-time commissioners or supervisors who in some jurisdictions still head departments—also could be an impediment. In some metropolitan areas, boundaries of a single county still provide insufficient geographic coverage to deal effectively with regional issues.

States such as California, New York, Florida, Virginia, and Maryland have authorized their counties to perform municipal-type functions and have given them home rule. Led by county executives or chief administrative officers, separately elected or appointed by the governing board, these "urban" counties possess both the structure and power to serve as area-wide or regional governments, especially where their boundaries are coterminous with those of the metropolitan area. The urban county movement has not swept the country, in part due to the reluctance of county boards and state associations to seek empowerment by the state constitution or legislature, as well as concerns on the part of municipal officials about usurpation of their authority and competition for visibility and prestige.

Special Districts

Special district and public authorities are pragmatic and popular. Their relative ease of creation, ability to draw boundaries around problem-sheds, avoidance of debt limits, and pay-as-you-go approach to finances are powerful inducements to local officials to seek budget relief through these means, as the figures of 1952–2002[16] structural trends underscore. Special districts have been criticized as being "invisible" or "shadow" governments, in that their boards of directors have a low profile with the voters and thus rate poorly on citizen accountability values. Most special districts provide a single service to a single jurisdiction, which makes it difficult to undertake comprehensive, integrated approaches to problems. Area-wide and multipurpose districts and authorities are not common. Only 9 percent of the 35,052 special districts in existence in 2002 performed more than one function, and 13 percent were area-wide (multicounty). About two-thirds of the area-wide districts covered two counties.

Area-wide Planning and Coordinating Bodies

Partly in response to continued fragmentation of local government structure and unwillingness on the part of local officials to develop effective collaborative problem-solving approaches, the national and some state governments assumed regional leadership roles. Beginning with a 1959 amendment to Section 701 of the Housing Act of 1954, federal funds were provided to encourage the formation and support of the operation of regional planning commissions and councils of governments (COGs)—more generally, regional councils—to provide comprehensive planning and technical assistance to local units whose elected officials comprised the majority of the members of COG governing bodies. COGs were not intended to be regional service providers and only a few have taken on this role, usually performing services for constituent local governments rather than directly to citizens. They were established primarily to serve as neutral data collectors and information providers, catalysts for interlocal communications between elected officials, comprehensive planners for future development in the region, reviewers of proposed projects against the contents of these plans and commentators thereon, and providers of technical assistance to member jurisdictions on grant-in-aid applications and other types of technical assistance needs. Although federal funding has been greatly reduced, more than 500 of these multipurpose bodies remain. According to a 1993 National Association of Regional Councils survey: 322 were designated as economic development districts; 304 served as clearinghouses for federal and state aid applications; 245 engaged in land-use planning; 227 assisted in allocating federal and state revolving loan funds for wastewater and drinking water facilities; 181 were designated metropolitan planning organizations (MPOs) for regional transportation; and 163 were organizations on aging, providing direct or indirect services to the elderly.[17] Most studies of regional councils concluded that they generally fulfilled these expectations, despite occasional friction between the members and opting out by some jurisdictions.[18]

Single-purpose functional planning and regulatory organizations also have been formed in metropolitan areas as a result of federal "carrots-and-sticks." During the 1970s, these bodies proliferated, covering functions such as environmental protection, law enforcement, health care, and economic development. They were responsible chiefly for planning activities, but grant coordination, standard-setting, and regulation also were among the tasks. In many cases these organizations were separate from regional councils. Metropolitan transportation agencies (MPOs) established under the Intermodal Surface Transportation Efficiency Act (1991)—and its successors, the Transportation Equity Act for the twenty-first Century (1998) and the Safe, Accountable, Flexible, Efficient, Transportation Equity Act: A Legacy for Users (2005)—together with air quality districts organized pursuant to the Clean Air Act (1990) are currently the most visible and authoritative of the federally supported regional organizations.

During the 1960s and 1970s, many states organized their own area-wide planning and development districts for state purposes, to meet federal requirements under the Intergovernmental Cooperation Act of 1968, and to assist localities within their boundaries. Most of these organizations focused on planning, economic development, and transportation. Despite their collaborative and coordinative benefits, multiple federal and state initiatives to create and support area-wide organizations added to the fragmentation of government structure in some metropolitan areas.

To sum up, over the past five decades, local government officials have had a large number of "tools" at their disposal to tackle tough problems and needs crossing their boundary lines. Availability of horizontal and vertical intergovernmental options has permitted local officials to sidestep the constraints of external structural fragmentation and internal organizational weakness. However, public officials and citizens continued to witness persistence and growth of sprawl, interlocal social and economic disparities, infrastructure decline, environmental degradation, and service deterioration. The consolidationist, choice, or collaborationist schools of thought have not successfully addressed the realities confronted by many metropolitan and some nonmetropolitan areas. Neither market forces nor systematic restructuring have been applied broadly across the local landscape. In the view of some experts, bolder and more creative approaches, and even a new vocabulary focusing on "governance" and "networking," are in order.[19]

From Government to Governance

Future directions of local structure and relationships can be considered from two complementary perspectives: the internal organization and powers of local governments; and the dynamics of external relationships at the regional level.

Internal Strategies

There are at least three jurisdictional dimensions of internal strategy: periodic reviews; home rule; and reorganized and empowered county governments.

Periodic Review of Local Government Structure,
Powers, and Service Responsibilities

While the current mosaic of local governments seems to have worked satisfactorily or tolerably in many places, observers argue it will need to work better given the unmet needs, unsolved problems, and unaddressed opportunities. A periodic review of local structure, powers, and responsibilities could reveal needed adjustments or, alternatively, ratify the current situation. In addition to form of government, the scope of the review could encompass relationships between general-purpose and special-purpose units, such as school districts. Such reviews are particularly needed in rapidly growing areas where development has overrun the boundaries of local governments, special districts, and regional councils.

One approach is Montana's state-mandated review of local governments. A 1972 state statute requires each local government to place on the ballot at least once every ten years the question whether the form of government should be reexamined. If so, the voters may ratify that form, amend it, or discard it by majority vote.[20] In 1976, two consolidated city–county governments were approved by the voters—Anaconda-Deer Lodge County and Butte-Silver Bow County. Another approach is establishment of Regional Civic Organizations (RCOs) or use of university-based research centers to conduct examinations of governments in metropolitan areas and prepare "state of the region" reports for consideration by local officials.[21] A third option is to expand the powers of boundary review commissions (existing in twelve states) to enable these bodies to conduct such periodic reviews and propose consolidation, annexation, or dissolution of local governments experiencing economic distress or failing to meet financial or functional viability criteria. Among important implementation issues are frequency of the reviews, voter interest, cost, and destabilizing potential.

Local Empowerment

Variations exist from state to state and within each state in the extent to which local units have been granted home rule authority, the areas in which they may exercise discretionary authority, and the degree to which constitutional or statutory grants have been undercut in practice by judges, attorneys general, bond counsels, or legislators. Generally, cities and municipalities enjoy greater authority over more matters than other forms of local government. Significant restrictions are still in place in most states on local financial powers and on the ability of localities to assume new functional responsibilities. In states that have adopted the "Imperium in Imperio" approach, courts generally have interpreted broadly the areas in which there was a state concern, and narrowly those that were of local concern.[22]

It was noted in a preceding section that among the many prescriptions offered for improving local government and state–local relations, home rule for counties and cities usually ranks high on the list. Empowerment is a crucial condition to effective collaboration. Independent of the extent of jurisdictional or functional fragmentation, if local governments lack the authority to modernize and strengthen their form of government, manage their personnel, levy and adjust taxes and fees, and deliver a wide range of services—directly or indirectly—they will be unable to meet the expectations of citizens and businesses in an increasingly regional and global competitive context. Empowerment also can produce strong local partners to regional collaborative arrangements, which in turn are key to competing successfully in a global marketplace.

A more sweeping approach to local empowerment seeks to reduce the interpretive role of the judiciary and remove restrictions, such as limits on finances and referenda requirements, through a twofold strategy: (a) ensure that all classes of general purpose local units (including townships, towns, boroughs, and villages) possess a full range of powers, under a constitutional grant of "devolution of powers" subject only to preemption by the state legislature; and (b) removal of all constitutional debt, levy, and tax limits affecting local governments. Zimmerman proposed that these grants be accompanied by enactment of a code of restrictions on local powers, identification of local powers either totally or partially preempted by the state legislature, and establishment of minimum standards or levels of performance for major services.[23]

With respect to the internal dynamics of local structure, efforts could be undertaken to centralize administrative responsibility and focus accountability where home rule charters permit. Especially in large and medium-sized municipalities operating under the mayor-council form of government, chief administrative officers or city managers could be appointed by, and serve at the pleasure of, the mayor and/or governing body. The critical need for professional management is underscored by the prevalence of part-time elected officials, technical complexity of problems confronting localities, and intergovernmentalization and privatization of services.

Reorganized County Governments

Despite authorization of counties in some states to modernize their form of government and assume a range of municipal-type responsibilities, most counties continue to play their traditional role as arms of state government for limited purposes. Especially where borders of the metropolitan area and a single county are coterminous, or where a core county serves as the work destination of many residents of fringe counties, the county is a logical area-wide performance unit.

Reorganizing these counties to enable them to carry out functions that cross the boundaries of constituent units and which are amenable to achieving greater efficiency, effectiveness, and equity as a result of scale of delivery offers a number of advantages. Most urban counties usually require no local structural reorganization, they are derived from a unit of local government that is well-known to citizens, and have the capacity to facilitate inter-functional coordination. They also promote a more systematic approach to sorting out local from area-wide services and enable municipalities and other general-purpose units to contract with the county to deliver desired services while they continue to perform other local functions.

Reorganizing counties as full-service jurisdictions for planning, problem-solving, and functional performance requires adoption of home rule charters, broadening of functional and fiscal powers, and replacement of the commission form of government with elected county executives and/or appointed county managers or chief administrative officers. City officials will need to put aside historic concerns about competition from empowered counties and demonstrate a willingness to work together to avoid duplication and promote coordination of efforts. At the same time, county officials will need to put aside parochial mindsets and overcome fears of the "big city."

External Strategies

External strategies could include traditional tools for addressing regional and statewide needs, as well as innovative actions that have proven successful in some local governments and offer promise for successful application elsewhere. Three key traditional components are strengthened regional councils, reassignment/consolidation of functions, and regional special districts and public authorities.

Regional Council Strengthening

Many regional councils are performing responsibilities beyond data collection and comprehensive planning, including grant application reviews and financial services. While these activities are important, local officials could also support an "empowerment agenda" for councils of government. This agenda could entail resurrecting and strengthening the consultation processes established by the Demonstration Cities and Metropolitan Development Act of 1966 and the Intergovernmental Cooperation Act of 1968, which were implemented in 1969 through U.S. Office of Management and Budget Circular A-95. The latter established a system of statewide and regional clearinghouses. Federal agencies were required to notify regional clearinghouses about applications for grants-in-aid made by constituent local governments. These were reviewed and commented on regarding their consistency with regional comprehensive plans. During the Reagan administration, the A-95 process was made discretionary owing to concerns about regulatory burdens.

This review process could be extended by state law or gubernatorial executive order to all local government applications for state aid for projects covered by the regional plan. Besides reviewing and commenting on proposed projects for consistency with regional plans, clearinghouse approval could be required prior to consideration by state funding agencies. Building on current roles, many regional councils play as economic development districts, area-wide agencies for the aging, and metropolitan transportation planning agencies, regional councils also could be relied upon to conduct other federally sponsored area-wide programs, such as monitoring air and water quality.

Regional councils could also be authorized to perform a wider range of services and to offer them to local units on a contractual or fee basis. For example, in Virginia, regional councils are authorized to assume service-delivery roles with the concurrence of constituent local governing bodies, and in Michigan, regional councils may offer to provide services to localities that are not available from the private sector.

Regional councils could play new or expanded roles in drug and alcohol prevention and awareness programs, Geographic Information System (GIS) mapping, and technical assistance in mediation and conflict management. Regional councils also could be looked to for leadership in conducting regional benchmarking studies of infrastructure, condition, social and economic disparities, and environmental quality. They could be authorized to prepare growth management plans and development controls and monitor their implementation in states where they are required.

Changes aimed at bolstering the area-wide effectiveness of regional councils may require parallel adjustments in representational and voting arrangements in order to succeed. Especially critical will be the political "balancing act" between central cities and other large jurisdictions that seek to avoid being outvoted by more numerous rural and suburban officials who do not want the agenda and priorities of the council/clearinghouse dominated by big-city interests. Regional councils also will need to give attention to the appropriate involvement of private and nonprofit sector interests in the regional decision-making process.

Reassignment of Functions

Localities have been active in pursuing "functional regionalism." A 1975 national survey of this activity conducted by Zimmerman focused on municipalities with more than 2,500 population. The survey found that 31 percent of the respondents (51 percent of central cities, 30 percent of suburbs) had voluntarily transferred full or partial functional responsibility to another municipality, county, special district, state, or regional council.[24] More recently, states have taken on, or assumed responsibility for or mandated shifts of, functions to geographically larger units in such areas as transportation, courts, corrections, welfare, and mental health. Another trend is privatization of local functions, with general-purpose units retaining policy direction, control, and monitoring roles and other organizations (either for-profit or nonprofit) responsible for implementation.

Regional Special District and Public Authority Creation

Despite proliferation of special district governments over the past four decades, the number of these bodies serving more than one jurisdiction and/ or providing more than one service is relatively small. A pragmatic response to pressures for collective action in a metropolitan area would be creation of regional special-purpose districts or authorities. These bodies would not be restricted by existing local boundaries in defining their "problem shed," and they would provide a single function—such as mass transportation, schools, water supply, sewage treatment, solid waste disposal, public housing, libraries, and hospitals—to localities or directly to citizens within their territory on a "pay-as-you-go" basis and not be subject to debt limits and other financial constraints on general purpose local units. An extension of this approach would involve broadening the scope of authorized services to include those that local officials agree could best be provided by an authoritative area-wide body, such as ports, economic development, and mass transit.

In no case would the regional district or authority become a government with directly elected area-wide council members. The limited regional single-service or multiservice districts would remain creatures of the local government governing bodies that created them, which would appoint their board members, approve their budgets, and review plans and projects.

Four Innovations

These traditional responses, despite their relatively nonthreatening nature in terms of local government structure, have not been widely embraced. Progress has occurred ad hoc and incrementally, and the pace of reform has been deliberate except in jurisdictions confronted by economic distress, service-delivery crisis, state or federal mandates, or a loss of citizen confidence in elected leadership.

These traditional approaches may not go far enough. At least four innovations offer promise for more authoritative regional action: liberalized annexation; tax-base growth sharing; state incentives for collaboration; and elected regional or metropolitan services districts/authorities.

Liberalized Annexation

Rusk has presented convincing empirical evidence that "inelastic" cities—surrounded by incorporated jurisdictions or unable to readily annex adjacent unincorporated territory due to referenda requirements and other restrictions—fare worse than "elastic" cities on several measures of fiscal and service quality. "Inelastic" cities fare even more poorly on segregation by wealth and race measures. While forty-one states have authorized annexation, most of these grants of authority also restrict the city's ability to initiate such action by local ordinance and subject any proposed annexations to approval by a majority of the residents of the area involved.

Rusk proposes, as part of a model state annexation statute, that cities be permitted to initiate proceedings as well as respond to landowner petitions, and that governing body actions determine the fate of the proposal in lieu of a public referendum.[25] Local governments that are not already completely surrounded by incorporated jurisdictions could become more "elastic" and expand their boundaries to include new populations and tax bases.

Tax-Base-/Growth-Sharing

Pioneered by the Minnesota legislature in 1971, tax-base- or growth-sharing plans established a fund into which a percentage of the new property tax revenues generated by industrial or commercial property development within the Minneapolis and St. Paul region is paid (40 percent in the Twin Cities). Remaining tax revenues go to the jurisdiction within which the industry or business is located. Pooled funds are distributed to all general-purpose local units within the region on a formula basis that reflects need and population size. Base-sharing seeks to reduce fiscal disparities among localities and lessen competition among localities that use costly tax abatements, training programs, infrastructure improvements, and other incentives to attract new businesses. Existing local tax bases are not affected, only new commercial and industrial property tax revenues resulting from economic growth. In addition to creating "win-win" local financial arrangements, regional collaboration of this nature sends positive signals to corporate leaders. Until recently, however, interest in tax-base sharing has been evident in only a few places, including Allegheny County, Pennsylvania (a Regional Asset District uses proceeds from a 1 percent county-wide sales tax for cultural facilities, such as the zoo, parks, libraries, and for a professional football stadium); Dayton, Ohio (a voluntary tax-base-sharing program funds economic development projects and provides some regional financial equity); and Denver, Colorado (a Scientific and Cultural Facilities District distributes regional sales tax revenues—one tenth of 1 percent—to support the zoo, museums, performing arts center, botanical gardens, and other civic facilities and attractions, while another tax district raised funds to construct and operate a stadium for the professional baseball team).[26]

State Incentives

In view of official and general public resistance to consolidating structures and reassigning functions, some state legislatures at the behest of coalitions of local officials, business executives, civic leaders, and chambers of commerce, have considered bills providing state financial incentives for regional activities.

In 1996, for example, the Virginia General Assembly approved the Regional Competitiveness Act developed by the Urban Partnership. Under its terms, localities became eligible for a share of a regional development incentive fund that would grow to $200 million annually when they: (a) voluntarily joined in regional partnerships with other stakeholders in the region; and (b) developed regional strategic plans to guide policy development and collaborative arrangements for the delivery of services. These steps could be taken through an existing organization like a regional council or state-designated planning and development district, or through a new entity such as a nonprofit organization. In reviewing plans, state agencies awarded points for different activities ranging from parks and recreation and libraries (2 points) to human services (8 points) to education (10 points). Regional revenue or growth-sharing arrangements also received 10 points. The strategic plans had to include provision for monitoring service performance and for issuing periodic "regional report cards." Local participation was not mandated, but the financial incentives were expected to be strong inducements to collaboration.

Proponents stressed that regional competitiveness was an indication of healthy local communities and that the state's incentives were important facilitating factors.[27] In the early years of the new century, however, the General Assembly decided to discontinue funding the measure because of Virginia's fiscal crisis and competing budget interests. Though not repealed, the Regional Competitiveness Act remains unfunded at time of writing.

Elected Regional Multipurpose Districts

Perhaps the boldest outside strategy is modeled on experience in Portland, Oregon. In 1970, a Portland Metropolitan Services District (MSD) was established by the state legislature to provide area-wide planning and limited services (e.g., zoo, solid waste disposal) in the metropolitan area encompassing three counties, twenty-four municipalities, and half of the state's total population. The legislature intended MSD to be a flexible structure that could assume other responsibilities desired by Portland area citizens or state legislators. In November 1992, a home rule charter was adopted by citizens of the metropolitan area consolidating MSD with the regional council of governments and making "Metro" the only directly elected regional government in the country. Seven members serve on the nonpartisan council, together with an executive officer elected at large.

In addition to its core planning responsibility, described in the charter as the "primary function," Metro is responsible for a wide range of functions including solid waste collection, recycling, and disposal; air and water quality; operation of the Washington Park Zoo; construction and management of the Oregon Convention Center; allocation of federal highway funds; and oversight of the regional transportation system (Tri-Met). As part of its regional land use planning and growth management responsibilities, Metro also is authorized to resolve inconsistencies between local plans and its "Regional Framework Plan" and land use standards, and to establish the Urban Growth Boundary for the region.[28]

Creation of a multipurpose district as a third- or fourth-tier does not require consolidation or restructuring of existing local governments. Instead, it is an extension of the metropolitan special district proposal, but with a clearly defined multifunctional charge, capacity to handle regional equity issues, and emphasis on public accountability. Voters have the opportunity to select a charter that specifies the powers and functions of the district, and that can be expanded or contracted by the electorate or state legislature. Regionally elected officials are visible and can be held accountable, in contrast to the largely invisible nature of traditional special districts and public authorities with governing bodies appointed by local officials. The regional multipurpose district could be phased in, with locally appointed governing board members leading the initial stages of implementation. Once the district is fully operational, possibly three to five years later, elections could be held for the regional council and executive.

Like tax-base- or growth-sharing arrangements, this proposal could have limited appeal; it may take time to develop elected official comfort with it and citizen understanding of it. It could easily be miscast as "metropolitan government." A regional multipurpose district will have to overcome other high political hurdles, including voter distrust of "big government," racial minority group fears that their political strength will be weakened, and unwillingness of leaders of large municipalities and counties to share visibility and prestige with regional elected officials. However, it may also offer political advantages, especially giving the region more clout in dealing with the governor and state legislature.

Enhancing Prospects for Success

There is no formula to ensure that the next stage in the evolution of local structure and relationships will be successful. Problems like sprawl, disparities, deteriorating services, and environmental degradation are formidable, and the weapons that local officials have in their arsenal are not very powerful relative to the severity and persistence of these problems. Substantial obstacles to regional governance also must be overcome, especially racial divisiveness, local official parochialism and coveting of home rule, political resistance by suburban voters, and citizen distrust of big government. These and other realities suggest that new and renewed strategies for working across local boundaries will be essential.

Research studies and lessons from experience elsewhere suggest that the following guidelines could be helpful to the architects and advocates for improvements in local structure and relationships. Prospects for successful implementation are enhanced when collaborative approaches to regional governance are:

- recipients of sustained leadership by local elected officials;
- inclusive of all affected units as well as nongovernmental stakeholders;
- influenced by long-term priorities and leadership of the business community;
- encouraged or enhanced with incentive funds from state or federal authorities;
- capable of ensuring financial, political, and ethical accountability to citizens and local elected officials;
- consistent with a systematic allocation of key functions to the regional, local, neighborhood levels;
- likely to promote some interjurisdictional equity;
- well-coordinated, both horizontally and vertically;
- able to establish levels of trust among stakeholders;
- provided with stable and flexible long-term financial resources;
- strong enough to persist despite occasional setbacks;
- clear in goals and objectives, costs and benefits, as well as performance and results; and
- amenable to public understanding and support.

Structural fragmentation and blurred boundaries will likely continue to be key characteristics of American local government. Given the obstacles to change of the status quo, local government officials will need to navigate a variety of stakeholder networks in their communities. They will need to bring both vision and patience to the task of improving local structure and relationships, and to exercise strong and skillful leadership in building coalitions to advance regional governance strategies.

Notes

1. This chapter is a revised and updated version of a paper on "Structuring Local Government Units and Relationships," published in Joe Ohren, ed., *The Future of Local Government in Michigan: Symposium Proceedings* (Ann Arbor: Michigan Municipal League Foundation, 2000).

2. Throughout this chapter, "local structure" refers to the forms of organization and patterns of general-purpose local governments and special purpose units in metropolitan and nonmetropolitan areas. "Relationships" refers primarily to interlocal relations, and secondarily to relationships between localities and state and federal authorities. Drawing on William Dodge's definition, the term "governance" refers to "… (1) All community interests affected by challenges and necessary to their resolution, not just government institutions,

and (2) the collaborative problem-solving mechanisms needed to design timely strategies as well as the government institutions and other service-delivery mechanisms needed to implement them." The term "region" refers to "a central core city and its contiguous suburbs and future growth areas or a rural area that is commonly influenced or impacted by crosscutting economic, physical, and social development challenges." This term is often used interchangeably with "regional," "areawide," or "multijurisdictional." See William R. Dodge, *Regional Excellence: Governing Together to Compete Globally and Flourish Locally* (Washington, DC: National League of Cities, 1996), 38.

3. U.S. Bureau of the Census, *2002 Census of Government, Volume 1, Number 1, Government Organization* (Washington, DC: U.S. Government Printing Office, 2002).

4. David Rusk, *Cities Without Suburbs* (Washington, DC: Woodrow Wilson Center Press, 1993), 5–49; Neal R. Peirce, *Citistates: How Urban America Can Prosper in a Competitive World* (Washington, DC: Seven Locks Press, 1993), 17–27; Larry Ledebur and William Barnes, *City Distress, Metropolitan Disparities and Economic Growth* (Washington, DC: National League of Cities, 1992); Myron Orfield, *Metropolitics: A Regional Agenda for Community and Stability* (Washington, DC: Brookings Institution Press/ Lincoln Institute for Land Policy, 1997), 1–73; Anthony Downs, *New Visions for Metropolitan America* (Washington, DC: Brookings Institution, 1994).

5. *City of Clinton v. Cedar Rapids and Missouri Railroad Company* (24 Iowa 455), 1868.

6. Joseph F. Zimmerman, *Measuring Local Discretionary Authority* (Washington, DC: U.S. Advisory Commission on Intergovernmental Relations, November 1981).

7. T.D. Mead, "Federalism and State Law: Legal Factors Constraining and Facilitating Local Initiatives," in *Handbook of Local Government Administration*, ed. J.J. Gargan (New York: Marcel Dekker, Inc., 1997). See also U.S. Advisory Commission on Intergovernmental Relations, *Local Government Autonomy: Needs for State Constitutional, Statutory, and Judicial Clarification* (Washington, DC: U.S. Government Printing Office, October 1993).

8. Dale Krane, Platon N. Rigos, and Melvin B. Hill, Jr., *Home Rule in America: A Fifty-State Handbook* (Washington, DC: CQ Press, 2001).

9. Joseph F. Zimmerman, *State-Local Relations: A Partnership Approach*, 2nd ed. (Westport, CN: Praeger Publishers, 1995), 1–84.

10. Krane, et. al., *Home Rule in America*, 11–14.

11. Joseph F. Zimmerman, *Pragmatic Federalism: The Reassignment of Functional Responsibility* (Washington, DC: U.S. Advisory Commission on Intergovernmental Relations, 1976).

12. Carl W. Stenberg III and William G. Colman, *America's Future Work Force: A Health and Education Policy Issues Handbook* (Westport, CN: Greenwood Press, 1994), 467–471.

13. See Victor Jones, *Metropolitan Government* (Chicago; University of Chicago Press, 1942); Robert L. Bish and Vincent Ostrom, *Understanding Urban Government: Metropolitan Reform Reconsidered* (Washington, DC: American Institute for Public Policy Research, 1973); David Y. Miller, *The Regional Governing of Metropolitan America* (Cambridge, MA: Westview Press, 2002), 89–98, 130–144; Dodge, *Regional Excellence*, 314–320.

14. See Dodge, *Regional Excellence*, 239–334; Frances Frisken and Donald F. Norris, "Regionalism Reconsidered," *Journal of Urban Affairs* 23, 5 (2001): 467–78.

15. See Dodge, *Regional Excellence*, 243–244; David B. Walker, "Snow White and the 17 Dwarfs: From Metropolitan Cooperation to Governance," *National Civic Review* 76 (January–February 1987): 14–28.

16. Bureau of the Census, 24, 43; G. Ross Stephens and Nelson Wikstrom, "Trends in Special Districts," *State and Local Government Review* 30, 2 (Spring 1998): 129–138; Kathryn Foster, *Political Economy of Special Purpose Government* (Washington, DC: Georgetown University Press, 1997).

17. "NARC Regional Council Survey: Some General Characteristics, NARC's 1993/4 Survey" (Washington, DC: National Association of Regional Councils, 1995), 2–3.

18. Nelson Wikstrom, "Metropolitan Government and Governance: A Suggested Agenda," *The Regionalist* 2, 1 (Spring 1997): 51; Howard J. Grossman, "The Case for National Substate Regionalism: Visioning the Future," *The Regionalist* 1, 1 (Winter 1995): 23–36; Bruce D. McDowell, "Regionalism: Where It Is, Where We Are, and Where We May be Headed," *The Regionalist* 1, 4 (Spring 1996): 1–6.

19. Peirce, *Citistates*, 1–37, Rusk, *Cities Without Suburbs*, 85–119; David Rusk, *Inside Game, Outside Game: Winning Strategies for Saving Urban America* (Washington, DC: Brookings Institution, 1999); David Rusk, *Baltimore Unbound: A Strategy for Regional Renewal* (Baltimore: The Abell Foundation, 1996); Orfield, *Metropolitics*, 74–172; John Kincaid, "The End of Mainframe Consolidation," *The Regionalist* 2, 1 (Spring 1997): 57–60.

20. Melvin B. Hill, Jr., *State Laws Governing Local Government Structure and Administration* (Washington, DC: U.S. Advisory Commission on Intergovernmental Relations, March 1993), 3.

21. William Dodge and Carl Stenberg, "Preparing for the Century of the Region," *The Regionalist* 2, 4 (Winter 1997): 81–82; Lyle Wray, "Regional Civic Organizations: Strengthening Citizenship in Changing Times," *The Regionalist* 2, 2 (Summer 1997): 13–20; National Association of Regional Councils, *Toward A National Regional Agenda: Building Regional Communities for the 21st Century* (Washington, DC: The Association, June 1998).

22. Zimmerman, *State-Local Relations: A Partnership Approach*, 28.

23. Ibid., 195.

24. Zimmerman, *Pragmatic Federalism*, 120–121.

25. Rusk, Cities Without Suburbs, 99–100.

26. Henry G. Cisneros, *Regionalism: The New Geography of Opportunity* (Washington, DC: U.S. Department of Housing and Urban Development, March 1995), 23–25.

27. Roger Richman and James B. Oliver, Jr., "The Urban Partnership and the Development of Virginia's New Regional Competitiveness Act," *The Regionalist* 2, 1 (Spring 1997): 14–16.

28. Rusk, Cities Without Suburbs, 104; Cisneros, Regionalism, 21–22.

Chapter 6

Congressional Devolution of Power

Joseph F. Zimmerman

The current system of federalism in the United States is the most complex one in the world. It stands in sharp contrast to the relatively simple system during the early decades following the American inauguration of federalism in 1789 when interactions between the national government and the states mainly comprised the election of two U.S. Senators and members of the Electoral College by each State Legislature and state conduct of elections for members of the U.S. House of Representatives. The theory of dual federalism adequately explains this early phase of the system.

A slow change in the nature of federalism commenced when Congress in 1789 devolved its power to regulate marine pilots to states and in 1790 exercised two of its constitutionally delegated broad regulatory powers, reinforced by the supreme law of the land clause, to enact the preemptive *Copyright Act* and the *Patent Act*, removing from states all regulatory powers in these two fields.[1] In the second half of the nineteenth century, the complexity of the system was increased significantly by devolution statutes and preemption statutes partially removing regulatory powers from the states. The *Bankruptcy Act of 1843* and the *Interstate Communications Act of 1866* were the first manifestations of this new trend.[2] Nevertheless, Congress was slow in exercising its latent regulatory powers and had enacted only twenty-nine preemption statutes by 1900. The pace of enactment remained moderate until 1965. Thereafter Congress enacted such statutes, some including mandates and restraints, at a faster pace and in new regulatory fields. A total of 576 preemption acts had been enacted by May 1, 2007.

This chapter assesses the significance of congressional devolution of powers to states. Textbooks on the federal system explain the powers delegated by the U.S. Constitution to Congress and the president by Articles I and II, respectively, and the powers reserved to the states by the Tenth Amendment. Generally omitted from their coverage are powers devolved by the constitution to each state legislature to: (1) determine the times, places, and manner of holding elections for Senators and Representatives, subject to possible alteration by Congress; (2) enter into compacts with sister states with the consent of Congress; (3) appoint presidential and vice-presidential electors; (4) require Congress to call a convention for the purpose of proposing constitutional amendments; and (5) control intoxicating liquors.[3]

These constitutionally devolved powers are outweighed in importance by congressional ones devolving to states powers, including the grant of consent to interstate compacts allowing states to initiate actions that otherwise would be unconstitutional.[4] Did the framers of the U.S. Constitution contemplate the possibility that a future Congress would turn over one or more of its delegated regulatory powers to states? The historical records are silent on this subject and the constitution contains only one provision prohibiting congressional devolution of one of its powers to states. Section 8 of Article I delegates the power of coinage to Congress and section 9 forbids states to coin money.

Three types of power may be devolved by a general or superior government to one or more inferior governmental units: legislative, executive, and administrative. The latter authorizes lower tier units to administer program previously administered by the national government.[5]

As noted, Congress enacted its first devolution statute in 1789, and it continues to transfer some of its regulatory powers to state legislatures, governors, and attorneys general. The resultant increase in systemic complexity makes it extremely difficult for even the most informed citizen to determine which government or officer is responsible for a given regulatory function while augmenting the influence of well-funded interest groups, thereby raising questions of democratic accountability.

Devolved Powers

A detailed listing of devolved powers is necessary to determine the degree to which these powers increase the complexity of the federal system. There are ten forms of devolution: (1) a statute turning over regulatory responsibility to the states; (2) inclusion of a savings clause(s) in a preemption statute; (3) turn back of regulatory enforcement authority; (4) authorization for a national department or agency to delegate regulatory primacy to states; (5) reverse preemption; (6) exemption of uniform state laws from a preemption statute; (7) opt-in and opt-out provisions; (8) empowerment of governors to initiate actions not authorized by their respective state constitution and statutes; (9) grant of authority to each state attorney general to bring a law suit to enforce a federal preemption statute; and (10) authorization for a state agency to administer a federal program.

Marine Ports and Shipping

Congress in 1789 granted states power to regulate marine pilots.[6] The current *Shipping Statute* provides that "pilots in the bays, rivers, harbors, and ports of the United States shall be regulated only in conformity with the laws of the States."[7]

The *Port and Tanker Safety Act of 1978* mandates the Secretary of Transportation to require federally licensed pilots on all domestic and foreign self-propelled vessels "engaged in foreign trade when operating in the navigable waters of the United States in areas and under circumstances where a pilot is not otherwise required by state law."[8] This act also devolves power to states to prescribe higher "safety equipment requirements or safety standards" than federal ones for bridges and other structures on or in the navigable waters of the United States.[9]

The *Coast Guard Authorization Act of 1984* directs the Secretary of Transportation to develop standards for determining whether an individual is intoxicated while operating a marine recreational vessel.[10] In 1987, the Coast Guard, a unit of the Department of Transportation, encouraged states to adopt such standards by promulgating a rule adopting the state blood-alcohol-content (BAC) standard if it exists, but also establishing a national BAC standard of 0.10 percent in the absence of a state standard.[11]

Insurance Regulation

States historically regulated the business of insurance. The U.S. Supreme Court in 1868 opined that the business of insurance was not commerce and hence not subject to regulation by Congress under its delegated power to regulate commerce among the several states.[12] The court in 1944 reversed this decision by ruling the business of insurance involves interstate commerce.[13] Alarmed by the loss of revenue derived from regulating the insurance industry, states successfully lobbied Congress to enact the *McCarran-Ferguson Act of 1945* exempting state regulation of the industry from the antitrust statutes and devolving upon states the power to regulate the business of insurance.[14]

With the passage of time, the insurance industry grew increasingly frustrated with nonharmonious state regulations requiring a national firm to obtain regulatory approval for a new product in each of the fifty states and the District of Columbia, a process requiring up to eighteen months. In consequence, it lobbied Congress to preempt aspects of state regulatory authority. Congress responded with the *Gramm-Leach-Bliley Financial Modernization Act of 1999* that partially preempts thirteen specified areas of insurance regulation and threatened to adopt a national licensing system for insurance agents if a minimum of twenty-six states failed to adopt a uniform system, certified by the National Association of Insurance Commissioners (NAIC), by November 12, 2002.[15] A federal licensing system was averted when NAIC certified on September 10 that thirty-five states had adopted a uniform system.

Terrorists on September 11, 2001, attacked the World Trade Center in New York City and the Pentagon in Arlington, Virginia. These attacks impacted adversely on casualty and property insurance companies and raised the question whether they would provide coverage for business firms and individuals against potential terrorism acts. In response, Congress enacted the *Terrorism Risk Insurance Act of 2002* providing for a temporary national government program to ensure the availability at affordable premiums of casualty and property insurance for terrorism risk.[16] A clause preempts the regulatory authority of the states: "State approval of any terrorism exclusion from a contract for property and casualty insurance that is in force on the date of enactment of this Act shall be void to the extent that it excludes losses that would otherwise be insurance losses."[17] The act's sunset provision of December 31, 2005, was extended to December 31, 2007, by the *Terrorism Risk Insurance Act of 2005*.[18]

The 1999 act convinced NAIC that state legislatures must initiate action to make insurance regulations more harmonious. To guide them, it drafted the Producer Licensing Model Act providing for interstate reciprocity, which has been enacted by forty-seven state legislatures.[19] NAIC also drafted an interstate insurance products regulatory compact establishing a commission with authority to establish uniform policies for annuity, disability income for life, and long-term health care products.[20] Currently, thirty state legislatures have enacted the compact and supported establishment of a commission as a central filing and decision-making body, thereby expediting the process of obtaining regulatory approval for new insurance products.

Cable Television

The *Cable Communications Policy Act of 1984* devolves power to subnational governments to issue and renew cable television franchises subject to national franchise renewal standards that make denial of a franchise renewal request difficult.[21] Each subnational franchising authority is required to assess whether

A. The cable operator has substantially complied with the material terms of the existing franchise and with applicable law;
B. The quality of the operator's service, including signal quality, response to consumer complaints, and billing practices, but without regard to the mix, quality, or level of cable services or other services provided over the system, has been reasonable in the light of community needs;
C. The operator has the financial, legal, and technical ability to provide the services, facilities, and equipment as set forth in the operator's proposal; and
D. The operator's proposal is reasonable to meet the future cable-related community needs and interests, taking into account the cost of meeting such needs and interests.[22]

A cable operator denied franchise renewal is authorized to seek relief in a state court or the U.S. District Court, which may grant relief if "the adverse finding of the franchise authority with respect to each of the factors ... is not supported by a preponderance of the evidence."[23]

Citizens Band Radio

The State and Local Enforcement of Federal Communications Commission Regulations on Use of Citizens Band Radio Equipment Act of 2000 devolves authority upon a state legislature or a local government legislative body to enact a law prohibiting a violation of specified regulations promulgated by the Federal Communications Commission (FCC).[24]

Firearms

The *National Firearms Act of 1934* imposed an annual $200 firearms dealers' license tax.[25] The act was challenged as an encroachment upon the reserved powers of the states, but the U.S. Supreme Court in 1937 rejected the challenge and explained that an inquiry into the hidden motives that may move Congress to exercise a power constitutionally conferred upon it is beyond the competency of the courts.[26]

A 1994 amendment mandates that an individual intending to register for a license must include a photograph and fingerprints with the initial application and cannot operate the business if a state or local law where the business would be conducted prohibits the business.[27]

Gambling Activities

To assist states in the enforcement of their criminal laws, Congress in 1951 enacted the *Johnson Act of 1951* prohibiting the interstate transportation of gambling devices and containing a devolution provision; that is, the statute does not apply to a state if it enacts a law opting out of the prohibition.[28]

Congress in the *Revenue Act of 1951* employed its taxation powers to assist states to enforce their gambling statutes by levying a $50 gambler's occupational tax on individuals accepting wagers, who are required to register with the Collector of Internal Revenue, and penalizing those who fail to register and pay the tax.[29] The collector forwards the registration information to the appropriate state officer as *prima facie* evidence the individuals have violated state antigambling laws. The tax was challenged as an infringement of the reserved powers of the states, but the U.S. Supreme Court in 1953 in *United States v. Kahriger* upheld the constitutionality of the tax and rejected the argument the tax denied the privilege against self-incrimination guaranteed by the Fifth Amendment to the U.S. Constitution.[30]

The 1951 act also imposed a 10 percent tax on the gross amount of all wagers accepted by persons engaged in wagering, who are required to register with the Collector of Internal Revenue. Registrants were required to post in a conspicuous place tax stamps or carry the stamps on their person if they lacked a place of business. A convicted gambler appealed to the U.S. Supreme Court, which in 1968 reversed the conviction on the ground the tax violated the privilege of no self-incrimination guaranteed by the Fifth Amendment to the U.S. Constitution.[31]

The *Interstate Horseracing Act of 1978* devolves powers to states, including limited ones to preempt the federal prohibition of interstate offtrack wagering.[32] A court challenge was launched against the act on the ground of restriction of commercial free speech. In 1993, the U.S. District Court for the Eastern District of Kentucky granted summary judgment by opining the act violates the First Amendment's guarantee of freedom of speech, is unconstitutionally vague, and is an irrational means to achieve a permissible goal.[33] Reversing that decision in 1994, however, the U.S. Court of Appeals for the 6th Circuit ruled that the legislation does not regulate commercial speech. Since offtrack wagering can occur in the absence of simulcasting, the measure regulates a very narrow subject and hence a "less strict vagueness test" is applicable to it. Moreover the act "does not delegate legislative power to private parties."[34]

In 1987, the U.S. Supreme Court opined a state lacks authority to unduly restrict gaming on Indian lands.[35] Congress reacted to the decision by enacting the *Indian Gaming Regulatory Act* placing gambling on Indian reservations in three classes.[36] Class I games, primarily social gaming for small prizes, are regulated by Indian tribes. Class II games—bingo and bingo-type games, and nonbanking card games—are regulated by tribes subject to limited oversight by the National Indian Gaming Commission. Class III games are all other types, including casinos, prohibited in the absence of a tribal–state compact.

The act devolves authority to the governor to negotiate a compact with a tribe, and a compact typically provides for the sharing of the profits of gaming by the state and the tribe. The U.S. Supreme Court in *Seminole Tribe of Florida v. Florida* in 1996 invalidated a section in the 1988 act authorizing a tribe to sue a state in the U.S. District Court if the governor did not negotiate in good faith a tribal–state compact regulating gambling by ruling such a suit is blocked by the Eleventh Amendment to the United States Constitution.[37]

In 1992, Congress enacted the *Professional and Amateur Sports Protection Act* forbidding "a governmental entity to sponsor, operate, advertise, promote, license, or authorize by law or compact…a lottery, sweepstakes, or other betting, gambling, or wagering scheme based, directly of indirectly (through the use of geographical references or otherwise), on one or more competitive games in which amateur or professional athletes participate, or are intended to participate, or on one or more performances of such athletes in such games."[38] The act contains a grandfather clause stipulating that the prohibition does not apply to the named sports' gambling activities if they were in operation during specified dates.[39]

The *Coast Guard Authorization Act of 1996* contains two exceptions to preemption: (1) An amendment to the *Johnson Act of 1951* grants Indiana jurisdiction over the "repair, transport, possession, or use of a gambling device on a vessel on a voyage that begins in…Indiana and does not leave the territorial waters of that State…," and (2) a second amendment devolves power to Alaska to forbid "the use of a gambling device on a vessel while it is docked or anchored or while it is operating within 3 nautical miles of a port at which it is scheduled to call."[40]

Congress in 1994 devolved power by amending its anti-lottery statutes to allow interstate transportation of lottery tickets, provided the concerned business is permitted under an agreement between the concerned sister states.[41]

Low-Level Radioactive Wastes

Authority to dispose of low-level radioactive waste was devolved to states by a 1985 act granting consent in advance to encourage states to form interstate compacts to dispose of such wastes.[42]

Minimum Standards Preemption

This preemption type can be described as "contingent" complete preemption based upon the theory that states have to be coerced to initiate action to meet minimum national standards under the threat of losing primacy in a regulatory field. In 1965, Congress decided that several major regional problems could not be solved by state and local governmental actions encouraged by conditional grants-in-aid, and a new problem-solving approach was necessary.[43] To continue to exercise regulatory authority under a minimum preemption statute, a state must submit a plan containing standards at least as stringent as national ones to the appropriate federal agency for approval and demonstrate the state possesses qualified enforcement personnel and equipment.

Upon approving a plan, the agency devolves regulatory "primacy" to the state; that is, only the state inspects and enforces its standards and the role of the agency is to monitor the performance of the state. In other words, a state law under minimum standards preemption supersedes the corresponding national law if the state standards are equal to or higher than the national ones. If a state fails to submit an acceptable plan or returns "regulatory primacy" to the agency, the latter assumes responsibility for enforcing national regulations in the state.

Congress has enacted four minimum standards environmental regulatory acts: Water Quality Act of 1965 (now Clean Air Act), Air Quality Act of 1967 (now Clean Water Act), Safe Drinking Water Act of 1974, and Surface Mining Control and Reclamation Act of 1977.[44]

More Stringent State Standards

This type of devolution of powers differs from minimum standards preemption in that a state is not required to submit its standards to a federal agency for approval before the standards become effective.

The *National Traffic and Motor Vehicle Safety Act of 1966* completely preempts the field with one exception: A state or local government is authorized to establish "a safety requirement applicable to motor vehicles ... procured for its own use if it provides a higher greater protection than the federal standard."[45]

States are authorized by *The Federal Railroad Safety Act of 1970* to adopt railroad safety laws and standards that are more stringent than the counterpart federal ones "when necessary to eliminate or reduce an essentially local safety hazard, and when not incompatible with any federal law, rule, regulation, order, or standards, and when not creating an undue burden on interstate commerce."[46]

The *Occupational Safety and Health Act of 1970* employs slightly different wording: "Nothing in this Act shall prevent any State agency or court from asserting jurisdiction under State law over any occupational safety or health issues with respect to which no [federal] standard is in effect."[47]

The *Toxic Substances Control Act of 1976* permits states and their political subdivisions to continue to regulate chemical substances until the Administrator of the U.S. Environmental Protection Agency (EPA) promulgates a rule or issues an order applicable to a substance designed to protect public health.[48] A degree of state regulatory flexibility is permitted subsequent to the administrator's issuance of a rule or order by stipulating the administrator, upon the application of a state or a political subdivision, may exempt a chemical substance or mixture from the federal requirements if the subnational requirements provide a higher degree of protection than the federal requirements and do not "unduly burden interstate commerce."[49]

The *Natural Gas Policy Act of 1978* stipulates "nothing in this act shall affect the authority of any State to establish or enforce any maximum lawful price for the first sale of natural gas produced in such States which does not exceed the applicable maximum lawful price, if any, under title I of this act."[50] The *Port and Tanker Safety Act of 1978* contains a similar provision.[51]

The *Telephone Consumer Protection Act of 1991* empowers a state to impose, compared to federal standards, "more restrictive intrastate requirements or regulations" pertaining to the use of electronic devices to send unsolicited advertisements, automatic telephone dialing systems, or artificial or prerecorded voice messages, and telephone solicitations.[52]

The *Family and Medical Leave Act of 1993*, a preemption act, devolves authority to subnational legislative bodies to supersede the act's provisions if the subnational laws "provide greater family or medical leave rights than the rights established under this Act."[53]

The *Armored Car Industry Reciprocity Act of 1993* requires each state to honor licenses for weapons issued by other states to armored car crew members and supersedes a state or local law only to the extent of any inconsistency with the act.[54]

The *Gramm-Leach-Bliley Financial Modernization Act of 1999*, a major preemption statute, contains a section exempting from preemption state law provisions affording greater protection than the act against the disclosure of nonpublic personal information by financial institutions.[55]

The *Do-Not-Call Implementation Act of 2003* directs FCC to promulgate final regulations within 180 days governing intrastate telemarketing.[56] Such regulations were promulgated on June 26, 2003, and do not preempt more restrictive state do-not-call laws on the subject.

The *Hazardous Materials Transportation Safety and Security Reauthorization Act of 2005* permits states to establish more stringent procedures for the conduct of background checks for drivers hauling hazardous materials provided there is a state appeals process similar to the federal one.[57] This preemption act is the first one establishing a minimum procedural standard.

The *Patient Safety and Quality Improvement Act of 2005* authorizes subnational governments to provide "greater privilege or confidentiality protections than the privilege and confidentiality protections" provided by the act.[58]

The *Safe, Accountable, Flexible, Efficient Transportation Equity Act: a Legacy for Users of 2005* allows a state to establish more stringent procedures for a hazardous materials endorsement to a commercial driver's license holders provided the state has an appeals process similar to the federal one.

Quarantines

A 1796 statute, relating to foreign and interstate marine commerce, authorizes the president to direct fort commanders and revenue officers to cooperate with state officers in the enforcement of state quarantine and health laws.[59] A 1799 amendment grants the secretary of the treasury authority to direct federal officers to cooperate with state officers in enforcement of the same laws.[60] A second 1796 act and a 1797 act prohibit the shipment in interstate commerce of goods in violation of the health or quarantine laws of a state.[61] Congress in 1878 enacted a statute providing that vessels carrying passengers with a contagious disease may enter into ports only in accordance with the quarantine laws of the several states.[62]

To prevent the spread of yellow fever, the Texas health officer on March 1, 1899, imposed a quarantine on all persons and articles originating in places infected by yellow fever, and New Orleans on August 31, 1899, was declared officially to have a case of yellow fever and was covered by the quarantine.

The Louisiana governor sought leave to file in the U.S. Supreme Court a bill of complaint in equity against Texas, her governor, and her health officer alleging the City of New Orleans and its residents engaged in interstate commerce were injured by the quarantine. The court invoked its original jurisdiction, reviewed section 2 of Article III of the U.S. Constitution defining the judicial power of the United States, and concluded in 1900 the bill of complaint "does not set up facts which show that the State of Texas has so authorized or confirmed the alleged action of her health officer as to make it her own, or that which it necessarily follows that the two states are in controversy within the meaning of the Constitution."[63] The court sustained the Texas demurrer and dismissed the bill of complaint. Justice John M. Harlan explained Louisiana citizens may seek, in an appropriate court, judicial protection of their property and/or rights affected adversely by statutes of administrative action in a sister state.

The *Plant Quarantine Act of 1912* empowers states to quarantine the shipment of diseased or infested plants not subject to a federal quarantine.[64]

Savings Clauses

Congress in enacting regulatory laws often includes a variety of types of savings clauses: Declaration of intent not to preempt, inconsistency, absence of a federal standard, medical exemption, uniform state law, and unusually worded provisions.

The *Civil Rights Act of 1964* declares: "Nothing in this Act shall be construed as indicating an intent on the part of Congress to occupy the field in which any such title operates to the exclusion of state laws on the same subject matter, nor shall any provisions of this Act be construed as invalidating any provision of state law unless such provision is inconsistent with any of the purposes of this Act, or any provision thereof."[65]

The *Federal Environmental Pesticide Act of 1972* empowers a state to register "pesticides formulated for distribution and use within that State to meet special local needs if that State is certified by the [EPA] Administrator as capable of exercising adequate controls to assure that such registration will be in accord with the purposes of this act and if registration for such use has not previously been denied, disapproved, or cancelled by the Administrator."[66]

The *Professional and Amateur Sports Protection Act of 1992* forbids a governmental body to advertise, license, promote, or sponsor any type of gambling competitive games in which amateur and professional athletes participate, but contains a grandfather clause providing that the prohibition is not applicable to sports gambling activities in operation during specified dates.[67]

The *Newborns' and Mothers' Health Protection Act of 1996* regulates group health insurance plans by mandating benefits standards relative for mothers and newborns, but exempts health insurance coverage in states with a statute requiring (1) "at least a 48-hour hospital length of stay following a normal vaginal delivery and at least a 96-hour hospital length of stay following a cesarean section" or (2) coverage "for maternity and pediatric care in accordance with guidelines established by the American College of Obstetricians and Gynecologists, the American Academy of Pediatrics, or other established professional medical association," or (3) the attending physician, in consultation with the mother, determines her hospital length of stay.[68]

The *Electronic Signatures in Global and National Commerce Act of 2000* preempts the electronic signatures laws of forty-four states, but exempts a state if its legislature enacts the *Uniform Electronic Transactions Act* drafted by the National Conference of Commissioners on Uniform State Laws.[69]

The savings clause in the *Commodity Futures Modernization Act of 2000* stipulates: "No provision of State law regarding the offer, sale, or distribution of securities shall apply to any transaction in a security futures product, except that this sentence shall not be construed as limiting any State antifraud law of general applicability."[70]

The *Help America Vote Act of 2002* amends the *National Voter Registration Act of 1993* by allowing a state to remove a voter from the official list of eligible voters if the voter has not notified the applicable registrar of a change of address or has not voted in two or more consecutive general elections for federal office.[71]

The *Real Interstate Driver Equity Act of 2002* exempts from preemption (1) state and local government taxicab regulation, (2) an airport, bus, or train operator providing "preferential access or facilities to one or more providers of pre-arranged ground transportation service," (3) and state or local government required pre-licensing drug testing or a criminal background investigation of "any individual operating a vehicle providing prearranged ground transportation service originating in the state or political subdivision … "[72]

The *Captive Wildlife Safety Act of 2003* excludes from its preemption provisions "a state college, university, or agency, State-licensed wildlife rehabilitator, or State-licensed veterinarian."[73]

Opt-In and Opt-Out Provisions

As noted, the *Johnson Act of 1951* devolves authority to state legislatures to enact a law opting out of the act's prohibition of the interstate transportation of gambling devices.

The *Department of Transportation Appropriations Act of 1990* mandates state legislatures to enact a statute requiring revocation of the operator's license of a motorist convicted of a drug-related crime. State sovereignty is respected by allowing each state to opt out of the mandate by means of a legislative resolution adopted in opposition to the requirement and a letter from the governor to the U.S. Secretary of Transportation expressing concurrence with the resolution.[74]

The *Riegle-Neal Interstate Banking and Branching Efficiency Act of 1994*, a preemption statute, contains an "out-in" section permitting a state legislature to enact a law permitting interstate branching through *de novo* branches provided the law "applies equally to all banks, and expressly permits all out-of-state banks to establish *de novo* branches."[75] Furthermore, the act has an "opt-out" section permitting a state legislature to enact a law prohibiting interstate branching within the state otherwise authorized by the act.[76]

Rulings Precluding Preemption

Congress enacted two preemption statutes lacking explicit devolution provisions, but authorizing an administrative or judicial determination precluding preemption. *The Voting Rights Act of 1965*, designed to protect black citizens, is a contingent statute applicable to a state or a political subdivision if two conditions are met: A voting device such as a literacy test had been employed in 1964 and less than 50 percent of the electorate cast ballots in the preceding presidential election.[77]

A subnational government covered by the act may make no change in its election system unless the U.S. attorney general, within sixty days of submission of a proposed change to him or her, fails to register an objection or the U.S. District Court for the District of Columbia issues a declaratory judgment that the proposed change would not abridge the right to vote of citizens protected by the act.[78]

The *Transportation Safety Act of 1974* authorizes the Materials Transportation Bureau of the Department of Transportation to issue an administrative ruling addressing the question whether a state law or rule is precluded by preemption.[79]

Reverse Preemption

The *Costal Zone Management Act of 1972* (1) authorizes grants-in-aid to states for the development of a land and water resources-management program for submission to the Secretary of Commerce for approval, (2) requires federal agencies to ensure their development projects in coastal zones are consistent "to the maximum extent practicable" with federally approved state management programs, and (3) prohibits federal agencies to issue licenses or permits to a private applicant to undertake "an activity affecting land or water uses in the coastal zone" if the concerned state objects to the application.[80]

The Secretary can override a state's objection to the issuance of a license or permit by a federal agency if, upon appeal, the Secretary determines "the activity is consistent with the objectives of this title or is otherwise in the interest of national security."[81]

Powers Devolved to Governors

Sixteen congressional preemption statutes and implementing administrative rules and regulations and one presidential executive order devolve national powers to governors not granted to them by their respective state constitution or statutes. These devolved powers are designed to provide states with additional flexibility in solving problems, but also generate increased lobbying of governors by interest groups and are particularly important in states where the governor is weak in terms of formal constitutional powers. A governor of an eastern state wrote to the author in 1986 that "I don't think many students of federalism understand how important these changes are, not only in an intergovernmental sense, but to Governors themselves in the expansion of their responsibilities as chief executive within their respective States."

Plan Submission

The first type is a statutory authorization for a governor to submit a plan to a federal department or agency. The *Federal Environmental Pesticide Control Act of 1972* devolves authority to a governor to submit a plan to the U.S. Environmental Protection Agency (EPA) Administrator for state assumption of responsibility for certification of pesticides applicators.[82] The *Clean Air Act Amendments of 1977* directs the administrator, who is required to review each state implementation plan within eighteen months of its submission, to consult the governor prior to mandating a revision of the plan.[83]

Plan Certification

Congress in a number of acts grants power to governors to certify their respective state plans. For example, the *Federal Water Pollution Control Act Amendments of 1972* authorize only the governor or his/her designee annually to certify area-wide waste water treatment management plans if the state desires to retain regulatory primacy.[84]

Compliance Certification

Certification of state compliance with a national requirement is a third type of power granted by congressional devolution statutes to governors. The *Emergency Highway Energy Conservation Act of 1974* required states to establish a maximum speed limit of fifty-five miles per hour as a condition for the receipt of federal highway grants-in-aid and directed the Federal Highway Administrator to promulgate implementing regulations stipulating "each Governor shall submit to the Federal Highway Administrator ... a statement that the State" is complying with the nationally established maximum speed limit.[85]

Temporary Permits

Congress devolved power to governors to issue temporary permits as illustrated by the *Safe Drinking Water Act of 1974* that authorizes the EPA Administrator, upon the application of a governor, to issue "one or more temporary permits each of which is applicable to a particular injection well and to the underground injection of a particular fluid."[86]

Requirement Waiver

Congress, in establishing many new grant-in-aid programs in the 1960s, required that a single state agency be responsible for administration of each program in order to establish responsibility and avoid programmatic duplication. Many governors protested that states lost the ability to reorganize their respective executive branch to ensure the most effective and economical delivery of services. Congress responded by empowering governors to request the waiver of the federal single-agency requirement.

Assumption of Responsibility

The *Wholesome Meat Act of 1967* and the *Poultry Products Inspection Act of 1968* grants a governor authority to request state assumption of responsibility for a function.[87]

State Agency Designation

The seventh type is illustrated by the *National Health Planning and Resources Development Act of 1974* that grants each governor authority to designate a state department or agency as the state health planning and development agency for a preempted function.[88]

Appointments

The National Health Planning and Resources Development Act of 1974 requires members of the Statewide Health Coordinating Council to be appointed by the governor.[89]

The *Highway Safety Act of 1966* forbids the Secretary of Transportation to approve a state highway safety program that fails to provide that the governor is responsible for the administration of the program.[90] This authorization precludes the state legislature from placing responsibility for state highway safety programs in an agency independent of the governor.

Gasoline Allocation

President Jimmy Carter in 1979 issued an executive order granting authority to the governor of a state "to establish a system of end-use allocation for motor gasoline, a very important power when gasoline is in short supply."[91]

Nuclear Waste Site Veto

The Secretary of Energy is directed by the *Nuclear Waste Policy Act of 1984* to select a site for the construction of a high-level radioactive waste facility, but the site may be vetoed either by the concerned state governor or the state legislature.[92] Congress, however, may override the state veto, and in 2002 overrode the Nevada governor's veto of the Yucca mountain, Nevada, site.[93]

Each governor is authorized by the *Tandem Truck Safety Act of 1984*, after consulting concerned local governments, (a) to notify the secretary of transportation that specified segments of the interstate highway system in the governor's state cannot safely accommodate motor vehicles of the length permitted by the *Surface Transportation Assistance Act of 1982* or 102-inch vehicles other than buses, and (b) to request the secretary to prohibit travel by these vehicles on the specified segments.[94]

The grant of air pollution abatement powers by preemption statutes to the governor is the most important type. EPA was forced by court decisions in 1972 and 1973 to promulgate regulations forbidding states to permit significant deterioration of existing air quality.[95] To implement the courts' decisions, EPA promulgated in 1974 final rules and regulations for prevention of significant deterioration of existing air quality by establishing three classes of air zones.[96] New pollution, measured in terms of sulfur dioxide and total suspended particulate matters, is not allowed in Class I areas; a limited amount of development is allowed in Class II areas, provided such development would not cause "significant deterioration of air quality;" and deterioration up to secondary standards is permitted in Class III areas. Primary ambient air quality standards are national ones designed to protect the health of susceptible citizens. Secondary standards generally are more stringent and are designed to prevent adverse environmental effects such as damage to animals, climate, vegetation, and water quality.

The *Clean Air Act* was amended in 1977 to add a new "Part C: Prevention of Significant Deterioration of Air Quality." It contained provisions similar to EPA regulations with one major exception: Pollutants in Class III areas are limited to 50 percent of the amount allowed by secondary standards.[97] Each state governor is allowed to redesignate areas from Class I to Class II with certain specified exceptions, principally national parks and wilderness areas.[98] The EPA Administrator may invalidate a redesignation only if procedural requirements were not followed. In effect, redesignation allows a governor to balance the need for economic development with preservation of air quality, provided pollutants emanating from new developments do not exceed national standards.

The amendments also authorize a governor, subject to the agreement of the federal land manager, to grant a variance from the maximum allowable increase in sulfur dioxide by a proposed major emitting facility denied certification under the standard certification procedure for a Class I area, provided the owner or operator of the proposed facility can convince the governor, after a public hearing, that a variance "will not adversely affect the air quality related values of the area (including visibility)."[99]

The EPA Administrator also is directed to delete from a transportation control plan a requirement for the tolling of bridges upon the application of the governor of the concerned state.[100] This provision was inserted in the amendments after intense lobbying by New York City and New York State officers. In compliance with this, the requirement was deleted with regard to East River bridges in New York City on the request of Governor Hugh L. Carey of New York on October 19, 1977.[101]

Amendments enacted in 1990 direct the governor of a state with regulatory primacy to submit to the EPA Administrator "a list of areas (or portions thereof) in the State designated as nonattainment, attainment, or unclassifiable, ..."[102] An entire metropolitan statistical area or consolidated metropolitan statistical area is classified as a nonattainment area if the ozone or carbon monoxide air quality in any subarea is classified as a serious, severe, or extreme. The administrator is directed to grant the application of the governor for exclusion of the portion from the area designated as nonattainment provided the governor can demonstrate to the administrator that sources of air pollution in "a portion of a metropolitan statistical area or consolidated metropolitan statistical area," ... do not contribute significantly to the violation of air quality standards.[103]

The amendments impact the coal industry whose influence is detectable in the section authorizing the governor, "with the written consent of the

President or his designee," to "prohibit any such major fuel burning stationary sources (or class or category thereof) from using fuels other than locally or regionally available coal or coal derivatives to comply with implementation plan requirements."[104]

Ozone Transport Commission

The 1990 amendments authorize a governor to petition the EPA administrator to establish a transport commission if "the interstate transport of air pollutants from one or more States contributes significantly to a violation of a national ambient air quality standard in one or more other States, …[105] In response to a petition, the administrator established the Ozone Transport Commission whose members are representatives of twelve northeastern states and the District of Columbia.

National Guard Duty

A 2007 statute devolves power to each governor, with the consent of the secretary of defense, to "order a member of the National Guard to perform Active Guard and reserve duty" as defined by the act.[106]

Enforcement Powers Devolved to
Attorneys General

Historically the U.S. attorney general and district attorneys brought lawsuits when necessary to enforce congressional statutes. According recognition to the desirability of state enforcement assistance, Congress in a number of complete preemption statutes devolved authority to state attorneys general to bring suits in court to enforce the statutes.

The *Federal Environmental Pesticide Control Act of 1972* authorizes the EPA administrator to enter into cooperative enforcement agreements with state attorneys general and provide grants to states to cover part of their enforcement costs.[107]

The *Telephone Consumer Protection Act of* 1991 empowers a state attorney general to bring a civil action against any person violating the act and regulations promulgated under its authority.[108] Congress enacted a partial preemption statute, the *Telephone Disclosure and Dispute Resolution Act of 1992*, devolving authority on a state attorney general to bring a civil action on behalf of his/her citizens in the U.S. District Court to enforce compliance with rules and regulations promulgated under the act by the federal communications commission.[109]

A complete preemption act—The *Telemarketing and Consumer Fraud and Abuse Prevention Act of 1994*—authorizes each state, as *parens patriae*, to "bring a civil suit in an appropriate District Court of the United States to enjoin such telemarketing, to enforce compliance with such rule of the [federal communications] commission, to obtain damages, restitution, or other compensation on behalf of" its residents.[110]

In 1996, Congress enacted the *Consumer Credit Reporting Reform Act* devolving authority to each state attorney general to bring an action in the U.S. District Court to enjoin a violation of the act, and also exempts from preemption any state law "relating to the prescreening of consumer reports" and other specified state laws in effect in 1996."[111]

The *Children's Online Privacy Protection Act of 1998* grants each state attorney general authority to bring a *parens patriae* civil suit in the U.S. District Court if he or she believes "an interest of the residents of that state has been or is threatened, or adversely affected by the engagement of any person in a practice that violates any regulations of the commission" (federal trade commission).[112]

State attorneys general under provisions of the *Controlling the Assault of Non-Solicited Pornography and Marketing Act of 2003* may bring a civil suit to protect state residents who have been or are "threatened or adversely affected" by an individual who violates the act.[113]

Similarly, the *Junk Fax Prevention Act of 2005* empowers state attorneys general to bring a civil suit in the U.S. District Court to enjoin unsolicited messages.[114]

Limited Regulatory Authority Turn-Backs

The turn back of limited regulatory authority to states may be initiated under provisions of four complete preemption statutes and one partial preemption statute. The *Atomic Energy Act of 1946* was amended in 1959 to grant authority to the former Atomic Energy Commission (now Nuclear Regulatory Commission) to enter into agreements with states under the requirement of allowing them to assume specified regulatory responsibilities.[115] The agreement with the state program requires that a state radiation-control program be compatible with, and not necessarily identical to, the commission's regulatory program. In contrast, a minimum standards preemption statute assigns regulatory responsibility to states, provided they adopt standards as high as, or higher than, federal standards and enforce them.

The *U.S. Grain Standards Act of 1968* authorizes the administrator of the Federal Grain Inspection Service to devolve power to state agencies to perform official inspection and weighing.[116]

The *Federal Railroad Safety Act of 1970* authorizes a limited turn back of regulatory authority allowing states to cooperate in railroad safety enforcement by means of state inspection of railroad equipment and facilities in accordance with national standards.[117]

The *Hazardous and Solid Waste Amendments of 1984* allow states to assume responsibility for EPA's hazardous-waste program that had been partially preempted by Congress in 1976.[118]

Cooperative Enforcement

Congress enacted several statutes, in addition to ones devolving powers upon state attorneys general, providing for cooperative federal–state enforcement of preemption statutes.

The *Age Discrimination in Employment Amendments Act of 1986* grants the Equal Employment Opportunity Commission authority to sign cooperative enforcement agreements with state and local government fair employment agencies.[119]

States are authorized by the *Oil Pollution Act of 1990* to enforce on their respective navigable waters only "the requirements for evidence of financial responsibility" of the party responsible for a ship transporting oil as cargo or fuel.[120]

A complete preemption statute—The *Anti Car Theft Act of 1992*—directs the U.S. attorney general and his district attorneys "to work with State and local officials to investigate car thefts, including ... armed carjacking ... "[121]

State and local government law enforcement officers are allowed by the *Antiterrorism and Effective Death Penalty Act of 1996* to arrest an illegal alien or a person convicted of a felony in the United States who was deported or left the country after conviction, subject to obtaining information from the immigration and naturalization service on the status of any such person.[122]

The *Coast Guard and Maritime Transportation Act of 2004* authorizes state and local government law enforcement officers to enforce state criminal laws by arresting persons for violating a federal security zone regulation.[123]

Summary and Conclusions

The framers of the U.S. Constitution by delegating broad regulatory preemption powers to Congress and allowing it to devolve to states all but one of these powers ensured the federal system would be a flexible one able to respond quickly in most instances to emerging public problems. A democratic deficit, however, has been created by congressional enactment of numerous devolution and preemption statutes since 1789 that make it extremely difficult for citizens to determine which plane of government or officer is responsible for a given function or subfunction, thereby inhibiting their ability to hold elected officers accountable.

Enactment of 576 preemption statutes since 1790 removing regulatory authority from states has not converted the federal system into a unitary system, as an *Imperium in Imperio* system remains in effect with states possessing important reserved powers not subject to formal congressional preemption and other powers excluded from preemption statutes by savings and other clauses.

The most important type of devolved powers is minimum standards preemption acts encouraging states to exercise their reserved regulatory powers with a degree of flexibility while meeting national standards, in lieu of losing such powers completely. Individual savings clauses and related provisions in preemption laws, such as permission for more stringent state standards than national ones, in effect devolve national powers to states by exempting these standards from complete preemption.

Congress also devolved regulatory powers upon governors, state attorneys general, and state administrative agencies. Several powers devolved to governors are very important and authorization for state attorneys general to bring a suit in the U.S. District Court for enforcement of a congressional statute is a significant latent power.

A review of devolved powers reveals that Congress neither has established criteria for determining the powers to be devolved to states and the extent of power devolution nor monitored the execution by states of the devolved powers. Congress generally enacts devolution and preemption statutes in a conceptual vacuum on an *ad hoc* basis to respond to pressing problems.

A federal system modeled on the theory of dual federalism would allow citizens to determine readily the plane of government—national, state, or local—responsible for failures to achieve desired goals or incompetent performance of duties. The current system produces citizen confusion attributable in part to (1) numerous types of devolution provisions such as savings clauses (2) multiple preemption provisions, often including separate acts, applicable to a variety of regulatory areas in a single appropriations statute that is hundreds of pages in length, and (3) frequent congressional exercise of preemption powers *sub silentio* with respect to their reach, thereby necessitating judicial determination on a case-by-case basis of their effect.

Congress can initiate action to clarify the responsibilities of the individual planes of government. When partial preemption is deemed essential, Congress should enact a code of restrictions applicable to state and local government activities in the functional areas partially preempted. A similar code for each complete preemption statute would be beneficial since the exercise of the police power by states may be desirable and will not interfere with the achievement of national goals. Publication of a code of devolution provisions also would facilitate citizen understanding of the respective responsibilities of subnational governments and enhance the ability of electors to hold officers accountable.

In sum, congressional statutes devolving powers to state and local governments create fewer problems in terms of citizen understanding of the metamorphic and complex federal system compared to preemption statutes and empower these units to initiate action to solve many subnational problems.

Notes

1. 1 Stat. 54 (1789); *Copyright Act of 1790*, 1 Stat. 124, 17 U.S.C.§101; and *Patent Act of 1790*, 1 Stat. 109, 35 U.S.C.§1.
2. *Bankruptcy Act of 1843*, 5 Stat. 440; *Interstate Communications Act of 1866*, 14 Stat. 66, 45 U.S.C. §84.
3. *U. S. Constitution*, Art. I, §4; Art. II, §1; Art. V; Twenty-First Amendment.

4. Joseph F. Zimmerman, *Interstate Cooperation: Compacts and Administrative Agreements* (Westport, CT: Praeger Publishers, 2002).

5. For additional details, consult Colin Pickington, *Devolution in Britain Today* (Manchester: Manchester University Press, 2002); and Vernon Bogdanor, *Devolution in the United Kingdom*, new ed. (Oxford: Oxford University Press, 2001).

6. 1 Stat. 54 (1789).

7. *Shipping Statute of 1983*, 97 Stat. 553, 46 U.S.C. §8501.

8. *Port and Tanker Safety Act of 1978*, 92 Stat. 1475–476, 33 U.S.C. §1226.

9. Ibid., 92 Stat. 1475, 33 U.S.C.§1225.

10. *Coast Guard Authorization Act of 1984*, 98 Stat. 2862, 46 U.S.C. §2302(c).

11. "Adoption of State Blood Alcohol Concentration Levels," 33 CFR §95.025 (1987). For an explanation of the standards, consult the *Federal Register*, December 4, 1987, 47526–47532.

12. *Paul v. Virginia*, 75 U.S. 168, 8 Wall 168 (1868).

13. *United States v. South-Eastern Underwriters Association*, 322 U.S. 533, 64 S.Ct. 533 (1944).

14. *McCarran-Ferguson Act of 1945*, 59 Stat. 33, 15 U.S.C. §1011.

15. *Gramm-Leach-Bliley Financial Modernization Act of 1999*, 113 Stat. 1353, 11422, 15 U.S.C. §§6701(d)(2)(A), 6751.

16. *Terrorism Risk Insurance Act of 2002*, 116 Stat. 2322, 15 U.S.C. §6701.

17. Ibid., 116 Stat. 2334, 15 U.S.C. §6701(b).

18. *Terrorism Risk Insurance Act of 2005*, 119 Stat. 2660, 15 U.S.C. §6701.

19. "Members Certify GLBA Reciprocity Requirement Met," a news release issued by the National Association of Insurance Commissioners, September 11, 2002.

20. Joseph F. Zimmerman, "Achieving State Insurance Uniformity: The Interstate Compact," a paper presented at an Interstate Compact Symposium: Strengthening State Regulation of Insurance, San Diego, California, December 7, 2002.

21. *Cable Communications Policy Act of 1984*, 98 Stat. 2792, 47 U.S.C. §546.

22. Ibid.

23. Ibid., 98 Stat. 2800, 47 U.S.C. §555.

24. *State and Local Enforcement of Federal Communications Commission Regulations on Use of Citizens Band Radio Equipment Act of 2000*, 114 Stat. 2438, 47 U.S.C. §302(a)(f)(1).

25. *National Firearms Act of 1934*, 48 Stat. 1236.

26. *Sonzinsky v. United States*, 300 U.S. 506 at 513–14, 57 S.Ct. 554 at 556.

27. *Violent Crime Control and Law Enforcement Act of 1994*, 108 Stat. 2012–013, 26 U.S.C. §5802, 18 U.S.C. §923(d)(1)(F).

28. *Johnson Act of 1951*, 64 Stat. 1134 (1951), 15 U.S.C. §1172.

29. *Revenue Act of 1951*, 65 Stat. 452, 26 U.S.C. §3285.

30. *United States v. Kahriger*, 345 U.S. 22 at 28, 32, 73 S.Ct. 510 at 513, 515.

31. *Marchetti v. United States* 390 U.S. 39 at 49, 83 S.Ct. 697 at 703 (1968).

32. *Interstate Horseracing Act of 1978*, 92 Stat. 1813, 15 U.S.C. §3004.

33. *Kentucky Division, Horsemen's Benevolent & Protective Association, Incorporated v. Turfway Park Racing Association*, 832 F. Supp.1097 (E.D. KY, 1993).

34. *Kentucky Division, Horsemen's Benevolent & Protective Association, Incorporated v. Turfway Park Racing Association*, 20 F.3d 1406 at 1416–417 (6th Cir. 1994).

35. *Cabazon Band of Mission Indians v. California*, 480 U.S. 202, 107 S.Ct. 1083 (1987).
36. *Indian Gaming Regulatory Act of 1988*, 102 Stat. 2467, 25 U.S.C. §2710.
37. *Seminole Tribe of Florida v. Florida*, 517 U.S. 44 at 76, 116 S.Ct. 1114 at 1133 (1996).
38. *Professional and Amateur Sports Protection Act of 1992*, 106 Stat. 4228, 28 U.S.C. §3702.
39. Ibid., 106 Stat. 4228, 28 U.S.C.§3704.
40. *Coast Guard Authorization act of 1996*,110 Stat. 3901, 15 U.S.C. §§1175(b)(1)(C), 1175(b)(1)(c)(A). See also the *Johnson Act of 1951*, 64 Stat. 1134, 15 U.S.C. §1172.
41. *Violent Crime Control and Law Enforcement Act of 1994*, 108 Stat. 2126, 18 U.S.C. §1301.
42. *Low Level Radioactive Waste Policy Act of 1980*, 94 Stat. 3347, 42 U.S.C. §2021d.
43. Consult Joseph F. Zimmerman, *Congressional Preemption: Regulatory Federalism* (Albany: State University of New York Press, 2005), 108–115, 151, 187–188, 190.
44. *Water Quality Act of 1965*, 79 Stat. 903, 33 U.S.C. §1151; *Air Quality Act of 1967*, 81 Stat. 485, 42 U.S.C. §1857; *Safe Drinking Water Act of 1974*, 88 Stat. 1665, 42 U.S.C. §201; and *Surface Mining Control and Reclamation Act of 1977*, 91 Stat. 445, 30 U.S.C. §1201.
45. *National Traffic and Motor Vehicle Safety Act of 1966*, 80 Stat. 719, 15 U.S.C. §1392(d).
46. *Federal Railroad Safety Act of 1970*, 84 Stat. 971, 45 U.S.C. §431.
47. *Occupational Safety and Health Act of 1970*, 84 Stat. 1608, 29 U.S.C. §607.
48. *Toxic Substances Control Act of 1978*, 90 Stat. 2038, 15 U.S.C. §2617.
49. Ibid., 90 Stat. 2039, 15 U.S.C. §2617.
50. *Natural Gas Policy Act of 1978*, 92 Stat. 3409, 15 U.S.C. §3431.
51. *Port and Tanker Safety Act of 1978*, 92 Stat. 1475, 33 U.S.C. §1225.
52. *Telephone Consumer Protection Act of 1991*, 105 Stat. 2400, 47 U.S.C. §227(e).
53. *Family and Medical Leave Act of 1993*,107 Stat. 26, 29 U.S.C. §2651.
54. *Armored Car Industry Reciprocity Act of 1993*, 107 Stat. 276. 15 U.S.C. §5901.
55. *Gramm-Leach-Bliley Financial Modernization Act of 1999*, 113 Stat. 1442, 15 U.S.C. §6807.
56. *Do-Not-Call Implementation Act of 2003*, 117 Stat. 557, 15 U.S.C. §6101.
57. *Hazardous Materials Transportation Safety and Security Reauthorization Act of 2005*, 119 Stat. 1895, 49 U.S.C. §5103a(g)(2).
58. *Patient Safety and Quality Improvement Act of 2005*, 119 Stat. 427, 42 U.S.C. §299b–22.
59. 1 Stat. 474 (1796).
60. 1 Stat. 619 (1799).
61. 1 Stat. 474 (1796), 1 Stat. 619 (1797).
62. 20 Stat. 37 (1878).
63. *Louisiana v. Texas et al.*,176 U.S. 1 at 22–23, 20 S.Ct. 251 at 258–59 (1900). See also Joseph F. Zimmerman, *Interstate Disputes: The Supreme Court's Original Jurisdiction* (Albany: State University of New York Press, 2006).
64. *Plant Quarantine Act of 1912*, 37 Stat. 315, 7 U.S.C. §151.

65. *Civil Rights Act of 1964*, 78 Stat. 268, 2 U.S.C. §206.
66. *Federal Environmental Pesticide Control Act of 1972*, 86 Stat. 996–97, 7 U.S.C. §§136u–136v.
67. *Professional and Amateur Sports Protection Act of 1992*, 106 Stat. 4228, 28 U.S.C. §3704.
68. *Newborns' and Mothers' Health Protection Act of 1996*, 110 Stat. 2937, 29 U.S.C. §1185.
69. *Electronic Signatures in Global and National Commerce Act of 2000*, 114 Stat. 467, 15 U.S.C. §7002.
70. *Commodity Futures Modernization Act of 2000*, 114 Stat. 2763A–436, 15 U.S.C. §28(a)(2).
71. *Help America Vote Act of 2002*, 116 Stat. 1728, 42 U.S.C. §1973gg-6(b)(2).
72. *Real Interstate Driver Equity Act of 2002*, 116 Stat. 2342, 49 U.S.C. §14501(d)(3).
73. *Captive Wildlife Safety Act of 2003*, 117 Stat. 2872, 16 U.S.C. §3372((2)(B).
74. *Department of Transportation Appropriations Act of 1990*, 104 Stat. 2185, 23 U.S.C. §105.
75. *Riegle-Neal Interstate Banking and Branching Efficiency Act of 1994* 108 Stat. 2352, 12 U.S.C. §215.
76. Ibid., 108 Stat. 2343, 12 U.S.C. §1831u.
77. *Voting Rights Act of 1965*, 79 Stat. 437, 42 U.S.C. §1973.
78. *Voting Rights Act of 1965*, 79 Stat. 437, 42 U.S.C. §1973c. See also Joseph F. Zimmerman, "Election Systems and Representative Democracy: Reflections on the Voting Rights Act of 1965," *National Civic Review* 84 (Fall/Winter 1995): 288–309.
79. *Transportation Safety Act of 1974*, 88 Stat. 2156, 49 U.S.C. §1801. See also 49 CFR §170–79.
80. *Coastal Zone Management Act of 1972*, 86 Stat. 1282, 16 U.S.C. §1454.
81. *Ibid.*, 86 Stat. 1286, 16 U.S.C. §1456(d).
82. *Federal Environmental Pesticide Control Act of 1972*, 86 Stat. 983, 7 U.S.C. §136b(2). Consult also the *Emergency Energy Conservation Act of 1979*, 93 Stat. 759, 42 U.S.C. §8512.
83. *Clean Air Act Amendments of 1977*, 91 Stat. 722, 42 U.S.C. §7424.
84. *Federal Water Pollution Control Act Amendments of 1972*, 86 Stat. 841, 33 U.S.C. §1151.
85. *Emergency Highway Energy Conservation Act of 1974*, 88 Stat. 1046, 23 U.S.C. §154. See also 23 C.F.R. §658.6.
86. *Safe Drinking Water Act of 1974*, 88 Stat. 1676, 42 U.S.C. §300h.
87. *Wholesome Meat Act of 1967*, 81 Stat. 596, 21 U.S.C. §71, and *Poultry Products Inspection Act of 1968*, 82 Stat. 797, 21 U.S.C. §451.
88. *National Health Planning and Resources Development Act of 1974*, 88 Stat. 2242, 42 U.S.C. §300m.
89. *National Health Planning and Resources Development Act of 1974*, 88 Stat. 2247, 42 U.S.C. §300m-3.
90. *Highway Safety Act of 1966*, 80 Stat. 731, 23 U.S.C. §402(b)(1).
91. "Executive Order 12140 of May 29, 1979," *Federal Register*, May 3, 1979, 31159. This delegation of authority is based upon the power vested in the President by the *Emergency Petroleum Allocation Act of 1973* [87 Stat. 627, 15 U.S.C. §751] and his inherent powers.

92. *Nuclear Waste Policy Act of 1982*, 96 Stat. 2217, 42 U.S.C. §10125.

93. *Yucca Mountain, Nevada, High Level Radioactive Waste Repository Act of 2002*, 116 Stat. 735, 42 U.S.C. §10125.

94. *Tandem Truck Safety Act of 1984*, 98 Stat. 2384, 42 U.S.C. §2312.

95. *Sierra Club v. Ruckelshaus*, 344 F. Supp. 253 (D.D.C. 1972), and *Fri v. Sierra Club*, 412 U.S. 541, 93 S.Ct. 2770 (1973).

96. *Federal Register*, December 5, 1977, 61543. Consult also *New York State Air Quality Implementation Plan: The Moynihan/Holtzman Amendment Submission: Transit Improvements in the New York City Metropolitan Area* (Albany: New York State Department of Environmental Conservation and State Department of Transportation, 1979).

97. *Clean Air Act Amendments of 1977*, 91 Stat. 731, 42 U.S.C. §7470.

98. Ibid., 91 Stat. 734, 42 U.S.C. §7474.

99. Ibid., 91 Stat. 737, 42 U.S.C. §7475.

100. Ibid., 91 Stat. 695, 42 U.S.C. §7410.

101. *Federal Register*, December 5, 1977, 61543. Consult also the *New York State Air Quality Implementation Plan*.

102. *Clean Air Act Amendments of 1990*, 104 Stat. 2400, 42 U.S.C. §7407(d)(1)(B)(iii).

103. Ibid., 104 Stat. 2403, 42 U.S.C. §7407(d).

104. *Clean Air Act Amendments of 1977*, 91 Stat. 723, 42 U.S.C. §7425.

105. *Clean Air Act Amendments of 1990*, 104 Stat. 2419, 42 U.S.C. §7506a.

106. *John Warner National Defense Authorization Act for Fiscal year 2007*, 120 Stat. 2196, 32 U.S.C. §328.

107. *Federal Environmental Pesticide Control Act of 1972*, 86 Stat. 996–97, 7 U.S.C. §§136u-1336v.

108. *Telephone Consumer Protection Act of 1991*, 105 Stat. 2400, 47 U.S.C. §227(f).

109. *Telephone Disclosure and Disputes Resolution Act of 1992*, 106 Stat. 4190, 15 U.S.C. §5712.

110. *Telemarketing and Consumer Fraud and Abuse Prevention Act of 1994*, 108 Stat. 1548, 15 U.S.C. §6103.

111. *Consumer Credit Report Reform Act of 1996*, 110 Stat. 3009–451 to 3009–453, 15 U.S.C. §1681s(2)(b–c).

112. *Children's Online Privacy Protection Act of 1998*, 112 Stat. 2681–733, 15 U.S.C. §6504.

113. *Controlling the Assault of Non-solicited Pornography and Marketing Act of 2003*, 117 Stat. 2712, 15 U.S.C. §7706.

114. *Junk Fax Prevention Act of 2005*, 119 Stat. 359, 49 U.S.C §609.

115. *Atomic Energy Act of 1946*, 60 Stat. 755, 42 U.S.C. §2011; *Atomic Energy Act of 1959*, 73 Stat. 688, 42 U.S.C. §2021.

116. *United States Grain Standards Act of 1968*, 82 Stat. 769, 7 U.S.C. §71.

117. *Federal Railroad Safety Act of 1970*, 84 Stat. 971, 45 U.S.C. §431.

118. *Hazardous and Solid Waste Amendments of 1984*, 98 Stat. 3256, 42 U.S.C. §§6297–928, 6901–991; *Hazardous Materials Transportation Act Amendments of 1976*, 90 Stat. 2068, 49 U.S.C. Appendix §1805c.

119. *Age Discrimination in Employment Amendments Act of 1986*, 100 Stat. 3342, 29 U.S.C. §623.

120. *Oil Pollution Act of 1990*, 104 Stat. 506, 33 U.S.C. §2719.

121. *Anti Car Theft Act of 1992*, 106 Stat. 3384, 18 U.S.C. §2119.
122. *Antiterrorism and Effective Death Penalty Act of 1996*, 110 Stat. 1276, 8 U.S.C. §1252c.
123. *Coast Guard and Maritime Transportation Act of 2004*, 118 Stat. 1078, 46 U.S.C. §70119(a).

Part III

Inequality and Federalism

Chapter 7

Hurricane Katrina, Racial Federalism, and the American State: A Tale Foretold?

Kimberley S. Johnson

When Hurricane Katrina struck the Gulf Coast of the United States and devastated the city of New Orleans, the world witnessed the results of the decades-long "devolution revolution" of modern American federalism. The national government of the strongest nation in the world stood by while thousands of people fled for their lives or lived on the precarious edge of survival, waiting for help that was too slow in coming. State and local governments, the new pillars of federal devolution, seemed unable to cope with the destruction and chaos left in the storm's wake.

Among the many disturbing media images of the Hurricane Katrina disaster were those of the mostly poor or elderly African Americans who were trapped in New Orleans. Race became the most resonant and visible reason that was offered as an explanation for this failure in governance. The story of Hurricane Katrina is thus somewhat simple. New Orleans provides a fundamental example of the interrelationship of race and poverty that is a fact of life in most American big cities. At the time of the storm, it was a majority-minority city, with African Americans making up 67 percent of its population. It was also a poor city, 34 percent of whose residents lived below the poverty line.[1] Thus it was a statistical coincidence that those unable to leave the city to escape the effects of the Katrina disaster—because they lacked either the means or the money—were largely (though not exclusively) African Americans.

Yet the media also revealed another story about Hurricane Katrina that was based on race and on citizenship: nonwhites were "refugees" who were "looting" stores, while whites and others were "evacuees" who "searched" for food. These reverse images of citizenship were not simply the result of racism, whether intentional or not, but more fundamentally reflected the legacy of a federal system that was based on racial differences.

This chapter traces the ways in which American federalism has been shaped by race and by divisions over racial citizenship from the founding of the republic until today. Race, federalism, and citizenship are so deeply intertwined in the national fabric that the American system of government could be more accurately called a racial federalism.[2] Racial federalism is defined as a federal state in which the divisions of power between the center and the federation's constituent units are marked by the ability, or freedom, of each unit to use race as the criteria for determining citizenship rights (political, civil, and social) as well as public policy within the unit. Gender apart, the two most significant determinants of a person's status in the polity throughout U.S. history have been where one lived in the United States and one's racial designation. Racial citizenship in the American federal system in turn has shaped government policy and performance at the national, state, and local levels. In the case of the American federal state, government performance and citizenship have critically been intertwined with the issue of race.

Race was not simply the exception to the creation of the American federal state; it was fundamental to its development. Racial federalism, however, is both a function of time and of place.[3] As the federal structure has shifted over time, so too has the role of race. In many instances, shifts in federalism has been occasioned by shifts in racial policy, and vice versa. Racial federalism is also tied to region and place. For much of the nation's history, the South played the role of the federal state's veto player.[4] The existence of the South as a distinctive political economy from the nation's founding until the mid-twentieth century played a significant role in shaping racial federalism and racial citizenship. The institutions of American federalism were initially shaped and then used by the South in order to protect its regional interests, which primarily centered on the issue of race.

Race was a critical element in the shaping of the American federal state's political institutions and the fragmented bureaucratic and policy delivery structures that now characterize it. The Hurricane Katrina disaster unfolded the way it did because it was part of a much older, rooted pattern of racial and regional inequalities that shaped, and was in turn shaped by, the American racial federal state.

This chapter shows that the path of American racial federalism has not been a straight one. The nation's founding moment was marked by the creation of an American racial federalism as a constitutionally based racial federalism. This constitutionally based federalism was overturned by the Civil War and the consequent brief assertion of national power in the Reconstruction era. In turn, the Reconstruction experiment gave way to a judicially defined and sanctioned new racial federalism. The latter challenged and transformed by the Civil Rights movement of the mid twentieth century. What followed was the climactic assertion of national citizenship and national power that attempted to displace older patterns of racial federalism. By the turn of the century, however, this had given way to a new period of racial federalism whose patterns were vividly displayed in the Hurricane Katrina disaster.

Creating American Federalism

The American revolutionaries faced a difficult issue at the end of their war for independence from England: how could thirteen separate sociopolitical economies combine into a coherent and functional state? The first solution was the Articles of Confederation, which kept intact existing state polities while granting very limited powers to a proto-central government. With no enforcement mechanisms available to check themselves or each other, political and economic instability began to spiral out of control. The new states of the Confederation concluded that another form of national government needed to be developed.

The solution that the framers of the new U.S. Constitution settled on was composite. The new constitutional structure was less confederal than the first experiment in self-government but did not establish a fully centralized or unitary national state. It created a hybrid state that accommodated the significant social, political, and economic differences between the former colonies while providing for more centralized power and coordination, especially in matters of economic policy.[5]

Although the American Revolution created a new state, it did not immediately create a new nation. Key differences still remained between the former colonies, most notably over slavery. While some northern states perpetuated slavery that had been established when they were colonies, the South's economy was particularly dependent upon the "peculiar institution." Under the earlier Articles of Confederation, the lack of a central power as well as the continued independence of the individual states meant that the slavery issue could not and did not have to be addressed.[6]

Potentially, slavery could have been a key stumbling block for the Convention. Early on, however, the decision was made that there would be no attempt to abolish slavery in the proposed constitution.[7] Any discussion about the status of slavery in a free republic's future was put off until the future. Keeping the southern slave states in the union also meant assuaging their fears of minority status. Compromise on this issue resulted in the infamous three-fifths clause (Article 1, Section 2, Clause 3), in which enslaved blacks were partially counted in order to allocate seats in Congress, yet were denied full humanity, let alone citizenship.

The American federal state was forged on the agreement that although the national government reserved the right to determine and apply criteria for national citizenship or naturalization, states could determine citizenship within their own sphere, and that race could be the determining criteria for this. As race and slavery were almost entirely commingled by the time of the American Revolution, this racial federalism reduced southern blacks to noncitizenship and denied them full personhood status until the Civil War altered their status.

The South was remarkably successful in shaping the government powers issued to this new national government. First, at the time of the Constitutional Convention, representatives from the region achieved a postponement of a consideration of the slave importation issue until 1808 (Article I, Section 9). Due to the importance of the comity principle, which established the right of all federal citizens to have their citizenship rights respected by other states, the South was able to further protect its position. With the insertion of a fugitive slave clause in the Constitution (Article IV, Section 2, clause 3), the South was able to limit the ability of persons who escaped slavery to live freely outside of the South by limiting the ability of northern states to allow escaped slaves to live in freedom.[8] The property rights of Southerners had to be respected regardless of the wishes of non-slave states. While this clause underscored the noncitizenship status of slaves, it also highlighted the South's ability to use the federal system, and national power, to buttress their regional interest in the maintenance of slavery.

From the beginning, American racial federalism was based on two understandings. First, there was the acknowledgement that the slave states (by the turn of the nineteenth century almost exclusively located in the South, as Northern states moved toward abolition) could and did have a distinctive veto power that they could exercise within the new government. This veto power came from the representational resources (seats in the House) that were based on their slave population. Second, there was a clear understanding that the citizenship status of Africans in America was a right that was contingent on location. For blacks in the South, citizenship and the rights thereto rested in the hands of those most hostile to black interests.

The South then followed these constitutional victories with an early legislative victory: the Fugitive Slave Law of 1793. This law went further than the constitutional clause by making it a federal crime to assist escaped slaves and established a system of federal oversight over these cases. In response to this legislation and in an ongoing struggle over the rights of states vis-à-vis both each other and the federal government, non-slave states (primarily Northern) enacted personal liberty laws.[9]

The response of the Supreme Court to these state laws demonstrates the power of the South in shaping the dynamics of the American federal system that was based on constitutional differences over race. In 1842, it ruled in *Prigg v. Pennsylvania* (41 U.S. 539) that state personal liberty laws were unconstitutional.[10] This case was followed by a number of other similar judgments, a trend that culminated in 1856 with *Dred Scott v. Sandford* (60 U.S. 393). The Supreme Court ruled in *Scott* case that persons of African ancestry were not eligible for American citizenship anywhere.[11] This upended the balance of power within early federalism over the question of African American citizenship. It also gave southern states the ability to override the political wishes of non-slave states. In all of these cases, the Court was largely sympathetic to the desires of southern slaveholders and was willing to uphold the South's use of federal power to enforce local concerns. As a result, race, citizenship, and federalism became inescapably intertwined.

In addition to support from the judicial branch, the South's political power also rested on the dynamics of the American party system and the still fragile nature of the American federation.[12] To keep the American political system in equilibrium and the Union intact, congressional leaders brokered the Missouri Compromise of 1820 and later the Compromise of 1850. Under these two agreements, the admittance of new states into the union was calibrated against the desire to maintain the balance the power between the interests of the existing slave and non-slave states.[13]

As a result of the party system, the South was able to exercise an influence that was disproportionate to its size or population. A significant example of this was the enactment of the Fugitive Slave Act of 1850 (part of the Compromise of 1850), which exerted more pressure on non-slave states that attempted to evade the earlier Fugitive Slave Law of 1793 by endowing federal commissioners with enforcement powers.

The election of 1860 sundered this decades-long balancing act between both the South and the North and the national and local levels. For the first time in American history, a strong centralized state and executive briefly emerged.[14] Complementing this was the permanent excision of a persistent, though low-grade, source of instability to the American state: the threat of the South's "exit" from the Union. On the other hand, the survival of the constitutional structure of federalism with its implicit recognition of states rights counterbalanced and eventually undermined the new drive for centralization.[15]

Reconstruction and the Rise of the Modern Federal Racial State

Reconstruction in the South pitted different conceptions of state power and citizenship against each other. Although many issues were at stake during this era, clearly one of the most contentious was the still unsettled status of African American citizenship.[16] As a result of trying to resolve this issue, the United States developed three differentiated types of citizenship and citizenship rights that would be available to the recently enslaved, as well as, of course, to other Americans. The first, civil rights citizenship, rested on the "rights necessary for individual freedom," such as the right to freedom of speech, the right to own property, or the right to justice. This citizenship was accompanied by political citizenship, which provided the right to vote and to hold office. The final type of citizenship was social rights citizenship, defined as a "whole range from the right to a modicum of economic welfare and security to the right to share to the full in the social heritage and to live the life of a civilized being according to the standards prevailing in the society." This type could be concretely expressed as the right to education and other social services.[17]

Battles between a recalcitrant President Andrew Johnson and the Radical Republicans in Congress led to the enactment of a succession of laws that attacked the remnants of constitutional racial federalism and beat back attempts by the South via the enactment of Black Codes to create a regional variant of the earlier state of racial federalism. The Civil Rights Act of 1871 (Ku Klux Klan Act) and the Civil Rights Act of 1875 each contained further specifications of national citizenship. In an effort to combat racial terrorism, the former gave citizens the right to sue states for civil rights violations. The latter guaranteed the equality of all citizens by forbidding any state to abridge these rights and specified the right of all citizens to sit on juries, an important element of political and civil rights citizenship.

These legislative attacks on the old racial constitutional order were accompanied by three constitutional amendments, which formally ended the constitutional racial federalism of the pre-Civil War era: the Thirteenth, Fourteenth, and Fifteenth Amendments. The Thirteenth and Fifteenth Amendments were relatively brief and straightforward. The former abolished slavery, one of the foundations of regional difference and conflict, while the latter specifically affirmed that the suffrage rights of U.S. citizens could not be denied or abridged on grounds of race, color, or previous condition of servitude.

The Fourteenth Amendment was more complex and arguably had greatest long-term significance. It established a national basis of citizenship based on birthplace rather than parentage and made people citizens of their state of residence as well as of the United States. It prohibited states from abridging the "privileges or immunities," of U.S. citizens, or from depriving these citizens of "life, liberty, or property, without due process of law." It further stipulated that they could not deny to any person within their jurisdiction the equal protection of laws. Though never enforced, the second section of the amendment also linked the right to political citizenship with congressional representation. States or jurisdictions that denied or restricted the right of male citizens to vote would have their representation reduced in proportion to the number of citizens denied the vote.

By 1877, Reconstruction's limited attempt to rid the United States of its heritage of racial federalism waned. The reconciliation of the North and the South rested on a reformulation of American racial federalism. Each section was allowed to go its own way in regard to race policy and racial citizenship in exchange for national political reconciliation.[18]

The Republican Party, which enjoyed political ascendancy in the North, withdrew its support for protection of African American political citizenship in the South. While the party lost votes in the South from rapidly disenfranchised blacks and their white allies, nationally it would feel little negative effects from this decision. By the mid 1870s, Republican leaders recognized that the northern electorate was disillusioned with the use of military force to sustain what were regarded as corrupt and inefficient Republican regimes in the Southern states. Withdrawal of federal protection permitted Southern supporters of white supremacy to use intimidation to prevent African Americans from exercising their right to vote. With the black vote in decline, there were too few whites to sustain a politically competitive Republican party at the local and state levels in the South. The region consequently became a "solid" Democratic bloc from the late nineteenth to the mid-twentieth century.

Southern white elites consolidated their regional domination and hence their power in national politics through formal disenfranchisement, first of blacks and then poorer whites. The use of instruments such as literacy tests, grandfather clauses, and poll taxes to determine suffrage eligibility circumvented the letter if not the spirit of the Fifteenth Amendment.[19] The introduction of so-called Jim Crow laws also formalized a new system of racial segregation. By 1910, all of the southern states had either adopted new state constitutions or a host of new laws that put into place a hierarchy of citizenship based on race. African Americans were thereby reduced to political insignificance and stripped of their civil rights and political citizenship

Southern Redemption was not solely the work of white Southerners. It was also entrenched in the form of new judicially created racial federalism that replaced Reconstruction's brief attempt to create a new form of nonracial national citizenship. This served to limit the reach of not only the Fourteenth and Fifteenth Amendments to the Constitution but also the legislative acts at both the national and the state levels that had attempted to constrain racial federalism.[20] The onslaught began with the *Civil Rights Cases of 1883*, which reversed the Civil Rights Act of 1875, and culminated in the late 1890s. In *Plessy v. Ferguson* (163 U.S. 537, 1896), the Supreme Court provided judicial sanction for Jim Crow on the basis of the "separate but equal" doctrine that segregation was not necessarily discrimination. Shortly afterward in *Williams v. Mississippi* (170 U.S. 213 (1898)), it approved Mississippi's new constitution, which was openly designed to disenfranchise blacks. These two decisions reaffirmed the central interaction of race, place, and citizenship. States could make policy distinctions between citizens on the basis of race, and could use "color-blind" mechanism to limit political rights based on race without fear of judicial retribution.[21]

Judicial racial federalism limited the prospect for a national nonracial citizenship that was promised by the Fourteenth Amendment. It went even further by implicitly "federalizing" the Fourteenth and Fifteenth Amendments. By refusing to hear cases based on these constitutional claims, the Supreme Court effectively ruled that these elements of the nation's supreme law simply did not apply below the Mason-Dixon line. This judicial racial federalism would stand until overturned by the *Brown v. Board of Education* (347 U.S. 483) decision in 1954.

The political power of the "solid South" offered a further safeguard for racial federalism. Massive disenfranchisement and electoral demobilization produced a closed, noncompetitive and lily-white regional political system for much of the twentieth century. This became the basis of Southern power in national politics. Even though the presidential wing of the Democratic Party grew more liberal from the 1930s onward, conservative white Southerners continued to exert disproportionate influence in the congressional wing of the party through to the 1960s. Their electoral lock on the region's representation in the national legislature was not seriously challenged until the 1970s. Endowed with safe seats, conservative Southern Democrats gained considerable leverage over national congressional policymaking, thanks to the seniority convention that linked power in the committee system to unbroken tenure of office.[22] The rise of this powerful southern bloc coincided with and significantly shaped the growth and capacity of the national government in the late nineteenth and early twentieth century.

Southerners remained vigilant against any type of national policy that could have altered the region's political economy to the disadvantage of its white elites. They were hostile to any agricultural reform that benefited tenant farmers and sharecroppers over landowners, to labor reform that boosted workers rights, and antipoverty assistance that benefited African Americans.[23] The institutionalization of regional self-interest within the U.S. Congress ensured that the mid-twentieth-century growth of the national state occurred within intergovernmental channels. In other words, the new federal programs enacted in the New Deal era and beyond were largely managed through state and local administrative structures that ensured, in the case of the South, that national priorities did not threaten regional interest.[24]

The new racial federalism and the bureaucratic adaptations that emerged in its shadow fundamentally shaped the expansion of the American welfare state created by the New Deal. In particular, southern influence in Congress effectively served to remove farm labor, garment workers, domestics and retail workers—occupations in which African Americans were heavily concentrated—from the social insurance provisions of the Social Security Act of 1935.[25] Although all citizens were theoretically eligible from the expansion of the New Deal state, race and place combined to make the promised benefits of these national programs illusory to those who needed them the most: poor southern African Americans. The benefits of nationalization and its filtering through the prism of racial federalism did not stop with programs created during the Depression. The GI bill of 1944, with its education, job training, and housing benefits for veterans, were again powerfully shaped by race and place.[26] National policies such as urban renewal, housing mortgages, and highway construction directly and indirectly reproduced the color lines of the American federal state.

Nonetheless, racial federalism faced challenges during and after World War II. While the white South had used it to truncate citizenship rights for blacks, the North had not followed suit. Indeed the booming northern labor markets and continued oppression in the South generated a massive northern migration of blacks. Enjoying suffrage rights in the North, millions of these migrants became part of an increasingly important bloc of the New Deal coalition.[27] Cold war rivalry between the United States and the Soviet Union was also a force for racial change. In the battle for the "hearts and minds" of the world's nonaligned nations, the inequality of racial federalism became a cause of embarrassment for America and a source of propaganda for its communist enemy.[28] Encouraged by these developments, national and local civil rights groups grew more active in demanding equality for African Americans. As a result, a new civil rights movement came into being.

Economic and social transformation within the South, from "cottonbelt to sunbelt," also appeared to weaken racial federalism's link between race and place.[29] The collapse of the traditional southern agricultural economy was accompanied by the mechanization of what remained and the rise of a new modern service- and industry-based economy. The population of the region was in flux as blacks continued their outward migration, while whites from outside of the region began their inward migration. Thus the South was poised by the 1960s on the edge of a significant transformation that seemed to portend the end of its shaping influence on American federalism.

The Civil Rights Movement and the Promise of National Citizenship

The civil rights movement promoted a legal, political, as well as social revolution that transformed not only the nation but also, more significantly, the South. It was the culmination of decades-long activism that sought to restore the promise of the Fourteenth Amendment for African Americans and establish a national citizenship that would counteract the older patterns of racial federalism. The political strength of northern black voters helped in attacking racial federalism. Also important in the battle was the post-New Deal Supreme Court, which slowly backed away from the racial federalism of the post-Reconstruction era. The most striking blow against this was the *Brown v. Board of Education* (1954) decision, which struck down the "separate but equal" justification for segregation. It marked the beginning of an attempt to separate race from citizenship and to assert the role of the national government in determining the basis of citizenship.

Other initiatives to rectify past inequalities—some preemptive, others coercive—were also significant. For example, in an attempt to head off pro-integration forces, southern states in the late 1940s and early 1950s announced sweeping plans to equalize the funding gap between black and white schools. Still other racial improvements, such as the integration of public spaces, were made under the threat of lawsuits or the pressure from protest and demonstrations. However, the drive for change reached its peak in the 1960s as the civil rights movement thrust the issue of race and citizenship to the forefront of the national agenda.

The enactment of the Civil Rights Act of 1964 and the Voting Rights Act of 1965 ensured that for the first time since the Reconstruction era, African Americans could begin to exercise the multiple aspects of American citizenship in the South. Political citizenship, meaning the right to vote and hold office, was reestablished with the passage of the Voting Rights Act as well as the ratification in 1964 of the Twenty-Fourth Amendment, which outlawed the use of poll tax payment as qualification to vote in federal elections. The Civil Rights Act reestablished civil rights for blacks, while the Great Society programs enacted under the Johnson administration expanded social citizenship for African Americans.

The results of this struggle for African American rights were largely positive. For example, using *Baker v. Carr* (369 U.S. 186 (1962)) as its basis, Congress as well as state legislatures addressed the issue of political representation. New legislative districts were drawn to create opportunities for minorities to elect representatives of their choice. This legislative redistricting also had significant effects on state politics and policies by ending the dominance of state legislatures by conservative rural interests. In terms of individual-level policies, the Johnson administration's Great Society programs were the highpoint of this attempt to rectify the effects of racial federalism.[30] Among its initiatives was the launch of affirmative action that sought to ensure quality not only of opportunity but also of outcome for groups that had been disadvantaged under the pre-*Brown* racial federalism.

Nevertheless, the Second (racial) Reconstruction, like its predecessor, faced a backlash from those who thought it had gone too far, and too fast. This reaction formed the basis of a new racial devolutionary federalism that ultimately resulted in the tragedy of Hurricane Katrina.

Racial Devolutionary Federalism

The expansion of national citizenship and national government during the late twentieth century could not prevent patterns of racial federalism from being slowly getting reestablished. New Orleans, like most large cities throughout the nation, experienced massive waves of white flight that was centrally linked to beliefs that the civil rights movement violated the boundaries of the pre-*Brown* racial federalism.[31] Throughout the country, race and place took a new shape against the expanding backdrop of suburban America.

Whereas the pre-civil rights era racial federalism had involved the use of coercive government power to determine the basis of racial citizenship, the new racial federalism relied on putatively race-neutral mechanisms such as housing and labor markets to establish geographic boundaries of citizenship that some have called "America's apartheid."[32] In this new federalism, poverty and economic failure could be laid at the feet of the cities' majority-minority inhabitants rather than blamed on those who withdrew economic and social resources from the cities.

In terms of national policy, the origins of the new racial devolutionary federalism can be traced to the Nixon's administration's conviction that the Great Society's expansion of national government was the root cause of America's socioeconomic problems in the 1970s. To limit the reach of what conservatives increasingly dubbed the "Leviathan state," Nixon sought to enhance state and local discretion on the allocation of their federal funding through the use of block grants and "stringless" revenue sharing. This initiated a quarter-century trend of new "New Federalisms" as subsequent presidents attempted, through administrative and fiscal means, to shift responsibility for many domestic policy areas from the federal government to the states.[33] The fiscal crisis of the 1980s provided new impetus for this. Cutbacks in federal grants-in-aid under Ronald Reagan hit urban areas—and their African American and other minority populations—particularly hard. To some critics this was tantamount to Washington "abandoning the cities" to fend for themselves.[34]

Republican presidents also shifted their attention to the federal judiciary that had undone the pre-*Brown* racial federalism. The appointment of judges who would respect the boundaries of this earlier period became a conservative priority. As a result, the Supreme Court under the chief justiceships first of Warren Burger and then William Rehnquist engaged in something of a judicial counterrevolution that employed the color-blindness principle to overturn governmental efforts to rectify the effects of past racial federalism. In 1989 the Rehnquist Court produced seven rulings that critics dubbed "the civil rights massacre of 1989" because they made it harder to prove job discrimination and easier to challenge affirmative action programs. In a curious reversal of the mid-century trend of federal support for the expansion of equality and local Southern resistance to it, one of these judgments—*City of Richmond v. J.A. Croson Co.* (488 U.S. 469 (1989))—struck down Richmond's minority set-aside program on the basis that it violated the Equal Protection Clause. Six years later the Rehnquist Court ruled in *Adarand v. Pena* (515 U.S. 200 (1995)) that "all racial classifications, imposed by whatever federal, state, or local government act, must be analyzed by a reviewing court under strict scrutiny." In short, unless there was a compelling government reason, efforts to undo the effects of past racial federalism were not allowable unless it was "narrowly tailored to meet demonstrated need."

During the last decade of the twentieth century the devolution revolution appeared to receive the stamp of bipartisan consensus as the Democrats sought to maximize their appeal to white voters who had defected to the Republicans in the 1980s. Running for the presidency as a centrist "New Democrat" who was not beholden to the party's traditional commitments, Bill Clinton promised to "end welfare as we know it." This had significant consequences for racial liberalism. By the 1990s American welfare policy had become thoroughly racialized in the minds of many white Americans who equated getting welfare with being black.[35] Though African Americans made up a little over a third of the caseload of Aid for Families with Dependent Children (AFDC) from 1980 to 1996, welfare was deemed a program that exclusively supported a black underclass. Thus, Clinton's rejection of "welfare" was understood by much of the public as a signal that federal policy would no longer be dominated by permissive attitudes towards African American dependency on public assistance. Indeed the Clinton administration repeatedly stressed that state and local governments were best situated to handle local problems.

Enacted in cooperation with a conservative Republican-controlled Congress, the signature policy of the Clinton administration was the Personal Responsibility and Work Opportunity Act (PRWORA) of 1996. This overturned a nationally directed (though still locally administered) system of social support enacted during the New Deal in favor of a new policy that was increasingly directly controlled and funded by the states. Unfortunately, this invocation of localism masked the reality of long-standing and persistent racial and economic inequalities at the state and local levels that these governments were unable or unwilling to address.[36]

This devolution revolution is very unlikely to benefit blacks and other minorities. What James Madison warned in his *Federalist No. 10* holds true at the start of the twenty-first century. Small powerful interests can easily dominate state politics. The growth of the twentieth-century welfare state has not created an even playing field across the country as a whole because of this. The strength of interest-groups representing minorities and the poor varies hugely at the state level in contemporary America. As would soon become evident, they were notably weak and contrary interests were correspondingly stronger in many southern states.[37]

Racial Federalism and New Orleans

The history of Louisiana traces many of the familiar paths of racial federalism that has been previously discussed.[38] Post-Civil War Reconstruction had produced a brief but vibrant display of political citizenship on the part of black Louisianans. Nearly 80 percent of all eligible black men were registered voters, while dozens served as state senators and representatives. Blacks served as the state's lieutenant governor, and one African American, Charles E. Nash, was elected to the U.S. House of Representatives. Louisiana's Constitution of 1898 put an end to this political citizenship. The number of registered black voters fell to less than 1 percent by 1920, and no blacks were again elected to political office until the 1960s. The civil rights citizenship of Louisiana's blacks was also stripped away, often through violent means. The 335 lynchings of blacks that took place in Louisiana from 1882 to 1962 was slightly above the overall average of 275 black lynchings in the eleven states of the former Confederacy over the same period. Social citizenship was also restricted with the establishment of Jim Crow segregation. The failure of the test case brought against Louisiana's new train segregation law by Homer Plessy, a New Orleans resident who was 7/8 white, effectively legitimized public segregation not only in the state but also throughout the South.

The Jim Crow system extended its reach in New Orleans over the next five decades. Segregation had a notable effect on the geography of the city. Areas populated primarily by whites, whether affluent or not, were on higher ground. Those populated primarily by blacks were on lower ground. Among them was the Lower Ninth Ward, where the media recorded the most shocking images of abandonment and destruction in 2005.

Political citizenship returned more slowly to African Americans in Louisiana than in some other parts of the South as a result of the civil rights movement of the 1960s. By 1980 there were 60 percent of the black voting-age population who were registered to vote, double the level in 1964. In 1987 came the election of New Orleans' first African American mayor. In 1991 Louisiana returned its first African American congressman, since Reconstruction, to the U.S. House of Representatives.[39] These political gains came about not only because of the activism of the civil rights movement but also as a result of the creation and enforcement of new national citizenship rights via the Civil Rights Act and the Voting Rights Act.

Advances were also made in social citizenship and civil rights citizenship after the *Brown* judgment's challenge to segregation. The federal courts ordered the desegregation of New Orleans' parks and public transit in 1958. The same instrument was used to end segregation in the city's public schools. In a repeat of the more famous episode in Little Rock, Arkansas, in 1957, New Orleans provided vivid images to the nation and the world three years later of Ruby Bridges, an African American girl, integrating an elementary school. Bridges entered her new school accompanied by federal marshals who protected her from an abuse-screaming mob of white adults, while state and local police stood by without intervening. White parents withdrew their children from the school, and eventually from the public school system as a whole as it became wholly integrated. By 1968, the New Orleans public school district was 67 percent black, and by 2005, like many big city schools systems, it was 95 percent black.[40]

As was the case in metropolises throughout the nation, the integration of New Orleans' public facilities and spaces contributed to the already growing movement of whites to suburban areas. As Kevin Kruse notes in his work on suburban Atlanta, white flight from southern cities resulted from not only national government housing subsidies and changing employment patterns but also decisions made by whites to create an alternative to integration. Kruse argued that for many white southerners, suburbanization cloaked, justified, and explained their resistance to integration as a matter of "rights, freedoms, and individualism."[41]

The city that was devastated by Hurricane Katrina was largely black and poor. It was a city in which public services such as the police and education had experienced serious deterioration in quality and public confidence. As measured by crime statistics, New Orleans ranked as one of the nation's most violent cities and had one of the highest rates of incarceration. It was also a city that was the casualty of the new racial federalism. In company with the ideology of free markets and free choice, the "devolution revolution" of powers and its associated cuts in federal fiscal assistance to urban areas had left New Orleans isolated. The city's most impoverished racial populations were left to fend for themselves with the resources available in their jurisdiction.

The "legacy of inequality," as President Bush was forced to acknowledge in his speech on Hurricane Katrina, was the legacy of racial federalism. The post-Jim Crow racial federalism had returned citizenship rights to the residents of New Orleans, but these residents found to their dismay that their rights stopped at the borders of their flooded city.

Conclusion

As black residents from New Orleans walked out of their flooded city as a consequence of natural disaster, they were told by police officers of adjacent cities and towns to keep moving. The message to these New Orleans residents was simple: they were not citizens of these locales, thus they had no claim to any social or economic respite that these places may have offered to others.

The inability of the Bush administration, the Louisiana state government, and the city of New Orleans to effectively respond to this disaster was rooted within this long-standing pattern of American federalism. While poor African Americans had achieved political citizenship in twenty-first-century Louisiana, the Hurricane Katrina disaster revealed the tenuousness of social- and civil rights citizenship for African Americans. Enduring patterns of residential and racial segregation coupled with new patterns of service delivery means that race and place increasingly determine whether one can access needed services. American racial federalism has proved to be an enduring and adaptable institution.

Notes

1. On the state of New Orleans, see Arloc Sherman and Isaac Shapiro, *Essential Facts about the Victims of Hurricane Katrina* (Washington, DC: Center for Budget and Policy Priorities, 2005). See also Paul Frymer, Dara Z. Stolovitch, and Dorian T. Warren, "Katrina's Political Roots and Divisions: Race, Class, and Federalism in American Politics," *SSRC Forum on Understanding Katrina: Perspectives from the Social Sciences*, 2005. (http://understanding-katrina.ssrc.org/frymerstrolovitchwarren) (accessed September 24, 2007).

2. This definition of racial federalism is different from that offered by Michael Lind, who defines racial federalism as "democracy within races." See Michael Lind, "Prescriptions for a New National Democracy," *Political Science Quarterly* 110 (1995): 563. Anthony Marx offers the closest analogy to my definition of racial federalism. His work explores how federalism (albeit indirectly) and deference on racial equality to local demands were central to new national settlements in the United States (post-Civil War era), South Africa, and Brazil. See Anthony Marx, *Making Race and Nation* (New York: Cambridge University Press, 1998). For the notion of citizenship rights, I draw upon T. H. Marshall's tripartite conception of political, civil rights, and social citizenship. See T. H. Marshall and Tom Bottomore, *Citizenship and Social Class* (London: Pluto Press, 1992).

3. For an interesting theory of racial orders see Desmond King and Rogers Smith, "Racial Orders in American Political Development," *American Political Science Review* 99 (2005): 75–92. While they make a case for white supremacy enduring over time, I contend that racial citizenship is a function of both time and place.

4. On the concept of veto players, see George Tsebelis, *Veto Players: How Political Institutions Work* (Princeton: Princeton University Press, 2002).

5. On theories of American federalism, see for example Samuel Beer, *To Make a Nation: The Rediscovery of American Federalism* (Cambridge, MA: Belknap Press, 1993); William Riker, *Federalism: Origin, Operation, Significance* (Boston: Little, Brown, 1964); and, Barry Weingast, "The Economic Role of Political Institutions: Market-Preserving Federalism and Economic Development," *Journal of Law, Economics, & Organization* 11 (1995): 1–31.

6. The following works discuss the intersection of early American federalism and slavery, Robin L. Einhorn, "Slavery and the Politics of Taxation in the Early United States," *Studies in American Political Development* 14

(2000): 156–183; David F. Ericson, "The Federal Government and Slavery: Following the Money Trail," *Studies in American Political Development* 19 (2005): 105–116; Paul Finkelman, "Story Telling on the Supreme Court: *Prigg v. Pennsylvania* and Justice Joseph Story's Judicial Nationalism," *The Supreme Court Review* (1994): 247–294, and "Slavery and the Northwest Ordinance: A Study in Ambiguity," *Journal of the Early Republic* 6 (1986): 343–370; Robert S. Hill, "Federalism, Republicanism, and the Northwest Ordinance," *Publius* 18 (1988): 41–52; Earl M. Maltz, "Slavery, Federalism, and the Structure of the Constitution," *The American Journal of Legal History* 36 (1992): 466–498; and, Karen Orren, " 'A War Between Officers': The Enforcement of Slavery in the Northern United States, and of the Republic for Which It Stands, Before the Civil War," *Studies in American Political Development* 12 (1998): 343–382.

7. See Jack N. Rakove, *The Beginning of National Politics: An Interpretive History of the Constitutional Congress* (New York: Knopf, 1979).

8. Article IV, Section 2, clause 3: "No Person held to Service or Labour in one State, under the Laws thereof, escaping into another, shall, in Consequence of any Law or Regulation therein, be discharged from such Service or Labour, but shall be delivered up on Claim of the Party to whom such Service or Labour may be due."

9. See Maltz, "Slavery, Federalism," and Orren, "A War Between Officers."

10. See Finkelman, "Story Telling on the Supreme Court."

11. The case is discussed in Don E. Fehrenbacher, *Slavery, Law, and Politics: The Dred Scott Case in Historical Perspective* (New York: Oxford University Press, 1981).

12. See Riker, *Federalism; Origin: Operation, Significance.*

13. This political arrangement is explored by Charles Stewart III and Barry R. Weingast, in "Stacking the Senate, Changing the Nation: Republican Rotten Boroughs, Statehood Politics, and American Political Development," *Studies in American Political Development* 6 (1992): 223–271.

14. For a discussion of Civil War-era growth of federal government see Richard F. Bensel, *Yankee Leviathan: The Origins of Central State Authority in America, 1859–1877* (New York: Cambridge University Press, 1991).

15. See Daniel J. Elazar, "Civil War and the Preservation of American Federalism," *Publius* 1 (1971): 39–58.

16. This is based on Eric Foner's discussion of Reconstruction in *Reconstruction: America's Unfinished Revolution, 1863–1877* (New York: Harper & Row, 1988). See also, Bruce Ackerman, *We the People: Volume 1, Foundations* (Cambridge, MA: Belknap Press, 1991).

17. These definitions of citizenship are defined and discussed by Marshall in *Citizenship and Social Class,* 8.

18. On other "racial federalisms," see Marx, *Making Race and Nation.*

19. The establishment of the Jim Crow order is covered extensively by C. Vann Woodward, *The Origins of the New South, 1877–1913* (Baton Rouge, LA: Louisiana State Press, 1951). The establishment of the political foundations of Jim Crow is treated in J. Morgan Kousser, *The Shaping of Southern Politics: Suffrage Restriction and the Establishment of the One-Party South, 1880–1910* (New Haven: Yale University Press, 1974).

20. See Michael Klarman, *From Jim Crow to Civil Rights* (New York: Oxford University Press, 2004).

21. Indeed the Court even stripped away the fig leaf of "separate and equal" of *Plessy* by ruling in a subsequent case that the determination of whether equality was being met or not was entirely a state and local matter.

22. The institutionalization of Congress is defined and discussed in Nelson Polsby, "The Institutionalization of the U.S. House of Representatives," *American Political Science Review* 62 (1968): 144–168.

23. On the ability of the South to influence national politics and policymaking, see Richard Bensel, *Sectionalism and American Political Development, 1880–1980* (Madison: University of Wisconsin Press, 1984); Ira Katznelson, Kim Geiger, and Daniel Kryder, "Limiting Liberalism: The Southern Veto in Congress, 1933–1950," *Political Science Quarterly* 108 (1993): 283–306; and Sean Farhang and Ira Katznelson, "The Southern Imposition: Congress and Labor in the New Deal and Fair Deal," *Studies in American Political Development* 19 (2005): 1–30.

24. For discussion on development of the modern American state and federalism, see Kimberley Johnson, *Governing the American State: Congress and the New Federalism, 1877–1929* (Princeton: Princeton University Press, 2006).

25. On the intersection of race, federalism and social policy, see Robert Lieberman, *Shifting the Color Line: Race and the American Welfare State* (Cambridge, MA: Harvard University Press, 1998); and, Jill Quadagno, *The Color of Welfare: How Racism Undermined the War on Poverty*, (New York: Oxford University Press 1994).

26. On post–World War II federal social policy and race, see also Ira Katznelson, *When Affirmative Action was White* (New York: W.W. Norton, 2006); and, Suzanne Mettler, *Soldiers to Citizens: The G.I. Bill and the Making of the Greatest Generation* (New York: Oxford University Press 2005).

27. On the intersection of national party politics and race, see Richard M. Vallely, *The Two Reconstructions: The Struggle for Black Enfranchisement* (Chicago: University of Chicago Press, 2004); and Paul Frymer, *Uneasy Alliances: Race and Party Competition in America* (Princeton, NJ: Princeton University Press, 1999).

28. The impact of the cold war on civil rights is extensively covered in Mary L. Dudziak, *Cold War Civil Rights: Race and the Image of American Democracy* (Princeton: Princeton University Press, 2000).

29. On the South's economic transformation, see Bruce Schulman, *From Cotton Belt to Sunbelt: Federal Policy, Economic Development, and the Transformation of the South, 1938–1980* (New York: Oxford University Press, 1991).

30. For a discussion of this era, see James Sundquist, *Dynamics of the Party System: Alignment and Realignment of Political Parties in the United States* (Washington, DC, Brookings Institution Press, 1983).

31. On the intersection of race and postwar suburban growth, see for discussion, respectively, of the North, the South, and the West Coast: Thomas Sugrue, *The Origins of the Urban Crisis: Race and Inequality in Postwar Detroit* (Princeton: Princeton University Press, 2005); Kevin Kruse, *White Flight: Atlanta and the Making of Modern Conservatism* (Princeton: Princeton University Press, 2005); and Robert O. Self, *American Babylon: Race and the Struggle for Postwar Oakland* (Princeton: Princeton University Press, 2003).

32. See Douglas Massey and Nancy Denton, *American Apartheid: Segregation and the Making of the Underclass* (Cambridge, MA: Harvard University Press, 1998).

33. For an overview of modern American federalism, see Timothy Conlan, *From New Federalism to Devolution: Twenty-Five Years of Intergovernmental Reform* (Washington, DC: Brookings Institution Press, 1988).

34. On federal policy toward America's cities, see Demetrios Caraley, "Washington Abandons the Cities," *Political Science Quarterly* 107 (1992): 1–30.

35. On the racialization of welfare policy, see Edward G. Carmines and James A. Stimson, *Issue Evolution: Race and the Transformation of American Politics* (Princeton: Princeton University Press, 1989); Thomas Byrne Edsall and Mary D. Edsall, *Chain Reaction: The Impact of Race, Rights, and Taxes in American Politics* (New York: W.W. Norton, 1991); and Martin Gilens, *Why Americans Hate Welfare: Race, Media, and the Politics of Antipoverty Policy* (Chicago: University of Chicago Press, 1999).

36. See Sheryl Cashin, "Federalism, Welfare Reform, and the Minority Poor: Accounting for the Tyranny of State Majorities," *Columbia Law Review* 99 (1999): 552–627.

37. This is discussed in Joe Soss, Sanford F. Schram, Thomas P. Vartanian, and Erin O'Brien, "Setting the Terms of Relief: Explaining State Policy Choices in the Devolution Revolution," *American Journal of Political Science* 45 (2001): 378–395.

38. For an overview of African American politics in Louisiana, see Adam Fairclough, *Race and Democracy: The Civil Rights Struggle in Louisiana, 1915–1972* (Athens, GA: University of Georgia Press, 1995).

39. See Mildred L. Amer, *Black Members of the United States Congress: 1870–2004*, Congressional Research Service Report for Congress. Updated March 4, 2004 (Washington, DC: Library of Congress, 2004).

40. The students attending New Orleans public schools, 75 percent of whom were eligible for free, or reduced rates, lunch, were also predominantly poor. See Paul Hill and Jane Hannaway, "The Future of Public Education in New Orleans," *After Katrina: Rebuilding Opportunity in the New New Orleans* (Washington, DC: Urban Institute, January 2006).

41. Kruse, *White Flight*, 6.

Chapter 8

The Politics and Policy of the State Children's Health Insurance Program

Alex Waddan and Douglas Jaenicke

While President Clinton's failed attempt to enact national health insurance was probably the defining event of his presidency,[1] there were, nevertheless, other health care initiatives among which the State Children's Health Insurance Program (SCHIP) was the most significant. In his memoirs, former president Clinton described SCHIP as "the largest expansion of health insurance since Medicaid was enacted in 1965."[2] When legislated, the federal government allocated $40 billion for SCHIP over ten years. Enacted in 1997 as part of the bipartisan Balanced Budget Agreement (BBA), SCHIP sought to reduce the rate of uninsurance among children in near-poor families whose incomes were too high for Medicaid. SCHIP built on the Medicaid mandates enacted between 1988 and 1990 that granted Medicaid to all pregnant women and young children below six years whose family income did not exceed 133 percent of the federal poverty line (FPL) and also to children from six to eighteen years who lived in poverty, that is, whose family income was less than the FPL.[3] (In 2007, the FPL was $17,170 for a family of three and $20,650 for a family of four.) Even though the SCHIP legislation does not require states to provide health insurance for children whose family income is too high for Medicaid, all states have done so apparently in response to the financial incentive written into SCHIP. To spur states to create SCHIP programs, SCHIP provides each state with a capped matching grant, and a state's federal medical assistance percentage (FMAP) for SCHIP is greater than its Medicaid FMAP. Hence, for the 2006 fiscal year (FY), while the Medicaid FMAP for the fifty states and the District of Columbia ranged from 50 to 76 percent, the enhanced SCHIP FMAP ranged from 65 to 83.2 percent.[4]

Although SCHIP built on Medicaid, there are important differences between the two. Unlike the open-ended Medicaid entitlement, SCHIP has a capped federal budget. Also, because SCHIP does not create an individual entitlement, states may cap enrolment in SCHIP, may refuse to enroll children who meet the eligibility criteria, and may implement waiting lists.

In addition, SCHIP grants states discretion over benefits and especially eligibility. Furthermore, unlike Medicaid, SCHIP was only authorized for a limited period and hence needed Congressional reauthorization to continue beyond 2007. Finally, Medicaid dwarfs SCHIP both in terms of federal spending and the number of children covered. In 2005, about 80 percent of children with federally funded health insurance were covered by Medicaid, the other 20 percent, by SCHIP.[5] Similarly, in FY 2006, the $5.5 billion for SCHIP was less than 20 percent of the $30 billion the federal government spent on providing Medicaid for children and only 3 percent of the federal government's total Medicaid spending of $180 billion.[6]

This chapter first analyses the politics of SCHIP's enactment. In a context of not only divided government but also polarized congressional parties,[7] SCHIP was legislated as part of a broader budget agreement negotiated by Clinton and congressional Republicans. In addition, SCHIP embodied a bipartisan compromise of conservative and liberal features. The chapter then focuses on the implementation and effectiveness of SCHIP. Reflecting the discretion granted to states, SCHIP's implementation has entailed significant state-level variation. Thinking that SCHIP's hybrid nature might provide a template for a bipartisan approach for reducing uninsurance and even for ensuring health insurance for all Americans, Henry Aaron observed that SCHIP "appeals to important principles espoused by both parties ... It uses the conservative principle of permitting states latitude and independence to achieve the liberal goal of extending health insurance."[8] Supporting Aaron's interpretation, both national parties claimed credit for SCHIP in their platforms for the 2000 elections.[9]

Finally, the chapter analyses the politics surrounding the attempt to reauthorize SCHIP in 2007. Given SCHIP's success in reducing uninsurance among children, its survival was not in doubt, but the debate about whether to expand SCHIP exposed the underlying partisan cleavage, and hence the bipartisan quid pro quos that originally produced SCHIP, were not equivalent to consensus. Although the bipartisanship that Aaron hoped for vanished during the reauthorization debate, Democratic senators easily passed a reauthorization bill by attracting significant cross-partisan[10] Republican support for their proposed large increases in SCHIP spending and eligibility. In contrast, almost no House Republicans voted for the House Democrats' reauthorization bill, which passed that chamber on an overwhelmingly partisan vote. Later, resembling the cross-partisan Senate legislation, the conference bill was passed with comfortable majorities in both chambers because nearly unanimous Democratic support was coupled with support from a significant minority of Republicans. However, despite that cross-partisan support, there was not sufficient Republican support to override President Bush's veto.

The Politics of SCHIP's Enactment

Given that both parties later claimed credit for it, SCHIP's initial enactment in 1997 was more problematic than might have been expected. Three features contributed to SCHIP's passage. First, SCHIP addressed the problem of uninsurance among low-income children. Since children are not seen as responsible for their economic fate, they are considered to be innocent and therefore deserving of government protection especially if their families cannot afford health insurance. Agreement on that point was insufficient to enact legislation since there were significant disagreements about the appropriate policy response.[11]

Hence, a second significant aspect of SCHIP's enactment was its incorporation into a much larger piece of bipartisan legislation—the 1997 BBA. President Clinton insisted upon government-provided health insurance for some near-poor children as his price for the 1997 BBA that gave congressional Republicans tax cuts and spending cuts as well as a balanced budget. Furthermore, the budget agreement's projected reductions in Medicare and Medicaid spending of more than $120 billion as well as cuts in discretionary programs obviated any need to increase taxes to pay for SCHIP's originally agreed cost of $16 billion over five years. Far exceeding the new SCHIP spending, those cuts not only paid for SCHIP but also financed the Republicans' tax cuts and helped balance the budget.[12]

Although it is impossible to prove that SCHIP would not have been enacted as a stand-alone legislation, Daniel Palazzolo concluded that SCHIP was a policy that the "Republican Congress would not have passed on its own."[13] Reflecting on Clinton's failed attempt to guarantee health insurance for all Americans, Margaret Weir contended that the "context of sharp, partisan-based ideological opposition raises doubts about the possibilities for rational discussion and political compromise among elites."[14] Similarly, after analyzing Republican opposition to Clinton's health security bill and the congressional Republicans' later attempt at conservative "big bang" health care reform in 1995 and 1996, Jacob Hacker and Theda Skocpol concluded that the increased weight of antigovernment conservatives among congressional Republicans made more difficult even an incremental expansion of the government's role in providing health care.[15] Even so, congressional Republicans accepted a new government health care program for uninsured children as the price they had to pay in order to receive their priorities of tax and spending cuts and a balanced budget.

Third, while congressional Republicans were willing to pay a price, they were unwilling to pay any price, hence SCHIP's specific features embodied a range of partisan compromises. One issue was the discretion that states would enjoy when deciding how to use the new federal money to provide for uninsured low-income children. Congressional Republicans wanted the money to be given as a block grant that would give the states absolute discretion when deciding how to spend it on children's health and also would not require the states to spend their own funds. Senator Phil Gramm (R-TX) argued: "I believe Federal mandates are inefficient because they stifle innovation. With a block grant, we'd get much more innovation. We'd have 50 different programs."[16] In contrast, Senator John Breaux (D-LA) reflected: "There is a real argument about how we will give this money to the states.

Table 8.1 Partisan differentiation and cohesion on SCHIP-related votes

Legislation, chamber, date	Outcome	Partisan differentiation	Republican cohesion percentage	Democratic cohesion percentage
Democratic amendment to extend Medicaid entitlement to near-poor children, i.e., with family incomes up to twice the FPL, House, 1997	Defeated	199.2	99.6	100.0
Dominici (R-NM) amendment affirming agreement to spend up to $16 billion over five years on children's health care, Senate, 1997	Passed chamber	7.2	96.4	100.0
Kennedy–Hatch amendment to increase cigarette tax by 43 cents per pack in order to spend $35 billion on SCHIP over five years, Senate, 1997	Defeated	135.4	85.5	82.2
Kennedy's (D-MA) amendments to extend SCHIP and Medicaid to low-income parents, Senate, 2000	Defeated	185.0	92.5	100.0
		177.4	88.7	100.0
Cornyn (R-TX) amendment to emphasize that SCHIP should be used to insure children with family incomes not greater than twice the FPL and to limit SCHIP's coverage of nonpregnant adults, Senate, 2007	Defeated	158.4	79.2	100.0
Smith (R-OR) amendment to allow federal government to increase cigarette tax by 61 cents in order to increase SCHIP spending over five years by up to $35 billion, Senate, 2007	Passed chamber	130.4	73.5	91.7
Democrats' cross-partisan SCHIP reauthorization bill to increase SCHIP spending by $35 billion over five years, Senate, 2007	Passed chamber	126.6	63.3	100.0

Continued

Table 8.1 Continued

Democratic SCHIP reauthorization bill to increase SCHIP spending by $50 billion over five years, House, 2007	Passed chamber	186.4	97.5	95.7
Conference SCHIP reauthorization bill to increase SCHIP spending by $35 billion over five years, House, September, 2007	Passed	147.0	77.0	96.5
Conference SCHIP reauthorization bill, Senate, September, 2007	Passed	123.4	61.7	100.0
House vote to override President Bush's veto, October, 2007	Failed	153.8	77.8	99.1

Source: *CQ Weekly* 1997: 1236, 1552; 2000: 919, 1839; 2007: 914, 994, 2391, 2404, 2870, 2876, 3118.

I have real concern that if we give it to them as a block grant, it may or may not be used to insure extra kids."[17] Similarly, the White House worried that the states might use the extra money only to provide a limited range of health services for children so that important areas of children's health care would be neglected.[18]

While congressional Republicans eventually acquiesced in President Clinton's demand that states use the new SCHIP funds to provide health insurance, not just health services,[19] they steadfastly refused to create a new entitlement. For example, on a nearly perfect party line vote that produced nearly perfect partisan differentiation (table 8.1),[20] House Republicans defeated a Democratic proposal to substitute a Medicaid-based entitlement for the SCHIP-capped federal matching grant to the individual states. As a capped matching federal grant, SCHIP exemplifies the "post-entitlement welfare" initiated by the 1996 welfare reform.[21] On the other hand, although they would not concede a simple Medicaid expansion to cover near-poor children, Republicans were compelled to accept a Medicaid extension as one method available to states for delivering SCHIP.

Furthermore, Republicans favored state discretion in determining eligibility for SCHIP and also the quality of health insurance that was provided. Conceding state discretion over eligibility, President Clinton insisted that SCHIP limit state discretion over the quality of the health insurance that was provided by SCHIP.[22] Under SCHIP, the states and the District of Columbia have discretion over how to implement SCHIP: they may simply expand Medicaid, create a separate SCHIP program, or do both. A state that chooses a Medicaid expansion must provide SCHIP children with all Medicaid benefits. Alternatively, if a state opts for a separate SCHIP program, its benefits have to at least match one of a limited range of specified benchmarks: the standard Blue Cross/Blue Shield preferred provider option available to federal employees, the health benefits provided to state employees, the managed-care program with the largest non-Medicaid enrolment in a state, the comprehensive benefits provided by existing children's health programs in New York, Pennsylvania and Florida, or any other actuarially similar package of health benefits approved by the Department of Health and Human Services (HHS).[23]

There was also disagreement over the size of the federal government's allocation for SCHIP. Although the Republicans' original budget resolution provided $16 billion over five years, a proposal by senators Edward Kennedy (D-MA) and Orrin Hatch (R-UT) to increase the federal cigarette tax by forty-three cents per pack in order to provide an additional $20 billion for SCHIP over five years generated significant partisan conflict. During the debate on the Kennedy–Hatch amendment, the chair of the Senate Budget Committee, Senator Pete Domenici (R-NM), proposed an amendment affirming that, as agreed in the budget resolution, up to $16 billion would be spent over five years to provide health services for uninsured children. With all Democrats and all but two Republican senators voting for the Domenici amendment, it generated almost no partisan differentiation (table 8.1). However, Domenici explained that the Kennedy–Hatch amendment was unacceptable because it would simultaneously reduce the agreed tax cut included in the budget resolution by $30 billion and increase government spending. Calling that amendment a "deal buster," the Senate Majority Leader, Trent Lott (R-MS), warned that he would permit a vote on it only if its defeat was certain, if not, he would pull the budget resolution from the floor.[24] Yielding to Republican pressure, President Clinton reversed his earlier support for the Kennedy–Hatch amendment and now lobbied Democratic senators to defeat it. Even so, more than 80 percent of the Democratic minority voted for the amendment while the Republican majority was slightly more unified in opposing it, hence, partisan differentiation reached a moderately high 135.4 (table 8.1).

Refusing to abandon the fight for additional funding, Kennedy and congressional Democrats continued to press President Clinton until he agreed to insist upon $24 billion for SCHIP's first five years, with the increase financed by higher tobacco taxes.[25] In addition, with the Children's Defense Fund organizing "one of the most feverish grassroots lobbying campaigns ever on an issue," a group of Republican senators—led by Hatch and John Chafee (R-RI)—persuaded Lott for expediential electoral reasons to allow $24 billion over five years for SCHIP with an increase in the federal cigarette tax financing the additional $8 billion.[26] Once Lott yielded, a Democratic-led cross-partisan majority coalition wrote $24 billion for SCHIP into the Senate's budget proposal. Finally, under the "rule of two thirds" adopted by the budget negotiators, the final bipartisan budget agreement included $24 billion for SCHIP since both the president and the Senate supported the additional money and its method of financing while the Republican-controlled House adhered to the original $16 billion.[27]

SCHIP's Effectiveness and Limits

Prior to SCHIP, only eight states provided health insurance to children with family incomes at twice the poverty level.[28] In contrast, by 2006, forty-one states and the District of Columbia enrolled such children in either Medicaid or SCHIP.[29] Between 1997 and 2005, children covered by public health insurance increased from 18.7 percent to 27 percent.[30] As a result of both SCHIP and the earlier Medicaid mandates, the uninsurance rate for all children under eighteen years fell from 15.4 percent in 1998 to 10.9 percent in 2005.[31] According to Ku et al., the percentage of children in families with income not exceeding twice the FPL, without health insurance, fell from 23 percent in 1997 to 14 percent in 2005.[32] Using slightly different data, Dubay et al. concluded that 14.9 percent of low-income children were uninsured in 2005 compared to 22.3 percent in 1997.[33] In contrast, the uninsurance rate for children in families whose incomes exceed twice the poverty line and also low-income parents remained more or less the same.[34] Although the children with employer-sponsored health insurance fell from two thirds in 1997 to 59.4 percent in 2005, the rate of uninsurance among children declined in this period because of the expansion of public health insurance via Medicaid and SCHIP.[35] In addition to providing health insurance for about 6.1 million children in 2005, SCHIP also insured 639,000 adults,[36] but this adult coverage had negligible impact upon uninsurance among working-age adults.

The reduced rate of uninsurance among low-income children produced clear benefits. Compared to low-income children who lacked health insurance, low-income children who were enrolled in Medicaid and SCHIP were more likely to have a constant source of medical care and also regular access to preventive care, and they also were less likely to experience unmet medical needs.[37]

SCHIP's success should not obscure its limitations. First, despite both Medicaid and SCHIP, about 14–18 percent of low-income children in the United States remain uninsured. Second, in 2005, the number and percentage of uninsured children increased for the first time since 1998.[38] Third, there are huge state-by-state variations in the rates of uninsurance among children (next section). Fourth, twice as many uninsured children are eligible for Medicaid, as SCHIP might deter states from active outreach since the Medicaid FMAP is less than the SCHIP FMAP.[39] Fifth, since SCHIP is not an entitlement, states may (and do) freeze SCHIP enrolment especially when they experience budgetary stringency, as they did earlier in the decade.[40] Valuing the state-level discretion conferred by SCHIP, governors oppose SCHIP becoming a mandate.[41]

Furthermore, despite SCHIP's success in reducing uninsurance among children, it fails to address the problem of high rates of uninsurance among working-age adults (i.e., aged eighteen to sixty-four years) and especially poor working-age adults who often do not benefit from employment-related health insurance and cannot afford health insurance. In 2005, there were 43 percent of the working-age poor who were uninsured compared to only 3.9 percent of the elderly poor, 18.6 percent of poor children under eighteen years,[42] and 18.3 percent of low-income children under nineteen.[43] Also, while uninsurance for low-income children has been falling, uninsurance for low-income adults has increased.[44]

Finally, SCHIP's emphasis upon "innocent" children reinforces a cultural norm that obstructs extending government-provided health insurance to working-age adults. Reflecting that norm, the Republicans' 2005 Deficit Reduction Act (DRA) prohibited any new SCHIP waivers covering nonpregnant childless adults. To undermine the argument for a large increase in SCHIP funding, the Bush White House and conservatives draw a distinction between "deserving" innocent children and "undeserving" irresponsible adults by emphasizing that SCHIP currently provides health insurance for nonpregnant adults and that in some states adults outnumber children in SCHIP.[45] Even while defending the House Democrats' plan in 2007 to increase the federal government's spending on SCHIP by $50 billion over five years in order to increase enrolment in SCHIP, the Democratic chair of the House Energy and Commerce Committee that has jurisdiction over SCHIP reinforced the deserving–undeserving distinction: "We're not proposing to cover adults, parents or wealthy children."[46]

The Reality of Federalism: State-Level Variation in Delivering SCHIP

States have discretion over SCHIP eligibility since a state may cover children whose family income is twice the FPL or whose family income is 50 percentage points above the state's Medicaid threshold.[47] However, states may increase eligibility above those levels since they enjoy flexibility in defining income and especially may employ "income disregards" to increase SCHIP eligibility.[48] In 2006, twenty-six states set eligibility at 200 percent of the FPL ($34,340 for a family of three and $41,300 for a family of four), fifteen states above twice the FPL,[49] and seven at three times the FPL or higher while nine states restricted eligibility to children whose family income fell below twice the FPL. North Dakota, the state with the most restrictive eligibility, limited SCHIP eligibility to children whose family income was no more than 40 percent higher than the FPL. The most generous state, New Jersey, set eligibility at 350 percent of poverty,[50] and New York passed legislation in 2007 to grant SCHIP eligibility to children whose family income is up to four times the FPL.[51]

States also vary in how they deliver SCHIP. In 2006, thirteen states and the District relied exclusively upon Medicaid expansions to deliver SCHIP, seventeen states relied exclusively upon separate SCHIP programs, and nineteen states employed a combination of a separate SCHIP program and a Medicaid expansion. This difference in the mode of delivery matters because a separate SCHIP program may cap enrolment or increase premiums but a Medicaid expansion generally may not. A difference in federal funding explains why separate SCHIP programs possess such discretion while Medicaid expansions do not. Once a state's SCHIP Medicaid expansion has used up its federal SCHIP allotment, the federal government still continues to contribute to the cost of insuring SCHIP children enrolled in Medicaid but at the lower normal Medicaid FMAP rather than at the enhanced SCHIP FMAP.[52] However, once a state's separate SCHIP program has spent its federal SCHIP allotment, it has to pay all, not part, of SCHIP's costs unless it has unspent SCHIP funds available from the two previous years or unless it benefits from the redistribution of unspent SCHIP allotments from other states.

Since the 1997 legislation required states to ensure that SCHIP coverage did not "crowd out" private health insurance, most states implemented a waiting period for SCHIP in order to discourage low-income parents who pay for health insurance for their children from enrolling them in SCHIP. As of July 2006, fifteen states and the District had no waiting period for children's SCHIP eligibility; thirty-five states operated waiting periods varying between one and twelve months, with most states imposing a waiting period of either three or six months. When SCHIP began, only eleven states had no waiting period for children seeking to enrol in SCHIP. In addition, more states have reduced their waiting periods than increased them.[53]

Whether a state employs a waiting period for SCHIP eligibility varies somewhat according to the program type. While only six (42.9 percent) of the fourteen simple Medicaid-expansion-only states imposed a waiting period, sixteen (78.9 percent) of the nineteen states that combined a SCHIP-funded Medicaid expansion with a separate SCHIP program and fourteen (82.4 percent) of seventeen states that simply used a separate SCHIP program did.[54]

To reduce SCHIP's crowding out of private insurance and also to reduce the strain on state budgets, thirty-nine states require families to contribute to the cost of their children's SCHIP coverage while eleven states did not impose any cost-sharing.[55] The states that impose cost-sharing vary according to the type of cost-sharing, the size of any cost-sharing, and also the income level at which any cost-sharing is imposed.[56] For example, in 2006, eleven states charged premiums for children in SCHIP when a family's income just exceeded the poverty line, twenty-six when it was 50 percent higher than poverty and twenty-eight when family income was twice higher than the poverty line.[57] States also vary in whether they charge co-payments for non-preventive physician visits, emergency room visits, inpatient hospital stays, and prescription drugs.[58]

Furthermore, states exercise discretion over their enrolment procedures. To encourage enrolment by simplifying enrolment procedures, the District and forty-five states do not require face-to-face interviews by SCHIP applicants. In addition, forty-three states and the District only require children to renew their enrolment annually rather than more frequently. However, only sixteen states have adopted twelve months continuous eligibility for successful applicants, and only nine states do not require families to provide proof of family income in order to enrol children in SCHIP.[59]

In order to enrol adults in SCHIP, states usually have to apply for a waiver from the HHS Secretary.[60] The Clinton administration introduced waiver guidelines to permit states to use SCHIP to cover pregnant women and parents, and the Bush administration allowed states to use SCHIP to cover "unborn" children and childless adults. As of February 2007, only fourteen states had waivers to enrol some adults in SCHIP. Of these fourteen states, only Idaho covered all three categories of adults.[61] Although covering an entire family increases the enrolment of eligible children in Medicaid and SCHIP,[62] only eleven states extend SCHIP coverage to parents. Also, these states extend SCHIP eligibility to adults at different income levels.[63] Furthermore, while the states' SCHIP programs for children have built on the earlier Medicaid mandates, only six states have built on the earlier Medicaid mandate for pregnant women with family income less than 133 percent of poverty line.

That so few states extend SCHIP to adults—whether parents, pregnant women, or childless adults—probably reflects an economic disincentive as well as the cultural norm that adults are responsible for their own health insurance. A state that enrols adults in SCHIP may not "close enrolment, institute waiting lists, or decrease eligibility for children while the waiver [for adults] is in effect."[64] By limiting a state's policy options, that requirement might discourage states from expanding SCHIP to cover pregnant women and parents.

Reflecting the discretion delegated to the states by SCHIP as well as other factors, the rate of uninsurance for both children and low-income children varies significantly from state to state. Between 2003 and 2005, the uninsurance rate for all children was 11.7 percent but ranged from a low of 5.6 percent in Vermont to a high of 20.4 percent in Texas.[65] Furthermore, 18.3 percent of low-income children under nineteen were uninsured in 2005. However, that national average obscures large interstate variations. For example, the highest rates of uninsurance for low-income children occurred in New Mexico (30.5 percent), Florida (30.2 percent), Texas (27.7 percent), Colorado and Arizona (26.6 percent), Nevada (22.3 percent), Montana (21.6 percent), Delaware, California, and Utah (21.4 percent), New Jersey (21.3 percent), and Connecticut (20.6 percent) while the states with the lowest rates of uninsurance for low-income children were Massachusetts (5.6 percent), Hawaii (7 percent), Alabama (7.4 percent), Vermont (7.9 percent), Iowa (8 percent), New Hampshire (8.1 percent), Minnesota (8.2 percent), and West Virginia (8.8 percent).[66]

This variation cannot be explained simply as a function of a state's income eligibility for SCHIP since all of the above states, except Montana, set SCHIP eligibility at or above twice poverty.[67] Similarly, nor can it be explained simply as a function of whether a state delivers SCHIP via a Medicaid expansion, a separate SCHIP program, or a combination, since all three methods of delivering SCHIP can be found in states with low rates of uninsurance and also in states with high rates.[68]

Partisan Conflict over SCHIP in 2007

In 2007, three factors coincided to reveal substantial partisan disagreement about the future of SCHIP that in turn reflected the partisan cleavage about the government's role in providing health care: a crisis in SCHIP's funding, Democratic control of Congress, and the need to reauthorize SCHIP. The likely partisan divisions over SCHIP's reauthorization had been foreshadowed in 2000 when the Senate defeated Senator Kennedy's amendments to reduce the Republicans' proposed tax cuts in order to extend SCHIP and Medicaid eligibility to low-income parents. Kennedy's proposal generated high partisan differentiation of 185.0 and 177.4 since all Democratic senators voted for his amendments that were opposed by about 90 percent of Republicans (table 8.1). Hence, in 2007, even though SCHIP's termination was not on the agenda, the debate about the program was always likely to expose the partisan cleavage over the proper role of government in guaranteeing economic security, especially after the Democrats won control of Congress in the 2006 elections.

The circumstances in 2007 contrasted with those that had largely kept SCHIP's funding off the political agenda since 1997. Four reasons help explain the relative quiescence over SCHIP for nearly a decade. First, the states' full implementation of SCHIP programs required a number of years. Second, a state has three years in which to spend its SCHIP allotment for a particular fiscal year (FY). This ability of states to carry over unspent SCHIP funds for two further years was especially important in SCHIP's early years when states frequently spent less than their annual SCHIP allotments. Third, if any state did not spend its full SCHIP allotment for a particular fiscal year during the permitted three-year period, then the unspent SCHIP dollars could be redistributed to states that spent more than their SCHIP allotment. Finally, given their tax-cutting priorities and their preference for private health insurance, first a Republican Congress and later a unified Republican government had little incentive to increase SCHIP's funding. For example, in 2004 and 2005, unified Republican government permitted $1.4 billion of unspent SCHIP allotments from 2001 and 2002 to expire rather than to be used to increase SCHIP spending.[69]

After 2002, however, various factors coincided to create a fiscal crisis for many states' SCHIP programs. First, in order to comply with budget rules,[70] the annual SCHIP allotment dropped from $4.2 billion for FY 1998–2001 to $3.1 billion for FY 2002–2004 and then increased only to $4.1 billion for the next two years.[71] With that reduction in the federal government's annual SCHIP allotment, states regularly began spending in aggregate more than the total SCHIP allotment for a particular fiscal year.[72] Initially that reduction was cushioned by the states' ability to carry over unspent SCHIP funds and also by the redistribution of SCHIP funds from underspending to overspending states. Second, with SCHIP's maturation, most states spent more than their annual SCHIP allotment. For example, in FY 2006, forty states overspent and were eligible for redistributed SCHIP funds. As a result, there has been less and less money available for redistribution.[73] Third, even while the annual SCHIP allotment was reduced, and reduced even further in real terms by medical inflation vastly exceeding the ordinary rate of inflation, enrolment in SCHIP did not fall but only temporarily levelled off between 2003 and 2005[74] and then increased after 2005 albeit at a slower rate than between 1998 and 2003.[75] Hence, by 2005, any slack in SCHIP's funding had largely disappeared, and many states faced shortfalls in their SCHIP allotments.

Through 2006, the problem of states spending more than their SCHIP allotments was dealt with in a piecemeal manner by unified Republican government. Providing the states with some fiscal relief, the 2005 DRA temporarily increased the SCHIP allotment for FY2006 by $283 million. Significantly, like the original 1997 BBA, the Republicans' DRA paid for its temporary increase in SCHIP funding by a much larger $11 billion reduction in projected federal spending for Medicare and Medicaid.[76] A year later, when the lame-duck Republican Congress reconvened in December 2006, it again adopted a short-term fix for the problem of overspending by some states; without increasing the annual SCHIP allotment, the 2006 National Institutes of Health Reform Act speeded up the redistribution of $270 million from underspending to overspending states.[77]

The new Democratic majorities in Congress in 2007 immediately placed more federal money for SCHIP on the congressional agenda in order to permit expanded eligibility.[78] In contrast, President Bush initially proposed to freeze SCHIP spending in nominal dollars for FY 2008 and therefore to cut SCHIP in real terms.[79] Later, President Bush proposed a small increase in SCHIP funding of about $5 billion over five years, which was much less than the additional $14 billion that the Congressional Budget Office estimated was necessary to maintain SCHIP's existing enrolment.[80]

The fiscal crisis in SCHIP's spending at the state level led some Republican governors to join with Democrats to press for more SCHIP funding. Prior to the annual winter meeting of the NGA, thirteen governors sent a letter to congressional leaders urging them to make up shortfalls in SCHIP funding. Seven of the signatories were Republicans, including Sonny Perdue of Georgia, chair of the Republican Governors' Association, Tim Pawley of Minnesota, vice-chair of the NGA, and Haley Barbour of Mississippi, a former chairman of the Republican National Committee. At the NGA's winter meeting, governors from across the political spectrum called for an extra $745 million to prevent any closing of SCHIP rolls before October.[81] Later, the NGA called for increased federal funding, abandonment of the requirement that states ensure that SCHIP does not "crowd out" private health insurance, and increased state flexibility in determining SCHIP eligibility.[82] However, as the NGA's summer meeting underlined, while governors supported SCHIP's reauthorization and additional money for SCHIP, they did not agree about the size of any increase.[83]

The Democrats' commitment to additional SCHIP spending first bore fruit in the bipartisan supplemental spending package that was passed in May

2007; that bipartisan quid pro quo included an additional $600 million for SCHIP[84] that covered most, but not all, of the projected $921 million shortfall in SCHIP funding for FY 2007.[85] A 2006 study by the Congressional Research Service observed: "If Congress intends to prevent state shortfalls of federal SCHIP funds in FY 2007, legislative action will be needed. If, however, Congress decides that the intent of the original legislation was to ensure states did not treat the program as an open-ended entitlement, no action will be necessary."[86] Congressional Democrats and Republicans have largely adopted those conflicting positions. Proclaiming SCHIP's success and exploiting reauthorization as an opportunity to build on that success, Democrats seek to increase SCHIP's funding in order to expand eligibility for it; some Democrats even see SCHIP's expansion as a first step toward guaranteeing universal health insurance.[87]

Although congressional Republicans had originally favored state discretion in implementing SCHIP, President Bush and many congressional Republicans complained in 2007 that some states have gone beyond what they described as SCHIP's "original purpose" and had improperly used SCHIP to insure children above 200 percent of the FPL as well as some adults.[88] Reflecting this Republican preference for restricting SCHIP eligibility to near-poor children and near-poor pregnant women, Senator John Cornyn (R-TX) proposed to amend the Democrats' FY 2008 budget resolution to emphasize that SCHIP funds should be used to insure children with family incomes not greater than twice the FPL and that the use of SCHIP funds for nonpregnant adults should be limited. Generating a moderately high 158.4 partisan differentiation, 79.2 percent of Republican senators voted for Cornyn's amendment that was opposed by all Democrats (table 8.1).

Echoing the earlier partisan conflict over the 1997 Kennedy–Hatch amendment, Senator Gordon Smith's (R-OR) amendment to the FY 2008 budget resolution to permit the federal government to increase the federal cigarette tax by a maximum of 61 cents per pack in order to pay for a $35 billion SCHIP expansion over five years generated a moderately high partisan differentiation of 130.4.[89] While 91.7 percent of Democratic senators voted for Smith's amendment, 73.5 percent of Republicans voted against (table 8.1). Underlining the partisan cleavage, President Bush threatened to veto any appropriations legislation along the lines of Smith's amendment, and his spokesman declared: "Tax increases are neither necessary nor advisable to fund the program appropriately."[90]

Just prior to the August 2007 recess, congressional Democrats defied Bush's veto threat and passed their reauthorization bills to expand SCHIP. In the House, the Democratic bill would have provided an extra $50 billion for SCHIP over five years and would have been financed by a 45-cent increase in the tobacco tax and reduced payments to private insurers in the Medicare Advantage program; it passed by 225 votes to 204. With only five Republicans and ten Democrats voting against their respective party lines, the Democrats' bill generated a high partisan differentiation of 186.4 (table 8.1). Needing sixty votes to obviate a Republican filibuster, Democratic senators adopted a cross-partisan approach to attract sufficient Republican support. While increasing the federal tobacco tax by 61 cents per pack in order to pay for an additional $35 billion for SCHIP over five years, the Senate bill also would end SCHIP eligibility for childless adults, would reduce the federal reimbursement for parental coverage, and would not cut payments to private insurers in Medicare Advantage.[91] Generating a moderate-to-high partisan differentiation of 126.6 (table 8.1), which was significantly higher than the moderate-to-low differentiation of 80 produced by the Senate Finance Committee's original reauthorization vote,[92] the cross-partisan Senate bill was passed by a potentially veto-proof margin of 68 to 31 with eighteen Republicans joining all Democrats.

Some Republicans have expressed alarm that SCHIP's creeping expansion could culminate in national health insurance. HHS Secretary Mike Leavitt declared the Bush administration's opposition to SCHIP becoming an "engine that pulls the train of a national health insurance program."[93] Similarly, Novak portrayed the Democratic proposal to expand SCHIP as "the thin end of the wedge to achieve the longtime goal of government-supplied universal health insurance and the suffocation of the private system."[94] Contrasting with the 2000 Republican platform's claiming credit for SCHIP, Jack Kingston, a Republican representative from Georgia, complained: "The Children's Health Insurance Program has given Democrats a wide-open door for socialized medicine. The door was left open by Republicans, who were in the majority when we passed the original legislation in 1997."[95] Similarly, explaining his opposition to the Democrats' proposal to expand SCHIP's budget and eligibility, President Bush charged: "The Democrats' proposal is part of a larger strategy ... Their goal is to take incremental steps down the path to government-run health care for every American."[96]

Manifesting their preference for private provision and individual responsibility, Republicans also worry that any significant increase in SCHIP spending will lead to SCHIP "crowding out" private health insurance.[97] In contrast, some liberals asked why a near-poor family should "not have the option of using an available subsidy [SCHIP] and applying the money previously spent on health insurance [for children] to some other good use such as child care or food"?[98] Significantly, the NGA called for the elimination of SCHIP's requirement that states prevent SCHIP from crowding out private health insurance.[99]

In contrast to the conservative fear that SCHIP might "crowd out" private health insurance, liberals note that private insurance might provide less extensive benefits and also might impose higher costs upon near-poor families than SCHIP. Even though the health benefits provided by separate SCHIP programs are not necessarily as comprehensive as those provided by Medicaid, SCHIP programs still guarantee extensive benefits and have to meet high quality benchmarks. In contrast to the high quality benefits provided by SCHIP, both President Bush and his HHS Secretary view the government's role as limited to ensuring that all Americans have at least "basic" health insurance.[100] Yet, "basic" health insurance would leave Americans vulnerable to inadequate coverage and substantial costs.[101]

Underlining its concerns about SCHIP exceeding its "original purpose," the Bush administration issued new regulations in mid-August that would drastically restrict the states' ability to use SCHIP to cover children living in families with incomes above 250 percent of the FPL. First, reflecting fear of "crowd out," children in such families would have to be uninsured for a year before enrolling in SCHIP. Second, states would have to ensure that 95 percent of children from families below 200 percent of the FPL were enrolled in SCHIP before children in families above 250 percent could be enrolled. When this new administrative rule was issued, no state met this criterion. Defending its new regulations, the administration argued that they would return SCHIP to its original goal of insuring children in low-income families. In contrast, Senate Finance Committee Chair Max Baucus (D-MT) insisted that the administration's new rules threatened "coverage for tens of thousands of children in low-income working families."[102]

Dominated by Democrats, the conference committee that convened to reconcile the House and Senate SCHIP reauthorization bills included some Republican senators but excluded House Republicans.[103] In order to attract Republican support, the conference bill largely resembled the cross-partisan Senate bill and abandoned both the House bill's larger increase in SCHIP spending and also the related House provision cutting Medicare payments to private insurers—both of which were unacceptable to Republicans who supported or were willing to support the Senate bill.[104] However, transcending the original Senate bill, the conference bill largely eliminated the rules announced by the Bush administration in August that aimed to restrict SCHIP eligibility to children in families with incomes not exceeding 250 percent of FPL.

The conference bill passed both chambers comfortably, but the votes were still marked by significant partisan patterning. In the House, there was much greater Republican support for the conference bill than for the Democrats' original reauthorization bill, but the vote still generated partisan differentiation of 147.0: 96.5 percent of Democrats voted for while 77.0 percent of Republicans voted against. In the Senate, there was a veto-proof majority of 67 to 29 in favor of the bill. Here partisan differentiation measured 123.4: all Democrats voted in favor while 61.7 percent of Republicans opposed. After President Bush's veto, the attempt to override it fell 13 votes short in the House, because although six Democrats changed from opposition to support, no Republicans switched. Indeed, the vote to override generated a slightly higher partisan differentiation of 153.8 than the chamber's original vote on the conference bill. The six Democrats who switched from "no" to "yes" increased the Democrats' cohesion to 99.1 percent while Republican cohesion increased marginally to 77.8 percent (table 8.1).

Conclusion

Although SCHIP's incorporation into the 1997 BBA partially obscured its partisan nature, the 2007 debate over SCHIP underlined the partisan stakes involved in government-funded health programs. The parties embrace different understandings of the proper role of government and therefore have conflicting visions of how extensively government should be involved in providing health care. Indeed, the debate surrounding SCHIP in 2007 echoed earlier ideological arguments about national health insurance in the late 1940s and Medicare in the early 1960s. For example, attacking the Democrats' plans to expand SCHIP and simultaneously ignoring the reality of managed care, President Bush warned that "government-run health care ... would replace the doctor–patient relationship with dependency on people here in Washington, DC."[105] Also, although the states' discretion in implementing SCHIP has softened partisan differences, the huge variation in the rate of uninsurance among children in general, and low-income children in particular, underlines the cost of such discretion.

Despite its status as a capped matching grant, SCHIP has become an entering wedge for increased government provision of health insurance since states have a financial incentive to expand SCHIP in order to shift more of the cost of treating the uninsured and underinsured to the federal government. Faced with the choice of increasing their own contribution, reducing SCHIP eligibility in order to avoid exceeding their fixed SCHIP allotment, or lobbying the federal government for increased SCHIP funding, the states have opted for the latter and therefore have rejected the Bush administration's proposal that they curtail SCHIP to comply with its "original purpose" of covering near-poor children with family incomes not greater than twice poverty. Hence, despite its capped matching grant that congressional Republicans expected to act as a brake on its expansion, Democrats won politically with SCHIP's enactment. Even so, accepting and reinforcing the distinction between the "deserving" and "undeserving" recipients of government provision, SCHIP is unlikely to become an entering wedge for covering uninsured working-age adults.

Notes

1. T. Skocpol, *Boomerang: Health Care Reform and the Turn Against Government* (New York: W. W. Norton, 1997).
2. W.J. Clinton, *My Life* (London: Hutchinson, 2004), 620.
3. Because those Medicaid mandates were gradually phased in, 18-year-olds living in poverty gained a right to Medicaid only in 2002. Some states initially used some of their SCHIP funds to speed up the implementation of the earlier Medicaid mandates.
4. C. Peterson, *SCHIP Financing: Funding Projections and State Redistribution Issues* (Washington, DC: Congressional Research Service, May 8, 2006), 4.
5. L. Dubay, J. Guyer, C. Mann, and M. Odeh, "Medicaid at the Ten-year Anniversary of SCHIP: Looking Back and Moving Forward," *Health Affairs* 26, 2 (2007): 372.
6. L. Ku, M. Lin, and M. Broaddus, *Improving Children's Health: A Chartbook about the Roles of Medicaid and SCHIP* (Washington, DC: Center for Budget and Policy Priorities, 2007).

7. J. Aldrich and D. Rohde, "The Transition to Republican Rule in the House," *Political Science Quarterly* 112, 4 (1997–1998): 541–567; J. Bond and R. Fleisher, eds. *Polarized Politics* (Washington, DC: CQ Press, 2000); R. Fleisher and J. Bond, "The Shrinking Middle in the U.S. Congress," *British Journal of Political Science* 34, 3 (2004): (429–451).

8. H. Aaron, "Template for Health Care Coverage," *Washington Post*, November 25, 2002, A15.

9. *The 2000 Democratic National Platform*, www.democrats.org/pdfs/2000platform.pdf (accessed February 20, 2002); *Republican Platform, 2000*. www.rnc.org/gopinfo/platform (accessed February 20, 2002).

10. For the difference between bipartisan and cross-partisan, see C. Jones, *The Presidency in a Separated System* (Washington, DC: Brookings, 1994), 19–22.

11. D. Smith, *Entitlement Politics: Medicare and Medicaid, 1995–2001* (New York: de Gruyter, 2002), 210.

12. D. Palazzolo, *Done Deal? The Politics of the 1997 Budget Agreement* (New York: Chatham House, 1999), 50, 59, 77, 81, 118–119, 125, 130.

13. Ibid., 200.

14. M. Weir, "Institutional and Political Obstacles to Reform," *Health Affairs* 15, 1 (1995): 102–104.

15. J. Hacker and T. Skocpol, "The New Politics of U.S. Health Policy," *Journal of Health Politics, Policy and Law* 22, 2 (1997): 315–338.

16. R. Pear, "Capitol in Discord over Plan to Aid Uninsured Youths," *New York Times*, February 13, 1997.

17. Ibid.

18. Ibid.

19. Palazzolo, *Done Deal?*, 130, 176.

20. Measuring the degree of difference between the congressional parties on a legislative vote, partisan differentiation ranges from 0 to 200 where 0 indicates that there was no difference between how the congressional parties voted on a legislative issue and 200 indicates that all members of one party (who voted) voted against all members of the other party (who voted). D. Jaenicke, "Abortion and Partisanship in the US Congress, 1976–2000," *Journal of American Studies* 36, 1 (2002): 5–6.

21. S. Rosenbaum, K. Johnson, C. Sonosky, A. Markus, and Chris DeGraw, "The Children's Hour: The State Children's Health Insurance Program," *Health Affairs* 17, 1 (1998): 82.

22. Palazzolo, *Done Deal?*, 176.

23. Government Accountability Office (GAO), *Children's Health Insurance: States' SCHIP Enrollment and Spending Experiences and Considerations for Reauthorization, Statement of Kathryn G. Allen, Director, Health Care* (Washington, DC: GAO, March 1, 2007), 18.

24. Palazzolo, *Done Deal?*, 111–112.

25. Ibid., 175.

26. J. Gray, "Through Senate Alchemy, Tobacco is Turned into Gold for Children's Health," *New York Times*, August 11, 1997.

27. Palazzolo, *Done Deal?*, 183–184.

28. D. Ross and L. Cox, *Preserving Recent Progress on Health Coverage for Children and Families: New Tensions Emerge* (Washington, DC: Center on Budget and Policy Priorities, 2003), viii.

29. D. Ross, L. Cox, and C. Marks, *Resuming the Path to Health Coverage for Children and Parents: A 50 State Update on Eligibility Rules, Enrollment and Renewal Procedures, and Cost-Sharing Practices in Medicaid and SCHIP in 2006* (Washington, DC: Kaiser Commission on Medicaid and the Uninsured, 2007), 30.

30. Dubay et al., "Medicaid at the Ten Year Anniversary of SCHIP," 372–373.

31. United States Census Bureau, "Table HI01: Health Insurance Coverage Status and Type of Coverage by Selected Characteristics: 2005," http://pubdb3.census.gov/macro/032006/health/ho1_001.htm (accessed June 12, 2007).

32. Ku et al., *Improving Children's Health*, 7.

33. Dubay et al., "Medicaid at the Ten Year Anniversary of SCHIP," 370.

34. G. Kenney and J. Yee, "SCHIP at a Crossroads: Experiences To Date and Challenges Ahead," *Health Affairs* 26, 2 (2007): 356–369.

35. Dubay et al., "Medicaid at the Ten Year Anniversary of SCHIP," 373.

36. Congressional Budget Office (CBO), *The State Children's Health Insurance Program*, (Washington, DC: Congress of the United States, May, 2007), 5.

37. Ku et al., *Improving Children's Health*, 4–5.

38. Kenney and Yee, "SCHIP at a Crossroads," 363.

39. Ibid.

40. D. Ross and L. Cox, *Out in the Cold: Enrolment Freezes in Six State Children's Health Insurance Programs Withhold Coverage from Eligible Children* (Washington, DC: Center on Budget and Policy Priorities, 2003).

41. National Governors Association (NGA), *HHS-09. The State Children's Health Insurance Program (SCHIP)*, April 9, 2007, www.nga.org, (accessed July 13, 2007).

42. United States Census Bureau. "Table HI03: Health Insurance Coverage Status and Type of Coverage by Selected Characteristics of Poor People in the Poverty Universe: 2005," http://pubdb3.census.gov/macro/032006/health/ho3_001.htm (accessed June 12, 2007).

43. United States Census Bureau. "Table HI10: Number and Percent of Children Under 19 at or below 200% of Poverty by Health Insurance Coverage and State: 2005," http://pubdb3.census.gov/macro/032006/health/h10_000.htm (accessed June 12, 2007).

44. Kenney and Yee, "SCHIP at a Crossroads," 358.

45. M. Leavitt, "Congress Should Reauthorize SCHIP," *TheHill.com*, June 6, 2007 (accessed June 2, 2007); R. Novak "Socialized Medicine for Kids," *RealClearpolitics.com*, June 8, 2007 (accessed June 28, 2007).

46. K. Freking, "House Democrats Offer Child Health Plan," *Washington Post*, July 24, 2007.

47. CBO, *The State Children's Health Insurance Program*, 1.

48. Since "such income disregards have been imposed as high as 100 percent of FPL," "a family with an income equal to 300 percent of FPL is treated as if its income were 200 percent of FPL." GAO, *Children's Health Insurance*, 4.

49. From 2002 to 2006, Tennessee did not have a SCHIP program; however, in 2006, the Department of HHS approved its SCHIP plan to cover children and pregnant women up to 250 percent of poverty. Ibid., 31. Hence, in 2007, sixteen states had set eligibility above twice poverty.

50. Ross et al., *Resuming the Path to Health Coverage for Children and Parent*, 30.

51. R. Pear, "A Battle over Expansion of Children's Insurance," *New York Times*, July 9, 2007.

52. CBO, *The State Children's Health Insurance Program*, viii.

53. Ross et al., *Resuming the Path to Health Coverage for Children and Parent,* 32.

54. Ibid.; Kaiser Commission on Medicaid and the Uninsured, "Fifty State Comparisons," click "Medicaid + SCHIP," then "SCHIP Program Type," http://www.statehealthfacts.kff.org/cgi-bin/healthfacts.cgi?action-compare (accessed June 21, 2007).

55. GAO, *Children's Health Insurance*, 2–3.

56. Ibid., 19–21.

57. Ross et al., *Resuming the Path to Health Coverage for Children and Parents*, 59.

58. Ibid., 61, 65.

59. Ibid., 26.

60. A state may also cover parents if the state demonstrates that its coverage of parents is cost-effective; that is, that it is no more expensive to cover the entire family than it is to cover the eligible child(ren). That cost-effective condition is impossible to satisfy.

61. GAO, *Children's Health Insurance*, 24.

62. C. Mann, D. Rousseau, R. Garfield, and M. O'Malley, *Reaching Uninsured Children through Medicaid: If You Build it Right, They Will Come* (Washington, DC: Kaiser Commission on Medicaid and the Uninsured, 2002), 5.

63. GAO, *Children's Health Insurance*, 24.

64. V. Smith, J. Cooke, D. Rousseau, R. Rudowitz, and C. Marks, *SCHIP Turns 10: An Update on Enrollment and the Outlook on Reauthorization from the Program's Directors* (Washington, DC: Kaiser Commission on Medicaid and the Uninsured, May 2007), 12.

65. GAO, *Children's Health Insurance*, 11–12.

66. Figures calculated from data in United States Census Bureau "Table HI10: Number and Percent of Children under 19 at or below 200% of Poverty by Health Insurance Coverage and State: 2005" http://pubdb3.census.gov/macro/032006/health/h10_000.htm (accessed June 12, 2007).

67. Ross et al., *Resuming the Path to Health Coverage for Children and Parents*, 30.

68. Kaiser Commission on Medicaid and the Uninsured, "Fifty State Comparisons."

69. CBO, *The State Children's Health Insurance Program*, 6; M. Broadus and E. Park, *SCHIP Financing Update: In 2007 Seventeen States Will Face Federal Funding Shortfalls of $921 Million in Their SCHIP Programs* (Washington, DC: Center for Budget and Policy Priorities, November 28, 2006).

70. GAO, *Children's Health Insurance*, 26.

71. Peterson, *SCHIP Financing: Funding Projections and State Redistribution Issues*, 3.

72. Ibid.

73. GAO, *Children's Health Insurance*, 28.

74. Between December 2003 and December 2004, while SCHIP enrolment stagnated nationally, the overall national stagnation obscured state-level variations. SCHIP enrolment increased in most states, but that increase was offset by enrolment declines in other states, especially Texas and Florida. Kenney and Yee, "SCHIP at a Crossroads," 358.

75. CBO, *The State Children's Health Insurance Program*, 5.

76. S. Dennis, "House Clear $39 Billion savings Plan," *CQ Weekly*, February 6, 2006, 347.

77. CBO, *The State Children's Health Insurance Program*, viii.

78. D. Baumann, "Priorities and Pragmatism," *CQ Weekly*, February 10, 2007, 32–34.

79. M. Serafini, "A Dose of Pragmatism," *National Journal*, September 9, 2006, 54–55.

80. CBO, *The State Children's Health Insurance Program*, 14.

81. R. Pear, "Governors Worry over Money for Child Health Program," *New York Times*, February 25, 2007.

82. NGA, *HHS-09. The State Children's Health Insurance Program (SCHIP)*.

83. P. Prah, "Health Care, Energy Top Governors' meeting," July 23, 2007, http://www.stateline.org/live/details/story?contentId=226171 (accessed August 23, 2007).

84. S. Labaton, "Congress Passes Increase in the Minimum Wage," *New York Times*, May 25, 2007.

85. Broadus and Park, *SCHIP Financing Update*.

86. Peterson, *SCHIP Financing: Funding Projections and State Redistribution Issues*, 3.

87. R. Pear, "Expanded Health Program for Children Causes Clash," *New York Times*, April 1, 2007.

88. R. Pear and R. Hernandez, "States and U.S. at Odds on Aid for Uninsured," *New York Times*, February 13, 2007.

89. S. Dennis, "Chambers' Budget Resolutions Overlap," *CQ Weekly*, March 26, 2007, 902.

90. R. Pear, "Bush is Prepared to Veto Bill to Expand Child Insurance," *New York Times*, July 15, 2007.

91. Alex Wayne and Drew Armstrong, "The SCHIP Challenge," *CQ Weekly*, August 6, 2007: 2374–2375.

92. R. Pear, "Senate Panel Adds Billions for Health," *New York Times*, July 20, 2007.

93. C. Lee, "Children's Health Care on the Agenda," *Washington Post*, March 4, 2007, A8.

94. Novak, "Socialized Medicine for Kids."

95. Pear, "Expanded Health Program for Children Causes Clash."

96. G. W. Bush, "President Bush Discusses Health Care," June 27, 2007, www.whitehouse.gov/news/releases/2007/06 (accessed June 28, 2007).

97. Ibid.; Leavitt, "Congress Should Reauthorize SCHIP."

98. Rosenbaum et al., "The Children's Hour: The State Children's Health Insurance Program," 89.

99. NGA, *HHS-09. The State Children's Health Insurance Program (SCHIP)*.

100. Bush, "President Bush Discusses Health Care."

101. L. Ku, *Comparing Public and Private Health Insurance for Children* (Washington, DC: Center for Budget and Policy Priorities, May 11, 2007).

102. C. Lee, "New Bush Policies Limit Reach of Child Health Insurance Plan," *Washington Post*, August 21, 2007, A04.

103. R. Pear, "Veto Risk Seen in Compromise on Child Health," *New York Times*, September 17, 2007.

104. Pear, "Veto Risk"; and Alex Wayne, "Congress Defies Bush on SCHIP," *CQ Weekly*, October 1, 2007: 2854.

105. Bush, "President Bush Discusses Health Care."

Chapter 9

Criminal Justice Policy Across the United States: Due Process in the Punitive Turn

Andrew Davies and Alissa Pollitz Worden[*]

Introduction

Students of criminal justice policy and politics generally agree that the past three decades have witnessed a dramatic shift toward harsh policies and practices in the United States.[1] Capital punishment has returned to common usage, rehabilitationist policies have been turned to punitive purposes, and severe sentencing[2] legislation has been passed in most states. Incarceration rates have risen dramatically, accompanied by record levels of spending on law enforcement, the courts, and corrections. David Garland has named this policy-shift "the punitive turn," and a growing body of literature explores its manifestations, unintended consequences, and possible causes.[3]

From a federalist point of view, however, the fact that the nation has become more punitive is not the whole story. Criminal justice policy in the United States is primarily formulated at the state level. Empirical research has made it clear that although the signature trends of the punitive turn have appeared in most states, they have taken variable forms and appear to have been influenced by states' political cultures and ideologies.[4]

Most scholarly attention to this topic has focused specifically on punishment policies and practices—incarceration rates, three strikes laws, and the like. To the extent that researchers have considered other domains of criminal justice policy, including due process issues, they have tended to assume, or assert, that defendants' rights have been compromised to accommodate more punitive regimes. For example, Garland's enumeration of indicia of the punitive turn includes "relaxation of civil liberties offered suspects, and rights of prisoners."[5] Beckett and Sasson mention the Nixon appointments to the Supreme Court as evidence of deteriorating defendant rights, and suggest further that a third domain of crime policy, the emergence of the victim's rights movement, came at the direct expense of defendants' rights.[6] But the evidence on the issue is scarce enough to suggest we should restate this assumption as an empirical question: is there a zero-sum relationship between punitiveness and defendant rights? If states differ in their enthusiasm for punitive policies, might they also differ on other dimensions of criminal justice policy such as due process?

Hence, a federalist analysis of the punitive turn presents four questions. First, how do state levels of punitiveness vary? Second, are states internally consistent in their adoption of punitive policies, suggesting an underlying political orientation that drives policy choices? Third, are due process policies—policies that define defendants' and offenders' rights—internally consistent too? Finally, are punitive policies inversely related to due process ones? By examining whether states do in fact differ across the dimensions of punitiveness or due process orientation, we hope to increase scholarly understanding of the true nature of the punitive turn and the variety in states' experiences with this policy shift.

Punitiveness in Criminal Justice Policy across the States

It is well established that the United States has become more punitive since the 1970s, and that states vary significantly in how punitive they are. We briefly consider four indicators of punitiveness within states: the presence of capital punishment, the incarceration rate, the adoption of "three strikes" laws, and correctional spending per inmate. We discuss each variable before assessing the relationships among them, and consider their implications for the existence of a "punitive orientation" within states.

Both capital punishment and so-called "three strikes" laws are symbolically punitive policies directed against a small number of particularly violent or persistent offenders. Capital punishment has been legal in the United States since 1976, though only thirty-eight states, the Federal government, and the United States military presently license its use.[7] The first so-called "three strikes" law, by contrast, dates from 1993 when Washington became the first state to legislate that offenders with multiple prior violent offenses would be sentenced to a term of twenty-five years to life upon conviction for a third serious felony. Twenty-four states followed suit in the subsequent two years.[8]

Incarceration figures and spending on inmates, by contrast with the symbolic policies mentioned above, reflect the reality of the operation of correctional systems and their treatment of those whom they house. In general, the past thirty years have seen exponential growth in prison populations: at midyear 2006, a total of 2,245,189 people, or one in every 133 residents in the United States, were under custody—the highest figures ever recorded. This growth has occurred unevenly, however, with the result that half of this population is held by the federal government and just six states (California, Texas, Florida, New York, Georgia, and Michigan).[9] Prison expenditures, meanwhile, vary independently of prison populations, with

Table 9.1   Bivariate correlations among measures of state punitiveness

	State has Death Penalty (2002)	State Incarceration Rate (2002)	State Correctional Spending per Inmate (2004)	State has 3 strikes law (1997)
State has Death Penalty (2002)	1	.469 (.001)	−.427 (.002)	.210 (.143)
State Incarceration Rate (2004)		1	−.715 (.000)	.060 (.681)
State Correctional Spending per Inmate (2004)			1	−.057 (.694)
State has 3 strikes law (1997)				1

Note: Cells contain: Pearson Correlation (Significance, two-tailed).

around a third on average going toward operating costs including inmate healthcare, food, and utilities. Correctional spending per inmate can be regarded, therefore, as an approximate measure of how spartan a state's carceral regime is. In 2001, spending per inmate ranged from a high of $44,379 in Maine to a low of $8,128 in Alabama.[10]

Table 9.1 shows the correlations between the dimensions of punitive policy outlined above. From these results we can infer that the implicit hypothesis of the punitive turn literature, that states adopt a consistent "orientation" to punitive policymaking, is largely supported. In particular, the bivariate correlations indicate that states with the death penalty were more likely to have higher incarceration rates and to spend less per inmate. Three strikes laws, on the other hand, are only weakly associated with the presence of the death penalty in states and are unrelated to either incarceration rates or correctional spending. A number of explanations might be proposed for this, including the possibility that states adopt three strikes laws for their symbolic value but use them only occasionally, with the result that they have little explanatory value when applied to incarceration rates. This anomaly notwithstanding, however, we observe that table 9.1 provides substantial evidence that states have fairly stable orientations toward punitiveness, which are manifested in real policies and practices.

Due Process Policies and the Generalizability of the Punitive Turn Thesis

Scholars have generally assumed that, whatever its source, the increase in punitiveness is a highly generalizable description of the course of criminal justice policy over the last three decades. In general, however, the evidence adduced to support this contention concerns only those policies connected with punishing offenders such as those discussed in the previous section. Criminal justice policy includes much more than only sentencing and punishment, however. State legislators must also make decisions on the rights of victims, correctional administration, and the rights and obligations of defendants both during and subsequent to their detention.

In order to test the generalizability of the punitive turn thesis, we examine what we refer to as "due process" policies, or policies that serve primarily to define the rights of defendants in the criminal justice process. By performing analyses parallel to those discussed above, we seek to discover first whether states have a generalized "due process" orientation that is manifested in their policies and, second, whether due process protections are weakest in states where punitive policies are strongest. As a preliminary test of the latter hypothesis, we test for an inverse relationship across states in the early twenty-first century between measures of due process protections and punitive criminal justice policies.

Defining Due Process

"Due process of law" is a prescription for criminal justice administration that emphasizes specific rights for defendants, officials' conformity to established legal procedures and rules, and open, recorded proceedings. In one of the contemporary formulations of due process, Herbert Packer described the two "value systems that compete for priority": the due process model and the crime control model.[11] Packer styled the due process model as one that establishes a high threshold for prosecutorial performance and proof, assumes the fallibility of fact-finding authorities, and is committed to equal treatment of defendants. The crime control model, in contrast, prioritizes system efficiency, presumes factual guilt and certain punishment, and relies on courthouse practitioners to make quick but accurate assessments of the best procedures and outcomes for cases.

Packer stated that these "models" are just that: idealized versions of processes that illustrate different values, not attempts to describe a dichotomization of real processes and policies. Writing in the late 1960s, he observed that practitioners sense a tradeoff between due process values and crime control (not, specifically, punishment). For instance, Fourth Amendment search and seizure laws protect the privacy of citizens, including those who may have committed crimes, but can hinder law enforcement's ability to provide important evidence in criminal prosecutions.

Times have changed since 1968, and the contemporary discourse on crime control is often conflated with discourse on punishment, as punishment is increasingly described as the primary means by which society incapacitates, deters, or stigmatizes lawbreakers, thereby (in theory) reducing crime. Garland has argued that harsher sentencing policies are manifestations of fundamental shifts in rationales for sentencing, away from individualized rehabilitation, toward the utilitarian justifications of deterrence and incapacitation, as well as retribution.[12] These trends have been fueled, he argues, by disenchantment with rehabilitative philosophies and programs, and the replacement of a correctional system administered by professionals and experts with one shaped by elected officials. To the extent that greater punitiveness, then, represents one end of a continuum during this era, the opposite end would be represented by decline of rehabilitative policies and programming, along with reduced confidence in the professionals who had been responsible for implementing them.

Experts who have sought to understand the causes of the punitive turn observe that the same political and social forces that paved the way for new sentencing and punishment policies—racial tensions, middle-class anxieties about crime and disorder, changing family structures, and a generalized insecurity about social stability—also led to diminished tolerance for due process rights.[13] Tonry describes these cumulative pressures as "a series of moral panics that, among other things, has led to artificially heightened anxieties and fierce overreactions."[14] He, and others, suggest that "other things" include the rolling back of civil liberties and due process rights. Garland underscores this point in describing the victims' rights movement: "a zero-sum policy game is assumed wherein the offender's gain is the victim's loss," particularly when the notion of victim includes not only actual, but potential, victims of recidivists.[15] But although the sentiments underlying shifts in punishment, victims' rights, and due process protections can sound very similar—expressing social outrage with criminal behavior, and isolating criminals for the purposes of public safety—we suggest that variation in the policies that define due process rights can be identified and measured separably from variation in policies associated with punishment rationales.

Due Process Policies at the Turn of the Century

Many of what we shall call "due process policies" derive from the U.S. Constitution's civil liberties amendments.[16] The U.S. Supreme Court has made fairly explicit rulings in some of these areas (such as Fourth Amendment search and seizure provisions), but has left others (such as the right to counsel) largely up to states to define for themselves. We are particularly interested in those policies that are largely under the purview of the states.

We define due process policies broadly: we include state policies that create or restrict defendants' and offenders' rights to fair and impartial trial that operationalize the notion of "innocent until proven guilty," and that stipulate or restrict liberties beyond their court-imposed sentence. We would not claim that some such policies do not carry punitive connotations. But unlike policies that are primarily about punishment, they also (and perhaps primarily) establish boundaries around the notion of due process.

Table 9.2 Descriptive statistics

Policy	Description	Distribution	Data Source	Year data refer to
Indigent defense expenditures	$ per capita state and local expenditures on legal representation of criminal defendants.	Mean = $10.07 S. D. = $5.64 Range: $2.92 to $37.47	The Spangenberg Group	2002
Cameras in Court	State law permits cameras in trial court (0 = no, 1 = yes)	Mean = .76	Radio-Television News Directors Association	2005
Rape Shield Law	State law prohibits any testimony about prior victim-defendant sexual relationship (0 = no, 1 = yes)	Mean = .20	National Center for Prosecution of Violence Against Women	2005
Post-Conviction DNA Testing	State law permits convicted offenders to request DNA testing for potential exoneration (0 = yes, 1 = no)	Mean = .24	American Society for Legal and Medical Ethics	2005
Scope of DNA sampling	Additive index of 4 provisions for DNA: (1) Most/all felons (n = 47) (2) Some misdemeanors (n = 15) (3) Some juveniles (n = 36) (4) GBMI verdicts (n = 9) (5) Some arrestees (n = 12)	Mean = 2.32 S.D. = 1.04 Range: 1 to 4	National Conference of State Legislatures	2007
Sexually Violent Predator Law	State law provides for post-sentence civil commitment of serious sex offenders (0 = no, 1 = yes)	Mean = .38	Lieb and Gookin	2004
Public access to sex information	State law provides for sex offender information to be available to public through local libraries, police departments, and/or Web site (0 = no, 1 = yes)	Mean = .60	Adams	2001
Felon disenfranchisement	Additive index of conviction conditions that disqualify voting: (1) all inmates (n = 46) (2) persons on parole (n = 32) (3) persons on probation (n = 29) (4) all ex-felons (n = 15)	Mean = 2.44 S. D. = 1.39 Range: 1 to 4	The Sentencing Project	1999

Of the many policies that define the parameters of due process, we present eight of them below. We chose these eight because they represent a range of issues with relevance to civil liberties. Some involve policy questions of long standing, such as disenfranchisement of defendants and the right to counsel for indigent defendants. Others exist only because recent social movements or technological developments have raised questions or possibilities that were previously unforeseen. Examples of these include rape shield laws, which changed longstanding common law rules of evidence in rape cases during the 1970s and 1980s, and the creation of DNA databases and online sex offender registries, which greatly expand the potential powers of law enforcement. The descriptive statistics for each policy are contained in table 9.2.

Indigent Defense

States have been required to underwrite the defense of indigent persons hailed before courts in an increasing variety of circumstances over the course of the twentieth century. In 1932, the United States Supreme Court held that states were obliged to provide assistance of counsel to capital defendants.[17] This right was later extended to felony defendants,[18] juveniles,[19] and then to all defendants facing the possibility of imprisonment.[20]

Among all this litigation, however, the Court said relatively little about how the mandate of providing defense services to indigents should be fulfilled.[21] States were left with broad discretion on matters of implementation, including how to organize the provision of defense services to the poor, how to assure quality, and how well to fund them. As a result, states continue to vary in the generosity with which they fund these services.[22] In 2002, states spent an average of $10 per capita on indigent defense, though they ranged from a low of less than $3 to a high of $37. Existing work has already shown, furthermore, that variation across these dimensions is predictably associated with other characteristics of states' political and social environments.[23] We argue that states characterized by a due-process orientation to criminal justice policy will fund indigent defense policy generously.

Cameras in the Courtroom

Thirty-eight states allow access to cameras in criminal trials. Rarely is this access unfettered, however, with the photographing of witnesses frequently prohibited, and the consent of certain parties frequently required.[24] Defense advocates have consistently opposed the introduction of cameras into court on the grounds that their presence serves to sensationalize trials, intimidate witnesses and jurors, and increase the risk to defendants that they will be the victims of injustice. They are assumed to encourage harsh sentencing among judges and discourage compromise among prosecutors, both of whom will be conscious of the broad exposure their decisions will receive among voters.[25] We expect that states with stronger due process orientations will impose greater restrictions on the presence of cameras in court rooms and will be more inclined to exclude them altogether.

Rape Shield Laws

Rape shield laws are designed to protect victims of rape from having their personal sexual history used to impeach their credibility as witnesses. Critics of such laws argue that they violate the Sixth Amendment rights of defendants to "compulsory process," under which a court is obliged to compel witnesses for the defense to appear.[26] They also argue that they impinge upon a defendant's right to be confronted by witnesses against them. In both cases, critics argue, rape shield laws interfere with the defendant's right to due process by preventing them from using relevant information about a witness' character and sexual history to defend themselves.[27] While all states have some form of rape shield law, ten have not adopted the key provision of such laws—the barring of evidence about prior victim–defendant relationships. We argue that states sympathetic to defendants' rights on other dimensions will also tend to adopt relatively weak rape shield laws, allowing the use of prior victim–offender relationships in evidence

DNA Databases and the Right to Post-Conviction Testing

All states now maintain DNA databases that house the identifying information of known criminals. DNA evidence is now routinely used for law enforcement purposes, both as a detection tool in open cases and as a way of generating "hits" for cold ones.[28] It has also featured in a number of high-profile cases of wrongful conviction.[29] States vary considerably in the circumstances under which they gather such data, however. While all states require convicted sex offenders to provide samples, forty-seven also require it from those convicted of other felonies, thirty-six from some juveniles, fifteen from some misdemeanants, and nine in cases resolved by verdicts of not guilty by reason of mental illness.[30] A simple additive index suggests that most states impose two or three of these requirements. At the same time, thirty-eight states have provided statutes that set out the rights of defendants to exploit existing DNA databases after conviction to prove their innocence.[31]

Civil liberties advocates emphasize that the collection of DNA evidence by authorities is limited by the Fourth Amendment protection against unwarranted searches and seizures, and are worried both by the expansion of these databases to include additional classes of offenders and by the possibility that they may expand further to include all citizens.[32] We expect that states possessed of strong due process orientations will be less likely to adopt the requirement that large numbers of defendants submit DNA samples and are also more likely to have procedures in place for convicted offenders to utilize DNA technology in pursuit of a claim of wrongful conviction.

Sex Offender Notification Laws

States have been required to maintain sex offender registration programs by federal law since 1994. Since 1996, they have been required to make these registries publicly accessible.[33] States retain considerable discretion on their interpretation of this mandate, however, and differ widely in the types of information they make available, the types of offenders included, the length of time they are listed, and the accessibility of the information itself. In 2001, thirty states made sex offender information generally available through Web sites or listings held at public libraries or police departments. Others restricted access to law enforcement personnel or permitted access to members of the public on a "need to know" basis only.[34]

Broadly accessible sex offender registers are often argued to have negative consequences for defendants and defendant rights.[35] As such, we expect that the level of accessibility of sex offender registries in states will be related to other measures of state orientation to due process rights. Specifically, states with a stronger orientation toward protecting due process rights will impose greater restrictions on public access to sex offender registries.

Sexually Violent Predator Legislation

Sexually Violent Predator legislation is aimed at offenders approaching release and is designed to prevent them from ever being allowed back into the community. Although the civil commitment to sex offenders has a long history, the enactment of legislation designed specifically for this purpose began only recently, with Washington State becoming the first to enact such a law in the early 1990s.[36] By 2004, a total of seventeen states had passed Sexually Violent Predator legislation.[37] These laws have been criticized as nothing more than cynical, politically opportunistic attempts to detain sex offenders beyond their release dates as a way to "get tough" on crime.[38] We expect that states with a strong due process orientation will tend not to have enacted Sexually Violent Predator legislation.

Felon Disenfranchisement

At the turn of the century, all but four states prohibited inmates from voting while incarcerated for a felony offense.[39] Thirty-two denied the vote to ex-offenders on parole, twenty-nine to ex-offenders on probation, and fifteen to ex-offenders no longer under supervision. Two states, Kentucky and Virginia, prohibit voting by all persons ever convicted of a felony. Civil liberties campaigners have long opposed such policies on principle.[40] Opponents argue they are insupportable by traditional correctional arguments since they do not prevent the commission of future crimes, and that their symbolic consequences for the legitimacy of the criminal law are severe.[41] We expect that states with strong due process orientations will have less severe felon disenfranchisement laws. In such states, convicted felons will be more likely to retain the vote following conviction, or, if they lose it, will be more likely to have it restored when on probation, paroled, or released.

Data, Analyses, and Results

We gathered data on the policies discussed above from multiple sources. Table 9.2 presents detailed descriptions and distributions for these policy variables, as well as our sources. With the exception of indigent defense funding, which is an interval level variable, these variables are either ordinal or dichotomous measures, coded such that higher values represent weaker protections for defendants, and lower values represent stronger due process positions.

It is important to note two caveats. First, for the most part, these are complex policy issues from which we have attempted to extract only the most salient due process dimensions. Laws defining the use of cameras in courts, for example, vary in their details about the consent of parties, and the judicial option to screen some parties from the viewfinder. Whether or not cameras are allowed as a general rule in trial proceedings is the bellwether issue for due process, however, so we confine our analyses to that. When possible, we also ran analyses on secondary characteristics of these policies, and report those findings, where relevant, in the notes. Second, we were interested in assessing due process policy at a high point in the "punitive turn," so we tried to access information on policies between 2000 and 2005. However, not all policy variables could be accessed for the exact same year. Given the relatively incremental pace of state policy change, we do not believe these small differences in source year are likely to affect our findings.

We explored bivariate associations among these policy variables in order to assess whether they reflect a broad due process orientation to criminal justice policy within states. We present the results in table 9.3. These results offer little evidence to suggest that there is a single dimension underlying due process policies in the states as we have measured them. About half the comparisons produce coefficients in the direction opposite to that expected.

The policies analyzed here can be organized typologically into subcategories by their implications for defendant rights, though few associations between them suggest that such a typology is substantially important. First, policies on cameras in the court, rape shield provisions, and post-conviction DNA testing all concern defendant protections in the adjudication and conviction process. Among these, however, there are few strong associations. The only close association is in the opposite direction to that predicted: states that fund indigent defense more generously are more likely to have restrictive rape shield laws, giving defendants fewer opportunities to raise reasonable doubts in those cases.

Second, policies regarding the submission of DNA samples, civil commitment of sex offenders, and public access to sex offender registries all represent tradeoffs between public safety and defendant rights. Specifically, these include rights to the presumption of innocence, to determinate punishment, and to relative privacy following service of a term of punishment. At the bivariate

Table 9.3 Correlation matrix for due process policy measures

	Indigent defense $	Cameras at trial	Rape shield law	No post-conviction DNA	DNA index	SVP / civil commit	Public access	Disenfranchise
Indigent defense $		.184 (.204)	.330 (.021)	.105 (.477)	.107 (.463)	(–).030 (.838)	(–).073 (.616)	.076 (.605)
Cameras at trial			.110 (.551)	2.125 (.248)	.175 (.225)	2.114 (.134)	(–)1.480 (.191)	.282 (.047)
Rape shield law				.247 (.449)	(–).058 (.687)	(–)1.092 (.257)	.521 (.365)	.058 (.688)
No post-conviction DNA					(–).084 (.563)	(–).003 (.622)	.292 (.425)	(–).112 (.439)
DNA index						.434 (.002)	(–).103 (.476)	.104 (.925)
SVP/ civil commitment							(–)3.800 (.050)	.108 (.454)
Public access to SOR								.007 (.556)
Disenfranchisement								

Note: Cells contain measures of association and statistical significance, as a guide to substantive strengths of relationships. Indicia in parentheses indicate empirical direction of association. For comparisons of interval and ordinal level variables, correlations are presented. For comparisons of interval or ordinal variables with dichotomous variables, etas are presented. For comparisons of dichotomous variables, chi-squares are presented.

level, we find only one substantive association among these: states with more inclusive DNA databases are more likely to have civil commitment legislation.

Third, we considered policies that impose costs on offenders past the execution of their imposed sentences. These include the civil commitment statutes and the public information access laws mentioned above—both fairly recent innovations in state policy—as well as longstanding felon disenfranchisement policies. We note in passing that states that sustain harsher disenfranchisement policies are more likely to permit cameras in trial proceedings. However, there is little reason to conclude, from these correlations, that post-prison restrictions are similar manifestations of an underlying political dynamic. These policies do not co-occur at any sort of predictable level.[42]

One could strain to interpret elusive patterns suggested by these data, but the more empirically justified conclusion to be drawn is that there is not much evidence to suggest that states do not enact due process policies in keeping with a stable orientation to defendant and offender civil liberties. Even within our loosely defined subsets of variables—trial and conviction issues, public safety tradeoffs with due process rights, and post-conviction penalties—we see little coherence. In short, these data give us little reason, or capacity, to classify states as strongly due process oriented, or otherwise.

Due Process and the Punitive Turn: Related Policy Dimensions?

Given the last two decades of research on the rise of punitiveness in American culture, and some intriguing research into the variability of states on this

Table 9.4   Correlations between punitive measures and due process policies

	Factor score of death penalty, incarceration rate, and correctional spending	State has death penalty (2002)	State incarceration rate (2002)	Correctional spending per inmate (2004)
Indigent defense expenditures per capita	−.245 (.090)	−.263 (.068)	−.142 (.331)	.226 (.119)
Cameras allowed in criminal trials	.085 (.557)	−.096 (.505)	.157 (.276)	−.158 (.274)
Rape evidence on victim–offender relationship permitted	.071 (.623)	.047 (.747)	.035 (.807)	−.110 (.447)
No DNA post-conviction testing available	−.185 (.199)	−.342 (.015)	−.085 (.556)	.048 (.740)
Index of DNA sample requirements	−.059 (.685)	−.144 (.319)	.000 (1.0)	.007 (.962)
Sexually Violent Predator legislation enacted	−.092 (.525)	−.091 (.530)	−.062 (.668)	.071 (.626)
Sex offender registries not openly accessible	.316 (.026)	.210 (.143)	.255 (.073)	−.318 (.025)
Felon disenfranchisement index	.375 (.007)	.248 (.082)	.359 (.010)	−.315 (.026)

Note: Cells contain: Pearson Correlation (Significance, two-tailed).

dimension, we are prompted to ask whether states' acceptance of (or resistance to) national trends toward increasing punishment is associated with our indicators of due process. To that we now turn. Table 9.4 presents the relationships, at the state level, between our disparate due process measures and an aggregate measure of punitive policy and practices. This measure is the factor scale score that results from an analysis of (1) whether or not the state had the death penalty in 2002, (2) incarceration rate of citizens, and (3) inversely, spending per inmate for corrections.

Table 9.4 presents simple correlations between our eight measures of restrictive due process policy, and the factor score for punitiveness, along with its three components. Despite earlier researchers' suggestions that the period of the punitive turn also witnessed the rolling back of due process protections, this does not appear to be the case at the comparative state level. It is true that more punitive states invest less in indigent defense, are somewhat more likely to make sex offender information widely available, and more likely to restrict ex-offender voting. But all in all, there is little support here for the notion that the most punitive states have taken the biggest steps toward policies that infringe on due process rights, or that the states that have most refrained from more punitive policies have likewise held back on adopting policies that might present tradeoffs with those civil liberties.

Summary and Discussion

This chapter explores the dimensions of criminal justice policy across states. First, we noted that the last three decades have been an era of unprecedented growth in punitive policies and practices in the United States. Second, we observed that despite national figures that suggest exponential changes in punitive indicia, such as incarceration rates, states do vary significantly across this dimension. Therefore, third, at the state level we considered whether the "punitive turn" has carried other criminal justice policy with it, specifically policies and innovations that define due process. We noted in this regard that while most experts broadly assert that incursions on civil liberties have tracked with increases in punitiveness, there have been virtually no empirical studies of these changes over time or across states. Finally, therefore, we analyzed a set of key due process issues, and assessed (1) whether they held together empirically to suggest a due process policy dimension across states that mirrors the punitiveness dimension, (2) and whether they reflected state-level variation in punitive policy characteristics.

We found little evidence to support these expectations about due process policies. Due process policies do not cohere—states adopt some new ideas, but not others, and not in neat patterns. Whether or not they adopt new policies that cut into offenders' civil liberties (such as civil commitment, or public airing of names and addresses) is apparently unrelated to longstanding policy decisions, such as those about offender disenfranchisement. Policies that clearly define matters of fairness at trial, evidentiary advantages, or exoneration do not track together. Further, due process policies are not clearly inversely related to punitive policies. In short, if we are to consider states as the units of analysis, we cannot conclude that criminal justice policies—largely legislative policies—materialize as coherent packages that emphasize either crime control and punishment, or rehabilitation and due process.

Before we go too far in assessing the implications of this study for understanding state crime policy, we must acknowledge its limitations. We limited our analysis to matters that are largely legislative, so jurisprudential policymaking is absent from this report. It is of course true that one would not expect public opinion and culture to shape judicial opinions nearly as much as legislative ones, but all the same, many important due process issues are settled by constitutional interpretation in appellate courts. Second, we focused our attention on matters of court decision making—not law enforcement or corrections. This was in part because most studies of the punitive turn devote very limited attention to court policies, other than statutory sentencing.[43] There probably are important due process issues that shape police decisions and prison decisions, to which we have not attended here. Third, we are limited to a cross-sectional study of the states, without access to information on the politics that may have led to the ultimate adoption or rejection of the initiatives we study; hence we must be guarded in our inferences about what might account for state-to-state variation. Finally, we acknowledge that while this inquiry started at an exploratory stage, seeking to answer some fairly specific questions, it introduces a number of theoretical questions about the policy process at the state level. We cannot answer these questions conclusively, but we can entertain some potentially fruitful areas for future research.

However, none of these methodological and measurement caveats clearly explains our unexpected findings, so we are left to reassess theoretical explanations of state policy in order to develop hypotheses that might help us understand why due process policies are orthogonal to punishment policies. We offer three propositions for consideration.

First, the next step for this line of inquiry is an exploration of the political cultures that may help us account for policy variation. It is fairly well established that punitive policies are generated by politically conservative states.[44] We would propose a careful examination of the multiple dimensions of political ideology, beginning with Daniel Elazar's classic typology of political subcultures, based on historical immigration patterns.[45] One could readily imagine a moralistic subculture (defined in terms of high levels of political participation, social responsibility for self-government, and collective responsibility for social functions) adhering to rehabilitative sentencing policies, while nonetheless accepting considerable responsibility for monitoring the behavior of ex-offenders, justified in terms of public safety. But we would also recommend that scholars look closely at the core explanations for the punitive trend (and, possibly, its consequences for due process): racial tension, social disorganization, anxiety about crime and order. The central thesis of many students of the punitive turn is that these escalating public concerns created a receptive climate for politicization of crime issues—but that not all states were equally vulnerable.[46] A close examination of variability in these domains of public opinion might help us understand states' susceptibility to punitive policies.

Second, many of the signature policy issues we studied are of recent vintage, and therefore the real question to ask might be whether state legislatures have even been faced with floor votes on these initiatives. States that have aggressive policy entrepreneurs lobbying for these policies may have succeeded in getting them onto the floor—at which point it is unlikely that a legislature could vote them down.[47] On the other hand, states in which strong advocates for defendants' rights have access to key decision makers might have effectively blocked such innovations. We did not have data on these variables, but they may turn out to explain a great deal of policies that are, in fact, more symbolic than practical.

Third, we note that there is considerable discrepancy, perhaps particularly in the last three decades, between formal state policy and local practices. The literature on court decision-making is replete with evidence that judges, prosecutors, and defense lawyers arrive at decisions based more on local values and fundamental legal principles than on the latest state prescriptions.[48] Malcolm Feeley argued twenty years ago that attempts to change the ways that courts do business are rarely successful, for reasons that have as much to do with the settled values and decision-making processes of local actors as with the poorly conceived and implemented initiatives of state house policy-makers.[49] More generally, we suggest that state policy outcomes (such as incarceration rate) may result from shared values amongst the public and administrators, at least as much as formal policy prescriptions.

From the research presented here, it does not appear that states are possessed of a generalized orientation to due process issues or policy matters. The principal finding here, therefore, is that the "punitive turn" as a paradigmatic approach to understanding and characterizing criminal justice policy development over the last thirty years is limited in its descriptive generalizability. Whereas it encompasses a great deal in relation to recent upturns in punitive policy measures, its descriptive thesis is of limited use when it comes to tracking changes across different policy dimensions of criminal justice policy. Scholars within criminal justice would therefore be wise to think more broadly in terms of the policy areas to which they pay attention, and to be cautious when assuming that broad-brush theses such as that concerning the punitive turn can be applied across diverse policy areas.

Cases and Legal Codes Cited

Argersinger v. Hamlin *407 US 25 (1972)*
Betts v. Brady *316 US 455 (1942)*
Gideon v. Wainwright *372 US 335 (1963)*
Gregg v. Georgia*428 US 153 (1976)*
In re: Gault *387 US 1 (1967)*
Kansas v. Hendricks *521 US 346 (1997)*
Powell v. Alabama *287 US 45 (1932)*
Strickland v. Washington *466 US 668 (1984)*
U.S. Code: 42 U.S.C. 14071 Jacob Wetterling Crimes Against Children and Sexually Violent Offender Registration Program and Megan's Law.

Notes

* Authors are listed alphabetically to denote equal and indistinguishable contributions to this chapter. The authors express their appreciation to the many policy organizations who make state-level data on crime policy available in published form and online; and to Hilary Worden for assistance in data management. The authors bear sole responsibility for the opinions and conclusions expressed herein.

1. Katherine Beckett and Theodore Sasson, *The Politics of Injustice* (Thousand Oaks, CA: Pine Forge Press, 2004).
2. Bureau of Justice Statistics, "Expenditure and Employment Statistics" (2007), http://www.ojp.usdoj.gov/bjs/eande.htm (accessed Oct 2, 2007).

Nils Christie, *Crime Control as Industry*, 3rd ed. (London: Routledge, 2000).

3. David Garland, *The Culture of Control* (New York: Oxford University Press, 2001).

4. For example, Edward McGarrell and David Duffee, "Examining Correctional Resources: A Cross-Sectional Study of the States," in *Criminal Justice Theory: Explaining the Nature and Behavior of Criminal Justice*, ed. David Duffee and Edward Maguire (New York: Routledge, 2007).

5. Garland, *The Culture of Control*, 12.

6. Beckett and Sasson, *The Politics of Injustice*, 142.

7. *Gregg v. Georgia* (1976). Death Penalty Information Center, *Facts about the Death Penalty*, http://www.deathpenaltyinfo.org/FactSheet.pdf (accessed October 2 2007).

8. Trevor Jones and Tim Newburn, "Three Strikes and You're Out: Exploring Symbol and Substance in American and British Crime Control Politics," *Criminology* 46 (2006): 781–802. Franklin Zimring, Gordon Hawkins, and Sam Kamin *Punishment and Democracy: Three Strikes and You're Out in California* (Oxford: Oxford University Press, 2001). Jackson Williams, "Criminal Justice Policy Innovation in the States," *Criminal Justice Policy Review* 14, 3 (2003): 401–422.

9. William Sabol and Paige Harrison, *Prison and Jail Inmates at Mid-Year 2006*, Bulletin # NCJ217675 (Washington DC: Bureau of Justice Statistics, 2007).

10. James Stephan, *State Prison Expenditures, 2001*, Special Report # NCJ202949 (Washington DC: Bureau of Justice Statistics, 2004).

11. Herbert Packer, *The Limits of the Penal Sanction* (Stanford, CA: Stanford University Press, 1968), 153.

12. Garland, *The Culture of Control*.

13. Ibid.

14. Michael Tonry, *Thinking About Crime: Sense and Sensibility in American Penal Culture* (Oxford: Oxford University Press, 2004), 25.

15. Garland, *The Culture of Control*, 11.

16. We distinguish here between rights and privileges, although the distinction is not perfect. Defendants may be legally granted privileges (such as inmates' privilege to work in prison or to receive visits from family). The granting and withholding of such privileges is a matter of administration and discretion, especially insofar as withholding privileges can be used as a form of discipline.

17. *Powell v. Alabama*, 1932.

18. *Gideon v. Wainwright*, 1963.

19. *In re: Gault*, 1967.

20. *Argersinger v. Hamlin*, 1972.

21. Though, see *Strickland v. Washington*, 1984.

22. Steven K. Smith and Carol DeFrances, *Indigent Defense*, #NCJ158909 (Washington DC: Bureau of Justice Statistics, 1996).

23. Andrew Davies and Alissa Pollitz Worden, "State Politics and Indigent Defense: A Comparative Analysis," unpublished manuscript, 2007. Alissa Pollitz Worden and Andrew Davies, "Protecting Due Process in a Punitive Era: An Analysis of Changes in Providing Counsel to the Poor," unpublished manuscript, 2007.

24. Radio-Television News Directors Association, "Cameras in the Court: A State-by-State Guide" (2005), available at: http://www.rtnda.org/pages/media_items/cameras-in-the-court-a-state-by-state-guide55.php (accessed, May 15 2007).

25. Administrative Office of the United States Courts, "Judicial Conference Acts on Cameras in the Courts," *The Third Branch: The Newsletter of the Federal Courts* (April 1996), http://www.uscourts.gov/ttb/apr96/judconf. htm (accessed, Nov 24 2007). "New York State Committee to Review Audio-Visual Coverage of Court Proceedings," in *An Open Courtroom: Cameras in New York Courts* (New York: Fordham, 1997). New York State Defenders Association, "Cameras in NY Courtrooms White Paper" (1999), http:// www.nysda.org/Hot_Topics/Cameras_in_the_Courts/03_Cameras_in_ NY_Courts_NYSDA_1999_.pdf (accessed October 1, 2007).

26. Robert Meadows, "Rape Shield Laws: A Need for an Ethical and Legal Reexamination," *Criminal Justice Studies* 17, 3 (2004): 281.

27. Andrew Soshnick, "The Rape Shield Paradox: Complainant Protection amidst Oscillating Trends of State Judicial Interpretation," *Journal of Criminal Law and Criminology* 78 (1987): 644.

28. National Institute of Justice, *Using DNA to Solve Cold Cases*, Special Report # 194197 (Washington, DC: National Institute of Justice).

29. Barry Scheck, Peter Neufeld, and Jim Dwyer, *Actual Innocence: Five Days from Execution and Other Dispatches from the Wrongly Convicted* (New York: Doubleday, 2000).

30. National Conference of State Legislatures, *State Laws on DNA Banks: Qualifying Offenses, Others Who Must Provide Sample* (2007), http://www. ncsl.org/programs/cj/dnadatabanks.htm (accessed September 27, 2007).

31. American Society for Legal and Medical Ethics, *Survey of Post-Conviction DNA Testing Statutes* (2005), http://www.aslme.org/dna_04/grid/index. php (accessed October 2, 2007).

32. Rebecca S. Peterson, "DNA databases: When Fear Goes Too Far," *American Criminal Law Review* 37 (2000): 1219.

33. See the "Megan's Law" statute at 42 U.S.C. 14071(e).

34. Devon Adams, *Summary of Sex Offender Registries, 2001* NCJ #192265 (Washington, DC: Bureau of Justice Statistics, 2002).

35. Jill Levenson and Jill Cotter, "The Effect of Megan's Law on Sex Offender Reintegration," *Journal of Contemporary Criminal Justice* 21, 1 (2006): 49.

36. Eric Janus, "Sexual Predator Commitment Laws: Lessons for Law and the Behavioral Sciences," *Behavioral Sciences and the Law* 18 (2000): 5.

37. Roxanne Lieb and Kathy Gookin, *Involuntary Commitment of Sexually Violent Predators: Comparing State Laws*, Document # 05-03-1011 (Olympia, WA: Washington State Institute for Public Policy, 2005).

38. Rudolph Alexander, "The United States Supreme Court and the Civil Commitment of Sex Offenders," *The Prison Journal* 84, 3 (2004): 361.

39. The Sentencing Project, *Felony Disenfranchisement Laws in the United States* (2007), http://www.sentencingproject.org/Admin/Documents/publications/ fd_bs_fdlawsinus.pdf (accessed October 2, 2007).

40. Robert Crutchfield, "Abandon Felon Disenfranchisement Policies," *Criminology and Public Policy* 6, 4 (2007): 707.

41. Pamela Karlan, "Convictions and Doubts: Retributions, Representation, and the Debate Over Felon Disenfranchisement," *Stanford Law Review* 56

(2004): 1147. R. Anthony Duff, "Introduction: Crime and Citizenship," *Journal of Applied Philosophy* 22, 3 (2005): 211.

42. Of course, bivariate associations do not tell us whether there are underlying dimensions connecting more than two variables. We performed a factor analysis of these eight policy measures. The results substantially corroborate the picture that emerges from the bivariate analysis (results available from authors). The analysis of these eight variables produces four factors, of modest eigenvalues. The first factor marks states that have adopted broad authority to collect DNA samples, have adopted civil commitment provisions for some violent offenders, and have kept access to sex offender information relatively restricted from public view. The second dimension marks the difference between states that are relatively generous in funding indigent defense, and that yet have prohibited any testimony at trial about rape victims' relationships with accused defendants. The third scale suggests an association between permissive policy about courtroom cameras and restrictive policies about ex-offender voting rights. The last dimension taps the permissibility of cameras at trial and the denial of post-conviction DNA testing.

43. But see Stuart Scheingold, *The Politics of Law and Order: Street Crime and Public Policy* (New York: Longman, 1984).

44. McGarrell and Duffee, "Examining Correctional Resources."

45. Daniel Elazar, *American Federalism: A View from the States,* 3rd edition (New York: Harper and Row, 1984).

46. V. Barker, "The Politics of Punishing: Building a State Governance Theory of American Imprisonment Variation," *Punishment & Society* 8 (2006): 5–32.

47. Edmund McGarrell and Thomas Castellano, "An Integrative Conflict Model of the Criminal Law Formation Process," *Journal of Research in Crime and Delinquency* 28, 2 (1991): 174.

48. James Eisenstein and Herbert Jacob, *Felony Justice: An Organizational Analysis of Criminal Courts* (Boston: Little, Brown, 1977). Milton Heumann and Colin Loftin, "Mandatory Sentencing and the Abolition of Plea Bargaining: The Michigan Felony Firearm Statute," *Law and Society Review* 12 (1979): 393. Stuart Scheingold, *The Politics of Street Crime: Criminal Process and Cultural Obsession* (Philadelphia: Temple, 1991).

49. Malcolm Feeley, *Court Reform on Trial: Why Simple Solutions Fail* (New York: Basic Books, 1983).

Part IV

Uniformity and Diversity in Federalism

Chapter 10

Gay Rights, the Federal Marriage Amendment, and the States

Edward Ashbee

Although often represented as a state prerogative, the legal regulation of marriage has both played a part in shaping and has been shaped by federal–state relations. In 1862, Congress prohibited plural marriage. Utah and other western territories only won statehood by incorporating a ban on polygamy in their state constitutions. Later federal statutes used marriage and marital status to determine eligibility for particular federal benefits. Marriage came to the fore again as a problematic issue for American federalism in the final decade of the twentieth century with enactment in 1996 of the Defense of Marriage Act that defined marriage as a heterosexual institution. From 2001 onward, conservatives have increasingly pressed for the addition of a Federal Marriage Amendment (or Marriage Protection Amendment) to the U.S. Constitution. This chapter surveys the debate over this issue and explores why many conservatives support a federal ban prohibiting states from recognizing same-sex marriage in violation of their traditional concern for states' rights.

Same-Sex Marriage

From the 1970s onward, there were calls for the legalization of same-sex marriage or, at the least, the legal recognition of same-sex unions through, for example, provision of domestic partnership arrangements. However, relatively few Americans outside particular metropolitan regions, such as New York City and San Francisco, regarded these calls as a legitimate part of political discourse. Insofar as same-sex unions were ever considered, it was only at local and state rather than federal level.

A significant shift in the 1990s reflected changing public attitudes toward homosexuality in initiatives by local officials and court decisions. Calls for the legal recognition of same-sex unions, including both marriage and "marriage-lite" (as some dubbed domestic partnerships or "civil unions"), began to make an impact on the federal policy process. Countermobilizing efforts also made their mark. The issue was opened up in Hawaii by *Baehr v. Lewin* (which became *Baehr v. Miike* and at a later stage *Baehr v. Anderson*). In ruling on the case in 1993, the Hawaii State Supreme Court declared that the state had to show a "compelling state interest" if it was to deny marriage licenses to three same-sex couples.

Despite being circumvented by legal and political maneuvers that resulted in enactment of a constitutional amendment allowing the state legislature to define marriage as a heterosexual prerogative, the ruling set off shockwaves that extended far beyond Hawaii. It raised fears that if same-sex marriage was established in one state, constitutional mechanisms might well allow its "spread" to other states and jurisdictions across the United States. Such concerns centered on Article IV of the Constitution, which required that "Full Faith and Credit shall be given in each State to the public Acts, Records, and judicial Proceedings of every other State." Under its terms, the authorities in a particular state would seemingly be compelled to recognize a marriage ceremony conducted in Hawaii or another state.

These anxieties led to the rapid enactment of the Defense of Marriage Act of 1996 (DOMA) by overwhelming majorities in both the House of Representatives (342-67) and the Senate (85-14). President Clinton signed it into law just two months before the presidential election.[1] DOMA defined marriage as "a legal union between one man and one woman as husband and wife."[2] It also stated that "no State, territory, or possession of the United States, or Indian tribe" would be required to recognize a "record," "proceeding," or act "respecting a relationship between persons of the same sex that is treated as a marriage under the laws of such other State, territory, possession, or tribe."[3] In short, DOMA sought to establish that the Full Faith and Credit Clause did not extend to same-sex (or for that matter polygamous) unions. It therefore purported to protect states from developments in Hawaii or another like-minded jurisdiction.

Anxieties

Social conservatives and, in particular, the individuals and organizations that collectively constituted the Christian right remained fearful that DOMA could be struck down by the federal courts as unconstitutional. Even before its enactment, they had been deeply unsettled by the U.S. Supreme Court's ruling in *Romer v. Evans*. This struck down an amendment to the Colorado state constitution (which had been passed by Colorado voters in 1992) to prevent antidiscrimination measures being extended beyond categories such as race, ethnicity, and gender to include sexual orientation. To social conservatives, making sexual orientation a protected category would have created "special rights" for gays and lesbians and prevented anyone from declining to provide them a service on grounds of conscience or faith. As amendment supporters observed, a motel owner or landlord would have been compelled to provide a room for a same-sex couple.

The Supreme Court struck down the amendment because, according to the majority opinion written by Associate Justice Anthony Kennedy, it was directed toward a particular grouping. This constitutional change imposed "a special disability upon those persons alone. Homosexuals are forbidden the safeguards that others enjoy or may seek without constraint."[4] It failed the most basic form of "test" for assessing the constitutionality of measures that sought to redress the consequences of perceived discrimination or unequal outcomes between different social groupings. In Kennedy's assessment, the amendment lacked "a rational relationship to legitimate state interests" and seemed "inexplicable by anything but animus toward the class that it affects."

The Court was by no means united in this judgment. In a strongly worded dissent, Antonin Scalia (joined by Chief Justice William Rehnquist and Clarence Thomas) saw *Romer* as a denial of democratic principles insofar as it overruled majority opinion that had been expressed in a popular ballot and prohibited "a modest attempt by seemingly tolerant Coloradans to preserve traditional sexual mores against the efforts of a politically powerful minority to revise those mores through use of the laws."[5] Scalia also invoked principles of strict constructionist jurisprudence to argue that homosexuality and same-sex marriages were matters for the state legislatures or the ballot. In his opinion, these issues should have been subject to the democratic will because they were not addressed in the U.S. Constitution.

Pessimism

Rulings such as *Romer* and seeming public indifference toward President Clinton's relationship with Monica Lewinsky contributed to a growing sense of pessimism among many social conservatives. Indeed some, most notably those around Father Richard John Neuhaus and the "theoconservative" journal *First Things*, began to question the legitimacy of the U.S. political process. Others did not go so far, but started to doubt its usefulness. In a reference to the network that had marked the entry of the Christian right into the contemporary political process and defined social conservatism during much of the 1980s, veteran conservative organizer and Heritage Foundation founder Paul Weyrich suggested that there was no longer a "moral majority." Fearful that society had been corrupted, he urged moral-issue activists to "drop out of this culture, and find places... where we can live godly, righteous and sober lives."[6]

Although Neuhaus and Weyrich were minority voices, and their words attracted some criticism from others on the right, there was much to fuel the fears of social conservatives. From their perspective, the assault on "traditional culture" that had begun in the 1960s was continuing unabated. The "homosexual lifestyle" was being forced upon the nation. In 2000, following a ruling by the state Supreme Court, the Vermont General Assembly established civil unions. These and the domestic partnerships that were subsequently offered in some other states granted same-sex couples next-of-kin status and other rights provided for in state law. However, civil unions and domestic partnerships were not recognized in terms of federal law, so they lacked the status of marriage. To radical critics, they represented a "separate but equal" arrangement that the history of Jim Crow laws in southern states had proved by definition to be unequal.[7]

Social conservatives also had reason to doubt the resolution of their political allies. After initial hesitation, many within the Christian right threw their weight behind George W. Bush in the 2000 presidential election campaign. There was a sense of faith-based affinity between Bush and many white evangelical Protestants. As Texas governor and later as president, he was adept at using words and phrases that had a particular resonance with them. To the chagrin of leading social conservatives, however, Bush met with gay activists and talked in equivocal terms about gay issues during the 2000 campaign. Though anxious to keep strong ties with his activist base, he sought to strike a much more sympathetic pose toward gay activists than previous Republican presidential candidates. His running mate, Dick Cheney, had been more forthright. When asked about the prospect of same-sex marriage during the televised debate between vice-presidential candidates, he emphasized that marriage and other forms of same-sex union were a matter for the states alone:

> The fact of the matter is we live in a free society, and freedom means freedom for everybody. ... And I think that means that people should be free to enter into any kind of relationship they want to enter into. It's really no one else's business in terms of trying to regulate or prohibit behavior in that regard ... I think different states are likely to come to different conclusions, and that's appropriate. I don't think there should necessarily be a federal policy in this area.[8]

Coming in the wake of Bush's equivocations, Cheney's remarks—in the opinion of conservative columnist Rod Dreher—had left social conservatives "feeling shell-shocked by the men leading the party they thought was their home."[9]

Calls for a Constitutional Amendment

Calls for the Federal Marriage Amendment (or Marriage Protection Amendment as it was named in some versions) emerged against this background. From the perspective of social conservatives, developments in both the judicial and political arenas posed an imminent threat to the institution of marriage. In their eyes, it was very likely that courts in one or more states would "find" a right to same-sex marriage in the references to equality or liberty that were incorporated in many state constitutions. A federal constitutional amendment was therefore deemed necessary to protect the citizens of such states from a fundamental redefinition of marriage and, more importantly, prevent the subsequent "federalization" of a state judicial ruling.

Although social conservatives joined together in regarding same-sex marriage as a threat to the social fabric, they disagreed about the wording of a constitutional amendment. Some campaigners, particularly those associated with "outsider" organizations within the Christian right, such as the Traditional Values Coalition and Concerned Women for America, sought to block the legal recognition of all forms of same-sex union. In the version that they put forward, civil unions and domestic partnerships would be prohibited alongside marriage.[10]

Others within the conservative movement adopted a more pragmatic strategy. They insisted that an absolute prohibition on same-sex marriage should be written into the Constitution, but at the same time they made a concession to the spirit of federalism. The amendment that they put forward included a specific bar on the courts establishing civil unions/domestic partnerships on the basis of terms or clauses in the state constitution, but allowed state legislatures to create them. As the Republican Study Committee, a grouping of about a hundred Republican members in the House of Representatives, observed, "the Vermont legislature would still have the power to enact a statute extending marriage benefits to same-sex couples, but the Vermont Supreme Court could not *require* it to do so."[11] As Hadley Arkes, an influential campaigner, spelt out, this approach had a tactical rationale:

> We would oppose those devices to offer marriage under another name, but we would be prepared to debate the matter state-by-state, for a critical authority would indeed remain in the separate states to legislate on this issue in many ways.[12]

By 2004, most campaigners had rallied around the more pragmatic version of the Amendment that permitted civil unions and removed some of the textual ambiguities in some earlier versions:

> Marriage in the United States shall consist solely of the union of a man and a woman. Neither this Constitution, nor the constitution of any State, shall be construed to require that marriage or the legal incidents thereof be conferred upon any union other than the union of a man and a woman.[13]

"Federalization"

The case for a constitutional amendment was put in its most structured and developed form by Hadley Arkes, who is closely aligned with "theoconservative" Catholics such as Father Richard John Neuhaus, Michael Novak, and Robert P. George of Princeton University. "Theoconservatism," which draws upon notions of natural law, has, as noted above, come close to questioning the legitimacy of the American political process insofar as it is in breach of much that is enshrined in the defining tenets of natural law. In a forceful essay published in *National Review*, the flagship journal of the conservative movement, Arkes asserted that some clauses in the Constitution could ensure that same-sex marriage was imposed upon the entire country:

> As long as the Full Faith and Credit Clause remains in the Constitution, along with the clauses on Equal Protection and Privileges and Immunities, the Constitution itself will act as an engine to "federalize" the issue of marriage by bringing the matter into the federal courts.[14]

Arkes's emphasis on the Full Faith and Credit Clause in Article IV of the Constitution was familiar. As has been seen, concern that the clause might be used as a lever to "federalize" same-sex marriage if it was introduced in a particular state had led to the passage of DOMA by Congress and its signature by President Clinton. However, there were grounds for thinking that DOMA was constructed on solid legal ground insofar as it built upon long-established precedent that had spelt out and circumscribed the ways in which the "Full Faith and Credit Clause" was applied. In practice, the clause had not been understood to require that all marriages conducted in one state be accepted and recognized in another state. The principle of interstate comity has always been reined in by public-policy exceptions. This is because some states permitted marriages that provoked moral or cultural concerns in other states. Marriages between first cousins are permitted in some states but not others. The age at which marriage is allowed and the forms of parental consent that are required if minors seek to wed also differ between states. In practice, such marriages need not necessarily be honored by courts in another state.

For a long period, there was another public policy exception apart from marriages that involved issues of age or incest. Until the latter half of the 1960s, southern states felt no constitutional obligation to recognize inter-racial marriages that had been conducted in states where such unions were legal. However, decisions about the legal recognition of these were less straightforward than has often been acknowledged by commentators in the post-segregation years. As Andrew Koppelman has recorded, where couples married in another jurisdiction so as to evade the laws of their own state, the marriage was always invalidated by the southern courts. In contrast, where the status of an interracial marital relationship was the subject of litigation in a southern court because of, for example, inheritance issues, such marriages were "routinely upheld."[15] Even when marriage across racial lines was established as a constitutional right, public-policy exceptions remained intact. When in 1967 the Supreme Court considered the case of a couple who had evaded Virginia law by marrying in the District of Columbia (*Loving v. Virginia*) and struck down state laws prohibiting interracial marriage, it asserted that the Lovings could marry because Southern law rested upon an arbitrary and discriminatory denial of basic freedoms.

The *Loving* ruling was based upon the Fourteenth Amendment's assurance of "equal protection" and "due process of law."[16] It did not put the right of states to deny recognition to some marriage ceremonies performed in other states in jeopardy. On the basis of precedent, therefore, there were credible grounds for thinking that Congress had every right to pass DOMA and that its provisions simply bolstered the public policy exceptions that enabled states to determine themselves how the "Full Faith and Credit" clause should be interpreted. As Koppelman concludes:

> States have always had the power to decline to recognize marriages from other states, and they have been exercising that power for centuries … [T]here is not a single judicial decision that holds that full faith and credit requires states to recognize marriages that violate their own public policies concerning who may marry.[17]

The call by Arkes for a constitutional amendment did not, however, rest on the "Full Faith and Credit" clause alone. He also cited other clauses. "Privileges and immunities" can be found in both Article IV and the Fourteenth Amendment. Section 2 of the former states that "The Citizens of each State shall be entitled to all Privileges and Immunities of Citizens in the several States," Section 1 of the latter is directed specifically toward state governments. It establishes that "No State shall make or enforce any law which shall abridge the privileges or immunities of citizens of the United States."

Although fears about the use of "Privileges and Immunities" led to the passage of DOMA and Arkes cited the clauses in his rationale for the Federal Marriage Amendment, claims that these guarantees could be used to "federalize" same-sex marriage may have been an overstatement. The scope of the clauses is limited. First, although the Fourteenth Amendment (1868) was shaped by the politics of the Reconstruction era and an emphasis upon the rights brought about by national citizenship, there is uncertainty about the original purpose and the meaning of the privilege and immunity clauses because they lack clarity. Second, there have been widespread suggestions that insofar as they have a defined meaning, the clauses are redundant. Other clauses in the Constitution constrain the states and establish national rights of citizenship. Third, insofar as these constitutional provisions still serve a purpose, most commentators argue that they have only limited forms of application. They do not require the states to end all distinctions between residents and nonresidents (which all concede would be *reductio ad absurdium*) but only address important, particularly economic, issues.[18]

In his *National Review* article, Arkes also argued that the "equal protection" clause of the Fourteenth Amendment could be used to "federalize" same-sex marriage. This stipulates that no state shall "deny to any person within its jurisdiction the equal protection of the laws." Again, however, there are doubts about the extent to which such concern is justified. The "equal protection" clause had customarily been understood by the courts in different ways depending upon the form of discrimination that was alleged. A "strict scrutiny" test was applied when a "fundamental" constitutional right, particularly those in the Bill of Rights, seemed to have been breached or when a "suspect classification," most notably race, was involved. Federal, state, and local law or the actions of public officials had to serve a compelling governmental interest, be "narrowly tailored" so as to address a specific goal, and employ the least restrictive means for achieving that goal. If strict scrutiny was applied to laws restricting marriage to one man and one woman, these considerations would have to be addressed. However, strict scrutiny was the most rigorous form of judicial test. Other tests involving "classes," other than race, rest upon a less rigorous approach. Rational basis review simply asks whether a law or governmental action is a rational means of achieving and "reasonably related" to a particular goal that it is appropriate for government to seek. In *Romer v. Evans*, the Supreme Court appeared to state that it was basing its ruling on rational basis review:

> In order to reconcile the Fourteenth Amendment's promise that no person shall be denied equal protection with the practical reality that most legislation classifies for one purpose or another, the Court has stated that it will uphold a law that neither burdens a fundamental right nor targets a suspect class so long as the legislative classification bears a rational relation to some independent and legitimate legislative end.[19]

The federal courts were, therefore, not considering homosexuality as a suspect class alongside categories associated with race or gender. Lawmakers simply had to demonstrate a "rational basis" for measures. This seemed to provide scope for legislation that refused to regard homosexual and heterosexual relationships in the same way.

States' Rights

At first sight, therefore, the reliance by Arkes on the Full Faith and Credit Clause, the Equal Protection clause, and the Constitution's references to "privileges and immunities" seem to suggest a degree of hyperbole. These clauses only appear to provide a limited judicial basis for the "federalization" process that he feared. Accordingly, the case for a marriage amendment seems unproven. There are other reasons the conservative movement and Republicans might be reluctant to embrace it. They have customarily celebrated the principles associated with federalism. President Ronald Reagan, whose strategies and perceptions have in many ways shaped contemporary Republicanism, reaffirmed the importance of the Tenth Amendment and the principle of "states' rights" in Executive Order 12612, issued in October 1987:

> Federalism is rooted in the knowledge that our political liberties are best assured by limiting the size and scope of the national government ... In most areas of governmental concern, the States uniquely possess the constitutional

authority, the resources, and the competence to discern the sentiments of the people and to govern accordingly ... In the search for enlightened public policy, individual States and communities are free to experiment with a variety of approaches to public issues.[20]

The customary GOP reverence for Reagan's ideological legacy was not reflected in roll-call votes when Congress considered the Federal Marriage Amendment (FMA) proposal in 2004. A total of 191 House Republicans supported the measure and only twenty-seven opposed it. The corresponding figures in the Senate were forty-six in favor and six against.[21]

Republicans who opposed the FMA did so for different motives. Some, most notably Jim Kolbe of Arizona's 5th congressional district, were openly or semi-openly gay. Among them, there was sympathy for the "conservative case" for same-sex marriage. This was, however, put in its strongest and most developed form by former *New Republic* editor Andrew Sullivan and Jonathan Rauch, a columnist for *National Journal* and a frequent contributor to the libertarian magazine *Reason*. The latter argued that same-sex marriage would curb promiscuity and hedonism within the gay communities and encourage the acquisition of conservative values such as responsibility and stability:

> We want the licenses, the vows, the rings, the honeymoons, the anniversaries, the benefits, and, yes, the responsibilities and the routines. And who is telling us to just shack up instead? Self-styled friends of matrimony. Someday conservatives will look back and wonder why they undermined marriage in an effort to keep homosexuals out.[22]

Other Republicans believed that because the constitutionality of DOMA had not yet been brought before the federal courts, the FMA was premature. There were also those, such as Congressman Christopher Shays of Connecticut and Senator Olympia Snowe (Maine), who represented relatively moderate districts and states in the northeast. They may have been reluctant to associate themselves too closely with the Christian right. For his part, John Hostettler from Indiana opposed the FMA because he advocated a different strategic approach and instead promoted the Marriage Protection Act (HR 3313), which sought to remove marriage from the jurisdiction of the courts. There were also those who looked toward the libertarian tradition and saw the FMA as a further bolstering of federal power. Their ranks included Ron Paul from Texas's 14th congressional district, who sought the presidency in 1988 on the Libertarian Party's ticket and was a contender for the 2008 Republican nomination.

There were, furthermore, some fears about the wording of the Federal Marriage Amendment, despite the changes that were made since the proposal had first been put forward. An earlier version had stated that courts could not confer marital status or "the legal incidents thereof...upon unmarried couples or groups."[23] Opponents were quick to point out that this could have broader implications than its backers acknowledged. There were claims that, although not explicitly stated, it would have prevented state and local governments from passing laws establishing domestic partnerships or indeed recognizing "common law" claims arising between unmarried heterosexual couples. For his part, Eugene Volokh of the University of California at Los Angeles Law School argued that the amendment might not have prevented legislatures from creating civil unions but would make them legally unenforceable.[24] The wording of the FMA was changed and brought into line with President Bush's thinking. The revised version supposedly allowed the creation of civil unions by state legislatures and did nothing to invalidate common law claims between unmarried heterosexual couples, but critics continued to suggest that the legal implications were uncertain. Winnie Stachelberg, political director for the Human Rights Campaign, one of the leading gay and lesbian organizations in the United States, suggested that even with rewording "it remained murky whether the amendment would ban civil unions in Vermont, where the state allowed them in response to a judicial ruling."[25]

Commitment to federal principle also played its part alongside these concerns. There were echoes of the argument that Dick Cheney had put forward during the 2000 election campaign. One of Colorado's two Republican senators, Ben Nighthorse Campbell, stressed the prerogatives of the states. According to Campbell's press secretary, he "believes the decision to ban gay marriages should be left up to the states, and feels we should not tinker with the Constitution."[26] Former Congressman Bob Barr of Georgia, who had played a leading role in the impeachment proceedings against President Bill Clinton and had been a sponsor of DOMA, spoke in similar terms:

> Marriage is a quintessential state issue . . . A constitutional amendment is both unnecessary and needlessly intrusive and punitive. . . . As any good federalist should recognize, this law leaves states the appropriate amount of wiggle room to decide their own definitions of marriage or other similar social compacts, free of federal meddling.[27]

For his part, Senator John McCain later supported a constitutional prohibition on same-sex marriage in his home state of Arizona.[28] To the chagrin of Christian right activists, however, he asserted the importance of state authority in voting against the FMA: "The constitutional amendment we're debating today strikes me as antithetical in every way to the core philosophy of Republicans . . . It usurps from the states a fundamental authority they have always possessed and imposes a federal remedy for a problem that most states do not believe confronts them."[29]

Along with making the "conservative case" for same-sex marriage, Jonathan Rauch also invoked principles of federalism in its support. In his estimate, the FMA was a direct repudiation of federalism because it "would withdraw from states the power to permit same-sex marriage even if 100 percent of the voters and legislators of some state wanted to allow it."[30]

Rauch echoed Supreme Court Justice Louis Brandeis's celebrated dictum that the states should serve as "laboratories" that would, through the pluralism and diversity that federalism permits, allow social, political, and cultural experimentation. Without a federal diktat, he asserted, same-sex marriage would in all probability be introduced in some of the more liberal "blue" states. Policy conclusions could then be drawn from the consequences of change. Federalism would furthermore play a part in defusing cultural tensions. DOMA would ensure that same-sex marriage would not be imposed nationally, but states could still pursue their own policies based upon their own cultural traditions and beliefs. In other words, "same-sex marriage could be tried in a few places where people feel comfortable with it." According to Rauch, this operation of federal principle with regard to same-sex marriage would "avert culture wars." As he put it:

> Same-sex marriage should not be a federal issue. Conservatives, of all people, should not be attempting to make it one. They have been trumpeting the virtues of federalism for years. Here is a particularly compelling opportunity to heed their own wisdom.[31]

Little Backing

Why, however, did these arguments win so little backing within the conservative movement? Why did the majority of Congressional Republicans back the FMA in such numbers and why were the principles associated with federalism so readily trumped? There were six principal reasons.

In part, arguments for the FMA won the day because there was a sense of unprecedented crisis. Although some Republicans (and many Democrats) opposed FMA because DOMA had not been struck down and same-sex marriage was not at that stage an issue that had to be addressed through a constitutional amendment, social conservatives saw events and developments in very different terms. From their perspective, the crisis was such that it trumped the principles associated with "states' rights." Senator Rick Santorum of Pennsylvania put this case in graphic terms: "I would argue that the future of our country hangs in the balance because the future of marriage hangs in the balance. Isn't that the ultimate homeland security, standing up and defending marriage?"[32]

The sense of crisis can partly be traced back to the character of the issue itself. Efforts to legitimize homosexuality through the legal recognition of same-sex unions were deemed morally wrong because homosexuality was a sinful form of behavior. However, this having been said, many social conservatives had moved away from the language of retribution and punishment that characterized the Christian right during the late 1970s and 1980s. The forms of discourse used from the 1990s onward are unyielding but also place an emphasis on the importance of compassion. There is love for the sinner alongside hatred of the sin. There is increasing belief that "deviant" individuals can overcome homosexual impulses through prayer, counselling, and resolve. The legal recognition of same-sex unions impeded such a "healing" process by legitimizing the homosexual "lifestyle." However, social conservatives also believed that the issues of sexual orientation had much wider social and cultural ramifications that went beyond moral principle. Once marriage had been extended to gay and lesbian couples, the principles around which marriage was constructed would be weakened.[33] First, the "promiscuous" lifestyle that the Christian right considered an endemic feature of gay culture would undermine the principle of monogamy on which marriage and the family rest. Gay culture, it was said, tied to promiscuity and the seeking out of partners beyond the primary relationship. The marriage vows would be devalued. Second, if marriage was to be extended to all those who simply wished to affirm their love and commitment to each other and detached from childbirth and responsibility for the subsequent upbringing of children, it could logically be extended to all forms of relationships. Indeed, as Stanley Kurtz, a contributing editor for *National Review Online* and a fellow at the Hoover Institution argued, there would be no logical bar to incestuous or polyamorous marriages.

> Once we say that gay couples have a right to have their commitments recognized by the state, it becomes next to impossible to deny that same right to polygamists, polyamorists, or even cohabiting relatives and friends. And once everyone's relationship is recognized, marriage is gone, and only a system of flexible relationship contracts is left.[34]

Same-sex marriage therefore constituted a threat to heterosexual unions, and American society would reap the social whirlwind as a consequence. Without marriage and the family, children would be adrift. According to Bridget E. Maher of the Family Research Council, one of the principal organizations associated with the Christian right, children raised in a traditional family are less likely to put themselves at risk, will make greater educational progress, achieve more in life, and have better emotional and physical health. She affirmed: "Children raised by their biological married parents receive numerous social, health, and economic benefits, and these gifts benefit the whole of society. Conversely, it is through the breakdown of marriage that children and society are harmed."[35]

The sense of crisis was exacerbated by judicial developments. In the period preceding the retirement of Sandra Day O'Connor from the U.S. Supreme Court at the beginning of 2006, the Christian right and other social conservatives were fearful that there would be further rulings that, as they saw it, defied the Constitution and extended "rights" such as abortion. There were also concerns that although the Republicans had a majority in the Senate, which confirms presidential nominees, a lack of political will on the part of the Republicans, or Democratic maneuvers, might rob them of the opportunity to place conservative, "strict constructionist" nominees on the Supreme Court bench or in the lower federal courts when vacancies arose. A network of Christian right organizations, including the Family Research Council and Focus on the Family led by Dr James Dobson, convened a series of televised rallies that they dubbed "Justice Sundays." Their aim was to rally conservative opinion and put pressure on the White House to select a resolute nominee who was committed to the rolling back of earlier liberal judgments.

The passions and fears that inspired the Justice Sundays had firm foundations. Although the *Romer v. Evans* judgment had not placed discrimination against homosexuals on the same footing as race or gender, it nonetheless went beyond a rational basis test for considering the constitutionality of a particular statute or action. The Supreme Court asserted that the amendment to the Colorado state constitution preventing antidiscrimination legislation being extended to include sexual orientation should be struck down because it "seems inexplicable by anything but animus toward the class that it affects."[36] The ruling therefore seemed to lay down a further legal hurdle that legislation had to meet beyond the rational basis test. Legislation or public policy could not be motivated by "animus" toward a particular grouping. For social conservatives, "animus" seemed to refer to the feelings of all those who regarded homosexuality as immoral or socially dysfunctional. They were concerned that on the basis of what might be termed the "animus" test, gays and lesbians would become a "suspect" class. If this were to happen, efforts to differentiate between homosexuality and heterosexuality (such as a prohibition on same-sex marriage) would only be constitutional if they could withstand strict scrutiny.

Social conservative anxieties about the judicial process went far further than this. Although Hadley Arkes had warned of the implications of the Full Faith and Credit Clause, the Privileges and Immunities Clause, and the Equal Protection Clause, the implied right to "privacy" presented a much greater danger to social conservatives and strict constructionist jurisprudence. "Privacy" was established in *Griswold v. Connecticut* in 1965. The ruling struck down a state law prohibiting the sale of contraceptives to married couples. The court's reasoning, which emphasized the limits and constraints upon governmental power, was not rooted in a particular term or clause that was to be found in the Constitution. It instead looked beyond the specific words in the Constitution and asserted that "specific guarantees in the Bill of Rights have penumbras, formed by emanations from those guarantees that help give them life and substance."[37]

The right to privacy was then built upon in 1973 when, in the *Roe* ruling, the Court asserted that it extended to abortion. Then in June 2003, the Court went further. Overturning a precedent that was not two decades old, *Lawrence v. Texas* struck down state laws prohibiting consensual homosexual sex. The ruling drew upon notions of due process in the Fourteenth Amendment (that, it was said, not only established procedures that the authorities should follow in dealing with criminal suspects but imposed limits upon governmental power) and talked in much more expansive terms about freedom and liberty. Actions could not be restricted simply because they broke with the moral standards of the majority. According to the majority opinion penned by Anthony Kennedy:

> Freedom extends beyond spatial bounds. Liberty presumes an autonomy of self that includes freedom of thought, belief, expression, and certain intimate conduct ... The petitioners are entitled to respect for their private lives. The State cannot demean their existence or control their destiny by making their private sexual conduct a crime.[38]

The ruling seemed to open the way for same-sex marriage. In a strongly worded dissent, Antonin Scalia claimed:

> Today's opinion dismantles the structure of constitutional law that has permitted a distinction to be made between heterosexual and homosexual unions, insofar as formal recognition in marriage is concerned. If moral disapprobation of homosexual conduct is "no legitimate state interest" for purposes of proscribing that conduct ... what justification could there possibly be for denying the benefits of marriage to homosexual couples exercising [t]he liberty protected by the Constitution?[39]

The *Lawrence* ruling was followed five months later by *Goodridge v. Dept. of Public Health*, a ruling of the Massachusetts Supreme Judicial Court. This held that there was no rational basis for the denial of marriage rights to same-sex couples and gave the state legislature 180 days to pass legislation addressing the issue. The legislature complied by establishing the right of same-sex marriage in Massachusetts on May 17, 2004. The sense of acute crisis felt by social conservatives in the wake of the *Goodridge* ruling was intensified by the actions of local officials in San Francisco. Although the ceremonies were later rescinded, newly elected mayor Gavin Newsom authorized the marriage of more than 3,400 couples.[40] Many social conservatives consequently regarded the spread of same-sex marriage as inevitable unless halted by a constitutional amendment. Though successful in promoting enactment of "mini-DOMAs" at the state level that put the nonrecognition of same-sex unions into state law, and reinforcing these through the passage of state constitutional amendments, they feared that these measures, like DOMA itself, could be struck down by the state or federal courts.

This leads to a second reason why the FMA was embraced by the overwhelming majority of Republicans. Against a background within which same-sex marriage seemed to be advancing by the day, the Amendment was not represented as a repudiation of federalist principles. Marriage had become a federal issue because of the cases brought by gay and lesbian campaigners and court rulings that had extended the Constitution. For social conservatives, federalism and the prerogatives of the states were being placed in jeopardy by the federal and state judiciary. The Constitution, they asserted, would either be changed by the FMA or, if it was not adopted, by the courts who would, through the right to "liberty," find a right for same-sex couples to marry. At issue in their eyes was no longer whether the Constitution would be amended. As Senate Majority Leader Bill Frist of Tennessee declared: "The only question is who will amend it and how it will be amended. Will activist judges—not elected by the American people—destroy the institution of marriage? Or will the people protect marriage as the best way to raise children? My vote is with the people."[41]

Its eventual backing by the White House was another reason why Republicans rallied in favor of the FMA. At that juncture, George W. Bush still played an important leadership role within the party. In the 2002 midterm elections, the president's campaigning had contributed to Republican congressional victories. Bush not only ensured his own reelection but remained a significant electoral asset in November 2004. Within the context of an increasingly partisan and polarized political process, the Bush White House offered direction to the party. It promoted and secured passage of the No Child Left Behind Act in 2001 and involved itself in the removal of Trent Lott of Mississippi as Republican leader in the Senate after he made remarks that were construed as racist.

Though Bush's initial hesitance created a degree of frustration and impatience among the most active backers of the FMA, he made a public statement in its support in February 2004. Playing down the rights and wrongs of same-sex marriage itself, the president framed the issue instead as a response to unrestrained judicial activism and the likelihood that the full faith and credit clause would be used to "federalize" same-sex marriage. He declared:

> The Constitution says that full faith and credit shall be given in each state to the public acts and records and judicial proceedings of every other state. Those who want to change the meaning of marriage will claim that this provision requires all states and cities to recognize same-sex marriages performed any-where in America. Congress attempted to address this problem in the Defense of Marriage Act … Yet there is no assurance that the Defense of Marriage Act will not, itself, be struck down by activist courts. In that event, every state would be forced to recognize any relationship that judges in Boston or offi-cials in San Francisco choose to call a marriage.[42]

The Federal Marriage Amendment also drew great support from core Republican supporters. As table 10.1 suggests, the strongest party identifiers, many of whom were associated at least in broad terms with the Christian right, opposed same-sex marriage in disproportionate numbers. In this poll, 77.2 percent of "strong Republicans" disagreed or "strongly disagreed" with same-sex marriage compared with only 55 percent of the general population.

At the same time, while opposition to same-sex marriage played well with core Republican supporters, it was also reportedly seen by some Republican strategists as a "wedge issue" that could be used to attract some habitual Democrats. As table 10.2 indicates, almost a quarter of "not strong" Democrats and over a third of those dubbing themselves "independents" strongly disagreed with same-sex marriage.

Table 10.1 Attitudes toward same-sex marriage among strong party identifiers, 2004 (percentages)

	Strong Republicans	Strong Democrats	National
Strongly agree	2.3	22.5	12.1
Agree	8.8	23.6	19.1
Neither agree nor disagree	11.8	12.8	13.9
Disagree	18.3	22.3	20.6
Strongly disagree	58.9	18.8	34.4

Note: Question text: "Homosexual couples should have the right to marry one another." (National Opinion Research Center, General Social Survey, MARHOMO, 2004).

Source: http://sda.berkeley.edu/cgi-bin/hsda3

Table 10.2 Attitudes toward same-sex marriage among Democratic identifiers and independents, 2004 (percentages)

	Not strong Democrats	Independents
Strongly agree	13.4	9.2
Agree	26.3	20.4
Neither agree nor disagree	15.9	16.5
Disagree	19.9	18.4
Strongly disagree	24.5	35.5

Note: Question text: "Homosexual couples should have the right to marry one another." (National Opinion Research Center, General Social Survey, MARHOMO, 2004).

Source: http://sda.berkeley.edu/cgi-bin/hsda3

It was a strategy that many observers have suggested was adopted in the 2004 presidential election by Karl Rove, Bush's principal political advisor and campaign strategist. From this perspective, efforts to pass the Federal Marriage Amendment and the placing of referenda proposing to ban same-sex marriage on the ballot in eleven states mobilized "values voters" who leant heavily toward the Bush–Cheney ticket. According to journalists Debra Rosenberg and Karen Breslau, "Gay marriage was a key part of Karl Rove's turnout strategy, and stood out as one of the cultural fault lines dividing the two Americas."[43]

A final factor may also have been in play. Although the Republican Party has traditionally associated itself, and has often been associated, with calls for decentralization and has sometimes spoken in deeply hostile terms about federal government power, contemporary Republicanism has done little to advance a federalist agenda. Indeed, it often seems imbued with a centralizing spirit. As Tim Conlan and John Dinan have argued, the Bush administration "has been routinely dismissive of federalism concerns and frequently an agent of centralization."[44] In their view, this reflects a shift in the character of conservatism and the conservative movement. There is now much more of a commitment to activist government and the use of government to secure conservative ends.[45] The change has not been confined to the White House.

According to Sidney Milkis and Jesse Rhodes, federalism has been downgraded in "party rhetoric."[46] This was exemplified by congressional enactment of the 2001 No Child Left Behind Act, which sought to modernize and reform the American educational system.

Conclusion

The Federal Marriage Amendment was again put to congressional vote in 2006. Some social conservatives had hoped in vain that a swathe of Democrats, particularly freshmen, would back it in recognition of the strength of public feeling on the issue in the 2004 elections. However, it only received 236 votes in the House (forty-seven votes short of the two-thirds majority required for a constitutional amendment) and forty-eight votes in the Senate vote to invoke cloture.[47] With the Democratic victories in the Congressional elections of November 2006 (and the seeming reluctance of the courts to address the issue), efforts to secure a constitutional ban on same-sex marriage appeared to be off the political agenda.

Although the FMA increasingly appeared to be a lost cause, the "assault' on traditional values proceeded at a more limited pace than social conservatives had feared. By the beginning of 2008, eight states offered domestic partnerships to gay and lesbian couples, but fears that Massachusetts marriage laws might be "exported" to other states were not borne out in the way that social conservatives had feared. To some extent, the sense of social crisis receded. In part, this was because the political agenda changed and cultural issues were displaced, most notably by the Iraq war and anxieties about the economy. It was also because there was an uneasy stalemate on the frontlines of the culture wars. At the time of writing, DOMA remains intact. The Massachusetts Supreme Judicial Court upheld a 1913 state law that prohibited those from outside the state marrying in Massachusetts if their marriage would not be accepted in their own state. For the most part, the gay movement held back from judicial appeals and focused instead on the legislative process. They confined themselves to domestic partnership arrangements where majority public opinion was relatively solid and did not seek to "nationalize" the rights secured in Massachusetts through court action. Nor have leading Democrats been ready to extend their agenda. In August 2007, as the Democratic presidential candidates limbered up, *Newsweek* commented, "In the six and a half years since the Clintons left the White House, the landscape has altered dramatically for gays ... And yet the Democratic front runners' positions on major gay issues ... are identical to those taken by Al Gore and Bill Bradley eight years ago."[48]

Conversely, the campaign to amend state constitutions so as to bar same-sex marriage (and in many cases the language was broad enough to have potential implications for civil unions and domestic partner benefits) seemed to be losing some momentum. In November 2006, Arizona became the first state to reject a ballot proposal that would have entrenched the prohibition of same-sex marriage in the state constitution. At the same time, the retirement of Supreme Court Justice Sandra Day O'Connor and the eventual appointment of Samuel Alito in her place reassured social conservatives that there was less likelihood of DOMA being struck down, and it strengthened their hopes that some of the implied rights that had been established from the time of Warren Court onward might be reined in.

The stalemate in the "culture wars" will almost certainly be maintained. In general, Democratic and Republican candidates in the 2008 prenomination contests have seen few political gains in the issues that have defined the cultural conflicts of recent years. With exceptions only at the fringes, they have pledged themselves to civil unions but held back from endorsing, or have opposed, same-sex marriage. Given the ambiguities and tensions within American public opinion, the partisan character of contemporary congressional politics, the Christian right's loss of élan, and the hold that other issues have on the political agenda, the stalemate may continue for a period long beyond the 2008 election. Against this background, the prospects for a federal marriage amendment, with all its implications for federal–state relations, are very limited.

Notes

1. President Clinton did not record the signing of DOMA in his autobiography. See Bill Clinton, *My Life* (New York: Alfred A. Knopf, 2004).
2. The Library of Congress – THOMAS, *Defense of Marriage Act (Enrolled as Agreed to or Passed by Both House and Senate)*, H.R.3396, http://thomas.loc. gov/cgi-bin/query/D?c104:1:./temp/~c104WPK3xv:
3. Ibid.
4. U.S. Supreme Court, *Romer v. Evans, No. 94–1039*, FindLaw, http://caselaw. lp.findlaw.com/scripts/getcase.pl?court=US&vol=000&invol=U10179
5. Ibid.
6. Quoted in Alain Epp Weaver, "Drop-out Christianity," *Christian Century* (March 17, 1999), http://findarticles.com/p/articles/mi_m1058/is_9_116/ ai_54216295.
7. Civil unions or domestic partnerships were subsequently offered in California (2003), Maine (2004), Connecticut (2005), New Jersey (2006), New Hampshire (2007), Washington (2007), and Oregon (2008).
8. Commission on Presidential Debates, *Debate Transcript, October 5, 2000, The Lieberman–Cheney Vice Presidential Debate*, http://www.debates.org/ pages/trans2000d.html.
9. Quoted in Ted Olsen, "Weblog: GOP Ticket Seems to Give Thumbs Up to Gay Unions," *Christianity Today* (October 1, 2000), www.ctlibrary.com/ ct/2000/octoberweb-only/52.0.html.
10. I am grateful to Martin Durham (University of Wolverhampton, UK) for this distinction.
11. Republican Study Committee, *Legislative Bulletin*, September 30, 2004, 2, http://www.house.gov/hensarling/rsc/doc/LB%2009-30-04.pdf.
12. Hadley Arkes, "Gay Rights and Federalism: An improbable marriage," *National Review* (August 6, 2001), http://www.nationalreview.com/ comment/comment-arkes080601.shtml.
13. American Civil Liberties Union, *Text of the Proposed Amendment* (March 23, 2004), http://www.aclu.org/lgbt/gen/11926res20040323.html.

14. Hadley Arkes, "Gay Rights and Federalism."
15. Andrew Koppelman, *Same Sex, Different States: When Same-Sex Marriages Cross State Lines* (New Haven: Yale University Press, 2006), 112.
16. *U.S. Supreme Court*, Loving v. Virginia, 388 U.S. 1 (1967), *Decided June 12, 1967, FindLaw*, http://caselaw.lp.findlaw.com/scripts/getcase.pl?court=US&vol=388&invol=1.
17. Andrew Koppelman, *Same Sex, Different States*, 117–118. http://www.bsos.umd.edu/gvpt/lpbr/subpages/reviews/koppelman0307.htm.
18. University of Missouri-Kansas City School of Law, *Exploring Constitutional Conflicts – State Discrimination Against Non-Residents*, http://www.law.umkc.edu/faculty/projects/ftrials/conlaw/priv&immart4.htm.
19. U.S. Supreme Court, *Romer v. Evans.*
20. The National Archives – The Federal Register, *Executive Order 12612—Federalism*, http://www.archives.gov/federal-register/codification/executive-order/12612.html.
21. Human Rights Campaign, *Federal Marriage Amendment Vote*, H.J. Res. 106, Roll Call Vote 484, Sept. 30, 2004, http://www.hrc.org/Template.cfm?Section=Home&CONTENTID=34218&TEMPLATE=/ContentManagement/ContentDisplay.cfm.
22. Jonathan Rauch, "The Marrying Kind," *The Atlantic* (May 2002), http://www.theatlantic.com/doc/200205/rauch.
23. Alan Cooperman, "Little Consensus on Marriage Amendment: Even Authors Disagree on the Meaning of Its Text," *Washington Post*, February 14, 2004, A01, http://www.washingtonpost.com/ac2/wp-dyn/A40866-2004Feb13?language=printer.
24. Ibid.
25. Carl Hulse, "Amendment's Words Tweaked: GOP Backers Say New Version Lets States Permit Civil Unions," *SFGate.com* (March 23, 2004), http://sfgate.com/cgi-bin/article.cgi?f=/c/a/2004/03/23/MNGR15PLR91.DTL.
26. Scott Heiser, Proposed Constitutional Amendment Fires Up State, Local Leaders, *ColoradoDaily.com* (February 25, 2004), www.coloradodaily.com/articles/2004/02/25/news/news01.txt.
27. Bob Barr, "Leave Marriage To the States," *Washington Post*, August 21, 2003, A23, http://www.washingtonpost.com/ac2/wp-dyn?pagename=article&contentId=A23357-2003Aug20¬Found=true,
28. Elvia Díaz, "Gay-Marriage Ban Initiative Wins Support from McCain," *The Arizona Republic* (August 26, 2005), http://www.azcentral.com/arizonarepublic/news/articles/0826initiatives26.html.
29. CNN.com, "McCain: Same-Sex Marriage Ban is Un-Republican," *CNN.com* (July 14, 2004), http://edition.cnn.com/2004/ALLPOLITICS/07/14/mccain.marriage/.
30. Jonathan Rauch, "Leave Gay Marriage to the States," *Wall Street Journal*, July 27, 2001, http://www.jonathanrauch.com/jrauch_articles/gay_marriage_2_leave_it_to_the_states/index.html
31. Ibid.
32. *Religious Tolerance. Org, "Federal Marriage Amendment (FMA) to the U.S. Constitution," Events (July 2004–January 2005), http://www.religioustolerance.org/mar_amend9.htm.*
33. Edward Ashbee, "Polyamory, Social Conservatism and the Same-Sex Marriage Debate in the US," *Politics* 27, 2 (June 2007): 101–107.

34. Stanley Kurtz, "Beyond Gay Marriage: The Road to Polyamory," *The Weekly Standard* 8, 45 (August 4–11, 2003), www.weeklystandard.com/Content/Public/Articles/000/000/002/938xpsxy.asp.

35. Bridget E. Maher, *The Benefits of Marriage*, Family Research Council, http://www.frc.org/get.cfm?i=IS05B01.

36. U.S. Supreme Court, *Romer v. Evans.*

37. *U.S. Supreme Court,* Griswold v. Connecticut, 381 U.S. 479 (1965), *Decided June 7, 1965, FindLaw, http://caselaw.lp.findlaw.com/scripts/getcase.pl?court= US&vol=381&invol=479.*

38. Supreme Court of the United States, No. 02.102, *John Geddes Lawrence and Tyron Garner, petitioners v. Texas, 539 U. S.* (2003) June 26, 2003, http://www.law.cornell.edu/supct/pdf/02-102P.ZD.

39. Ibid.

40. CNN.com, *California court halts same-sex marriages,* May 5, 2004, http://edition.cnn.com/2004/LAW/03/11/gay.marriage.california/index.html.

41. Michael Foust, "Summary: What Senators Said During Debate Wednesday," *Baptist Press* (Jul 14, 2004), http://www.bpnews.net/bpnews.asp?ID=18686.

42. The White House – Office of the Press Secretary, *President Calls for Constitutional Amendment Protecting Marriage: Remarks by the President,* February 24, 2004 , http://www.whitehouse.gov/news/releases/2004/02/20040224-2.html.

43. Debra Rosenberg and Karen Breslau, "Culture Wars: Winning the 'Values' Vote," *Newsweek – Election 2004 / MSNBC.com,* http://www.msnbc.msn.com/id/6401635/site/newsweek/. This conclusion has however been widely questioned. See, for example, Gregory B. Lewis, "Same-Sex Marriage and the 2004 Presidential Election," *PS: Political Science and Politics* 38 (2005): 195–199, http://journals.cambridge.org/action/displayAbstract;jsessionid= DD45A0001A4993215E597B293BA350E9.tomcat1?fromPage=online&aid=296249.

44. Tim Conlan and John Dinan, "Federalism, the Bush Administration, and the Transformation of American Conservatism," *Publius: The Journal of Federalism* 37, 3 (2007): 280.

45. Ibid., 299–300.

46. Sidney M. Milkis and Jesse H. Rhodes, "George W. Bush, the Party System, and American Federalism," *Publius: The Journal of Federalism* 37, 3 (2007): 483.

47. CBS News, "House Rejects Gay Marriage Amendment: 236-187 Vote Ends For Another Year Congressional Debate Over Marriage," *CBS News* (July 18, 2006), http://www.cbsnews.com/stories/2006/07/18/politics/main1813421.shtml.

48. Jonathan Darman, "Show 'Em Whatcha Got," *Newsweek,* CL 7, August 13, 2007, 29.

Chapter 11

Clearing the Air: The New Politics
of Public Smoking

Christopher J. Bailey

A major change has occurred in the way governments in the United States have sought to deal with the problem of passive smoking. From the mid-1970s to the mid-1990s, governments tended to require the provision of designated smoking areas as the primary means of controlling exposure to Environmental Tobacco Smoke (ETS). The public spaces typically covered by this first phase of smoking control laws were relatively noncontroversial spaces such as hospitals, schools, elevators, and public transportation. From the mid-1990s onward, however, governments have proved increasingly willing to prohibit rather than restrict public smoking. An expansion of the range of public spaces covered by this second phase of smoking control laws has also been apparent. A greater readiness to ban smoking in controversial spaces such as private workplaces, restaurants, and bars has been evident.

In this chapter I argue that this increased willingness to ban smoking across a wide range of public spaces signals the emergence of a new politics of public smoking that challenges existing understanding of the issue. First, I argue that a transformation in the way the issue of public smoking is defined is the key to understanding the new politics of smoking control laws. A growing acceptance that public smoking is a significant *public* health problem rather than simply an annoyance to nonsmokers has created a momentum for smoking bans that transcends partisan/ideological factors and submerges economic considerations. In short, a paradigmatic shift in the definition of the issue has undermined the old politics of public smoking and ushered in a new era. Second, I argue that this new era is characterized by a complex web of intergovernmental relations. Although regulatory activity has been evident at all levels of American government, it is at the state and particularly the local level that most activity has been seen. This chapter will examine the driving forces behind this pattern of activity, and will conclude with some normative observations about the variation in the delivery of a public good such as health provision in a federal system.

ETS as a Public Health Problem

Many nonsmokers have long regarded ETS as a nuisance. King James I of England famously railed against smokers for "infect[ing] the air, when very often, men that abhor it are at their repast" in *A Counterblaste to Tobacco* published in 1604.[1] Even smokers have occasionally displayed sensitivity to the distress their actions might cause to others. Samuel Johnson accepted that "it is a shocking thing, blowing smoke out of our mouths into other people's mouths, eyes, and noses, and having the same thing done to us."[2] Growing epidemiological evidence that exposure to ETS poses a health risk to nonsmokers, however, has gradually transformed how the problem of secondhand smoke has been defined over the last thirty years. ETS has increasingly been viewed as a public health problem worthy of government action rather than simply an annoyance to nonsmokers that should be addressed at an individual level by asking a smoker to desist or by leaving a smoke-filled room.

Official recognition that exposure to ETS posed a health risk to nonsmokers in certain circumstances first appeared in the U.S. Surgeon General's 1972 report on smoking.[3] The Report warned that smoking in a closed room or car might lead to a buildup of dangerously high levels of carbon monoxide. A subsequent review of the literature on the health effects of exposure to "involuntary smoking" in the U.S. Surgeon General's 1979 report *Smoking and Health* confirmed that tobacco smoke could be a significant source of atmospheric pollution in enclosed areas, and could be annoying to nonsmokers even under conditions of adequate ventilation.[4] Further epidemiological studies during the early 1980s provided sufficient evidence of a link between ETS and health problems to allow the Surgeon General to release a report in 1986 that identified "involuntary smoking" as a cause of disease and death in healthy nonsmokers.[5] Not only did this constitute the first statement by a major public health agency that ETS was a cause of death and disease, but the Report also provided the first official acknowledgment that "involuntary smoking" was a public health problem. In the Preface to the Report, U.S. Surgeon General C. Everett Koop claimed that "measures to protect the public health are required now," and in language that mirrored the landmark 1964 U.S. Surgeon General's report on smoking and health,[6] called for "appropriate remedial action" to protect the nonsmoker from environmental tobacco smoke. Koop argued that such protection required restrictions on smoking in public places because simply separating smokers from nonsmokers within the same airspace failed to eliminate exposure to ETS.

Two government reports published in the early 1990s reinforced the message that ETS constituted a public health problem that required "appropriate remedial action." In 1991 the National Institute for Occupational Safety and Health (NIOSH) issued a report that concluded that ETS could cause lung cancer in nonsmokers and recommended that workplace exposures "be reduced to the lowest feasible concentration."[7] A report published by the Environmental Protection Agency (EPA) in 1993 also concluded that ETS caused lung cancer (and a range of other respiratory illnesses) in nonsmokers.[8]

In a significant development the report categorized ETS as a "Class A" carcinogen for which there is no safe level of exposure, and estimated that 3,000 nonsmokers died every year as a result of breathing someone else's smoke. The report noted that although the EPA did not have any regulatory authority for controlling ETS it expected its findings "to be of value to other health professionals and policymakers in taking appropriate steps to minimize peoples' exposure to tobacco smoke in indoor environments." Tobacco companies challenged the EPA report in the federal courts and secured an initial victory in 1998 when U.S. District Judge William L. Osteen ruled in *Flue-Cured Tobacco Cooperative et al. vs. US Environmental Protection Agency* that the methodology employed in the report was flawed. The EPA appealed the decision, and in 2002 the U.S. Court of Appeals (4th Circuit) dismissed the tobacco companies' suit. Two years earlier the National Institute of Environmental Health Sciences had included ETS on a list of known human carcinogens for the first time in its *9th Report on Carcinogens.*[9]

An important report published by the California Environmental Protection Agency in 1997 provided further evidence that ETS constituted a public health problem that needed to be addressed by identifying a link between exposure to ETS and heart disease.[10] The report indicted ETS as a cause of heart disease and concluded that passive smoking caused 53,000 deaths per year. In 1999 the National Cancer Institute gave the Cal-EPA report a national imprimatur by republishing it as a federal document.[11] The U.S. Center for Disease Control (CDC) proceeded to highlight the link between ETS and heart disease when it issued a warning in 2004 that even a short period of exposure to secondhand smoke creates an increased risk of heart attacks in vulnerable populations. Cal-EPA published a subsequent report in 2005 that identified additional links between ETS and ill health.[12] New findings in the report included a causal link between exposure to ETS and premature births, breast cancer in young women, asthma in adults, and a range of cardiovascular diseases.

Publication of the Surgeon General's report *The Health Consequences of Involuntary Exposure to Tobacco Smoke* in 2006 confirmed scientific findings that exposure to ETS had serious adverse health effects and declared that secondhand smoke constituted "an alarming public health hazard."[13] "The health effects of secondhand smoke exposure are more pervasive than we previously thought," stated Surgeon General Richard Carmona when introducing the report, "The scientific evidence is now indisputable: secondhand smoke is not a mere annoyance. It is a serious health hazard that can lead to disease and premature death in children and non-smoking adults."[14] The report concluded that "separating smokers from nonsmokers, cleaning the air, and ventilating buildings cannot eliminate exposures of nonsmokers to secondhand smoke," and called for the elimination of smoking in indoor spaces.[15]

Industry and Public Responses

The identification of ETS as a public health problem changed the way the problem of smoking is defined. Evidence of the adverse health effects caused by exposure to ETS provided antismoking advocates with the opportunity to bypass traditional arguments that smoking is a self-regarding action that concerns only the smoker, and focus instead on the harm that smokers do to others. The injunction not to "expose others to risks which they did not agree to take on themselves" replaced the libertarian claim of earlier years that "it's my body and I'll do with it as I please."[16] Some public health campaigners even described underaged exposure to ETS as a form of child abuse.[17] Growing public acceptance of the health risks associated with ETS meant that concern about the rights of nonsmokers increasingly dominated debates about smoking.

Big Tobacco industry recognized at an early stage the threat the identification of ETS as a public health problem posed to the industry. Internal industry documents reveal that tobacco companies began to identify ETS as a problem at least as early as 1973.[18] Two concerns, in particular, worried the industry. First, the tobacco companies understood that ETS undermined the traditional defense of the industry that smoking was a matter of "informed choice" and acceptance of risk that were matters for the individual not society. A Roper Organization report of 1978, commissioned by the Tobacco Institute, noted: "What the smoker does to himself may be his business, but what the smoker does to the nonsmoker is quite a different matter."[19] Second, the tobacco industry feared that successful efforts to restrict public smoking would lead to a decline in smoking rates.[20] Faced with ostracism in the workplace, restaurants, and public buildings, smokers might decide to abandon cigarettes totally.

The tobacco industry initially sought to combat the threat posed by ETS by challenging claims that secondhand smoke is dangerous to nonsmokers.[21] Early efforts to discredit links between ETS and adverse health effects simply advanced the crude idea that other pollutants were responsible for poor indoor air quality and associated ill health. Industry claims that "sick building syndrome" had nothing to do with ETS were typical of a strategy that sought to confuse the public and distract attention from smoking. Later efforts sought to provide more sophisticated rebuttals of the links between ETS and ill health. Research sponsored by the tobacco-industry-funded Center for Indoor Air Quality sought to show that factors such as genetic predisposition, diet, and stress played a more important role in the onset of lung cancer than ETS.

Opinion polls reveal that these industry efforts to challenge claims that ETS represented a significant public health risk fell largely on deaf ears. Prominent coverage of government reports in the media generated widespread public concern about the health risks associated with ETS. Between 1974 and 1987 the number of Americans who believed that passive smoking posed a health risk to nonsmokers rose from 46 percent to 81 percent.[22] This number has remained fairly constant, but annual Gallup Polls conducted from 1994 reveal significant changes in public perceptions of the nature of the risk involved (see figure 11.1). In a 2006 poll, 56 percent of respondents felt that secondhand smoke was "very harmful" and 29 percent "somewhat harmful" compared to 36 percent and 42 percent in these respective categories in 1994.

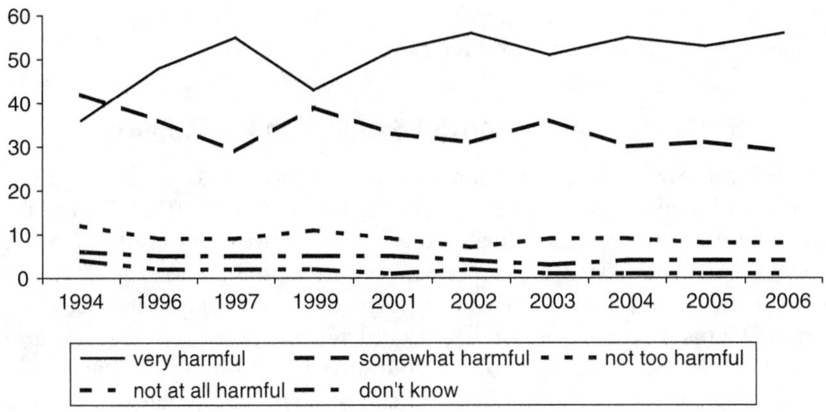

Figure 11.1   How harmful is secondhand smoke to adults

Source: Data from the Gallup Organization (2007), "Tobacco and Smoking," www.poll.gallup.com

An increased willingness to support stricter restrictions on public smoking has accompanied this growing perception of the hazards of ETS.[23] In a 2004 poll, 58 percent expressed support for bans on smoking in workplaces, restaurants, and bars in their state. Public support for stricter restrictions on public smoking is even more pronounced in state and local polls. Surveys in states as diverse as New York, Mississippi, Indiana, and Michigan, for example, typically reveal that 60 percent to 82 percent of those polled supported smoking bans in workplaces and restaurants.[24] Even smokers appear to believe that increased restrictions on smoking in public places are justified. In 2005, a Gallup Poll revealed that 59 percent of smokers supported such measures.[25]

The tobacco industry responded to polls showing public acceptance that ETS constituted a health hazard and support for bans on smoking in public places by seeking to reframe the debate in more favorable terms. First, it resourced a number of grassroots groups to champion smokers' rights in an effort to counter the stress on nonsmokers' rights that dominated arguments about ETS.[26] The National Smokers Alliance, created by Philip Morris in 1993, became the most prominent of these groups. Second, the tobacco industry claimed that smoking restrictions would harm the entertainment and hospitality industries. It has consistently asserted that bans on public smoking would lead to a 20–30 percent decline in business for restaurants and bars.[27] However, Big Tobacco's ability to define the terms of the debate has been limited. Arguments about the need to protect smokers' rights have not proved compelling to a public worried about the health effects of exposure to ETS, and evidence that most restaurants have not suffered economically when smoking bans have been introduced has undermined the industry's argument about the costs of restrictions on public smoking.[28] A paradigmatic shift in public understanding of the problem of public smoking has occurred that has left the industry struggling to find a way to counter demands for more pervasive and restrictive smoking bans.

Federal Action to Control Smoking in Public Places

The federal government's reaction to the identification of ETS as a public health problem has been limited. Although the *Healthy People* initiatives launched in 1990 and 2000 included goals to reduce exposure to ETS, the federal government has been hesitant to regulate public smoking beyond its own facilities and has concentrated instead on funding state and local action.[29] This pattern of action has been determined not only by the influence of Big Tobacco on Capitol Hill but also a belief among public health groups that federal action might harm the progress in combating ETS that has taken place at the state and local level. While the tobacco industry sought to protect its interests, public health advocates sought to prevent the federal government from preempting state and local government authority to enact tough antismoking laws.

Early federal efforts to restrict public smoking focused on interstate transportation largely because of the government's constitutional authority to regulate in this area.[30] In 1971 the Interstate Commerce Commission (ICC) required interstate buses and trains to have designated nonsmoking sections. Two years later the Civil Aeronautics Board (CAB) followed suit and ordered airlines to provide nonsmoking seating sections. No further regulatory activity occurred until publication of the 1986 Surgeon General's report on *The Health Consequences of Involuntary Smoking* prompted renewed federal interest in public smoking. Congress enacted legislation in 1987 that banned smoking on domestic flights lasting two hours or less, and in 1990 extended this ban to flights lasting six hours. The ICC also banned smoking on interstate buses and trains in 1990. A decade later, Congress passed a law that required all flights to and from the United States to be smoke-free.

Federal action to restrict public smoking in other public places has encountered strong opposition from Big Tobacco. In 1993 the Occupational Safety and Health Administration (OSHA) proposed a rule that sought to ban or limit smoking in workplaces, but opposition from the tobacco industry ultimately led to the defeat of this initiative.[31] Public health groups acquiesced in OSHA's decision to abandon the proposed rule out of a fear that federal action might preempt the tough laws that state and local governments had begun to enact against smoking in the workplace.[32] Efforts to restrict smoking in federal facilities, however, have encountered less opposition. Bans on smoking in government buildings began to be introduced in the late 1980s. Smoking was banned in all Department of Health and Human Services buildings in 1987, in Post Office buildings in 1993, and in indoor military facilities in 1994. President Clinton completed the process in 1997 when he issued an Executive Order that banned smoking in all indoor federal facilities under the control of the Executive Branch. Some action has also been taken to prohibit smoking in buildings that provide federal services.

The Pro-Children Act of 1994 banned smoking in buildings that provide federally funded educational, health, library, day care, or child development services to children under eighteen years of age.

Although the federal government has failed to regulate significantly public smoking beyond its own facilities, it has provided some financial and technical support for state efforts to reduce exposure to ETS. The American Stop Smoking Intervention Study (ASSIST) gave seventeen states a total of $128 million between 1991 and 1999 to develop effective strategies to reduce smoking.[33] Promoting smoke-free environments formed a central component of these strategies. The National Tobacco Control Program (NTCP), begun in 1999, expanded the funding and technical support given to sub-federal level efforts to reduce smoking.[34] Approximately $57 million per year has been available to help state, local, city, and county governments control tobacco, and this funding and technical assistance has helped boost state and local efforts to restrict public smoking.[35]

State Action to Control Smoking in Public Places

The response of state governments to the identification of ETS as a public health problem can be divided into two phases. From the mid-1970s to the mid-1990s, state governments gradually increased the range of places covered by smoking restrictions to include a broad array of public spaces. Prominent among the types of spaces covered by these restrictions were areas used for health purposes (hospitals, day care centers) and public transportation systems. A requirement to provide designated smoking areas constituted the vast majority of restrictions during this phase of smoking control. From the mid-1990s onward, however, a new phase in state action to control public smoking has been evident. Not only has the range of public spaces covered by smoking controls expanded dramatically as states have proved willing to extend the coverage of smoking controls to controversial places such as private workplaces and bars, but also the nature of these restrictions has changed. Laws that prohibit smoking entirely have increasingly superseded the limited restrictions of the first phase of smoking control.

State action to control smoking in public places on health grounds rather than to reduce the risk of fire began modestly in the wake of the 1972 U.S. Surgeon General's report that secondhand smoke might pose a health risk in certain circumstances.[36] Arizona enacted the first statewide controls on smoking in public places in 1973. This law restricted smoking to designated areas in theatres, museums, art galleries, and libraries. A year later Connecticut became the first state to restrict smoking in restaurants. Enactments increased in number and range in the late 1970s. Minnesota passed the first comprehensive Clean Indoor Air Act in 1975 "to protect the public health, comfort, and the environment by prohibiting smoking in public spaces and at public meetings except in designated smoking areas."[37] Utah, Montana, and Nebraska enacted similar wide-ranging legislation over the next five years. By 1980 a total of 36 states had enacted statutes that regulated smoking in at least one public place. This number increased rapidly in the wake of the publication of the 1986 U.S. Surgeon General's report, and rose further following publication of the EPA's 1992 report. By 2007 all states had introduced some restrictions on public smoking.

Increased comprehensiveness has been apparent in state smoking control laws.[38] Over the past three decades the number and nature of places where smoking is restricted or prohibited has increased steadily. Public transportation, hospitals, elevators, indoor recreational facilities, schools, public meeting rooms, and libraries were the most frequent targets of early state smoking controls. Growing concern about the health risks associated with exposure to ETS, however, has prompted greater efforts to impose more comprehensive controls on public smoking. Particular attention has been paid to workplaces, restaurants, and bars. Not only have studies shown that the workplace is the primary source of exposure to ETS for adult nonsmokers, but also they have revealed that levels of secondhand smoke are especially high in restaurants and bars.[39] The result is that states have proved increasingly willing to control smoking in private worksites, restaurants, and bars. By 2005 there were 30 states that had laws imposing some form of control on smoking in private workplaces, 33 states had laws controlling smoking in restaurants, and 11 had laws controlling smoking in bars.

An increased restrictiveness has accompanied the increased comprehensiveness of state smoking control laws. Restrictions rather than prohibitions characterized early state action to control smoking. Virtually all the laws simply required the provision of designated smoking areas in specific public places. Complete bans on smoking were very rare. Four states (Florida, Georgia, Massachusetts, and Washington) banned smoking entirely on public transport, and one state (Washington) banned smoking in theatres, museums, and indoor sports arenas. The 1986 Surgeon General's warning that merely separating smokers from nonsmokers within the same air space failed to eliminate the dangers of exposure to ETS, however, signaled the beginning of a new phase of state smoking controls characterized by efforts to create 100 percent smoke-free environments. California led with the enactment of a law in 1994 that banned smoking in restaurants and bars unless separately ventilated rooms were provided.[40] Utah went a stage further with a complete ban on smoking in restaurants in 1994. No further state action to prohibit smoking in public places took place until 2002 when South Dakota banned smoking in workplaces. A more significant event in 2002 occurred when Delaware enacted the first comprehensive statewide ban on smoking in public places. The law prohibited smoking in workplaces, restaurants, and bars. New York passed a similar law in 2003, and Massachusetts followed suit in 2004. Rhode Island, New Jersey, Montana and Washington enacted comprehensive statewide bans on smoking in public places in 2005, Hawaii and Ohio in 2006, and Arizona in 2007. Other states took action to prohibit smoking in specific areas but did not enact comprehensive bans. By the middle of 2007 a total of twenty-three states had enacted laws that banned smoking entirely in at least one of these areas (see table 11.1).

Table 11.1   State smoke-free laws, July 2007

100 percent Smoke-free in Workplaces, Restaurants and Bars	100 percent Smoke-free in Workplaces or Restaurants or Bars
Delaware (2002)	California (1994, 1998)
New York (2003)	Utah (1995, 2006)
Massachusetts (2004)	South Dakota (2002)
Rhode Island (2005)	Florida (2003)
Washington (2005)	Connecticut (2003, 2004)
New Jersey (2006)	Maine (2004)
Hawaii (2006)	Idaho (2004)
Ohio (2006)	North Dakota (2005)
Arizona (2007)	Vermont (2005)
	Montana (2005)
	Colorado (2006)
	Nevada (2006)
	Louisiana (2007)
	New Mexico (2007)

Source: Data from American Nonsmokers' Rights Foundation, "United States Population Protected by 100 percent Smoke-free Workplace and/or Restaurant and/or Bar Laws," www.no-smoke.org (accessed August 6, 2007).

The range and diversity of the states that have prohibited public smoking over the last decade is evidence that the politics of the issue has changed. The politics of public smoking has traditionally been explained in terms of political economy.[41] Variables such as ideology, partisanship, the size of the tobacco economy, health care costs associated with smoking, and the activities of antismoking groups have typically been seen as the key to explaining state action against public smoking. Recent developments, however, suggest that the issue can no longer be understood simply in terms of political economy. Changes in the way the issue is defined provide the key to explaining a new era of state smoking bans that has seen states as politically, economically, and culturally diverse as California, South Dakota, and Florida, for example, take action to ban public smoking. An acceptance that exposure to ETS is a health hazard to nonsmokers has created a demand for action that transcends partisan/ideological factors and submerges economic considerations.

Local Action to Control Smoking in Public Places

Local governments have led efforts to restrict public smoking in the United States. Over the past three decades, grassroots groups such as the Group Against Smokers' Pollution (GASP) and the California-based Americans for Nonsmokers' Rights (ANR) have succeeded in persuading local governments to pass antismoking ordinances that have generally exceeded federal and state laws in their range and restrictiveness.[42] Local governments have proved willing to *ban* smoking in places such as private workplaces and restaurants when the federal and state governments have only been willing to *restrict* smoking in less controversial public spaces. Over 110 local ordinances prohibiting smoking completely had been adopted, for example, before enactment of the first state law to do the same in the early 1990s.[43] Local governments have remained in the vanguard of the battle against public smoking ever since. Antismoking ordinances continue to be more comprehensive and effective than federal or state laws despite the flurry of activity seen at these levels over the past decade.

Local campaigns against public smoking began in California in the late 1970s. In 1977 Berkeley, CA, became the first community to limit smoking in restaurants and other public places, and in 1983 San Francisco became the first large city to pass an ordinance restricting smoking in workplaces. By 1990 over 200 Californian cities and counties had passed ordinances restricting public smoking.[44] Publication of the 1986 Surgeon General's report on the health consequences of exposure to ETS acted as a catalyst for local action in other states. Local governments in Massachusetts quickly followed California's lead in restricting public smoking, and other communities across the nation began to follow suit in the 1990s as further evidence of the dangers of passive smoking became known. By 2006 over 2500 ordinances restricting public smoking had been passed (see figure 11.2).

Greater comprehensiveness and restrictiveness accompanied the increase in the number of ordinances as local governments began to prohibit smoking in a wide range of public places. Publication of the EPA's 1993 Report that ETS is a "Class A" carcinogen for which there is no safe level of exposure proved a key event in the development of this less tolerant approach to public smoking. Widespread media coverage of this finding led to public demands for action that prompted local government action. Between 1993 and 1994 the number of ordinances that banned smoking completely in workplaces, restaurants, and bars nearly tripled from 47 to 114 (see figure 11.3). A period of relative inaction followed this alarmed response, with the number of ordinances prohibiting smoking remaining fairly constant until the end of the decade.

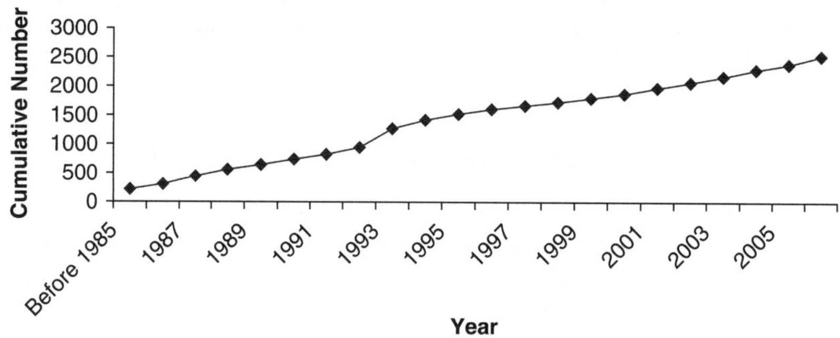

Figure 11.2   Cumulative number of local clean indoor air laws, 1985–2006

Source: Data from American Nonsmokers' Rights Foundation, "Municipalities with Local Clean Indoor Air Laws," www.no-smoke.org (accessed August 6, 2007).

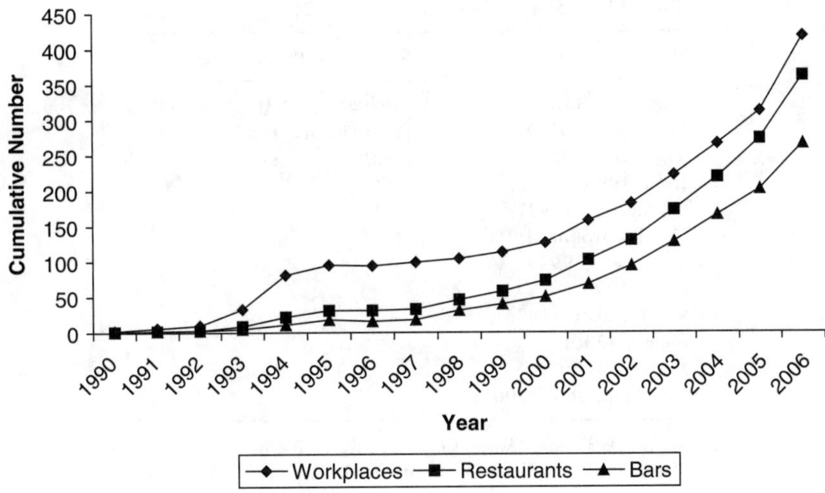

Figure 11.3 Cumulative number of local 100 percent smoke-free laws

Source: Data from American Nonsmokers' Rights Foundation "Municipalities with Local 100 percent Smoke-free Laws," www.no-smoke.org (accessed August 6, 2007).

Publication of further evidence about the health hazards associated with ETS, and increased federal, state, and private financial and technical assistance for local tobacco control programmes, produced a dramatic surge in the number of smoking bans after 2000. By 2006 there were 1046 ordinances that banned smoking in workplaces, restaurants, and bars.

Recent efforts to extend smoking bans to outdoor spaces show that local governments continue to play a leading role in the campaign against public smoking in the United States. Prompted by a desire to eliminate fire risks, reduce litter, and promote public health, local governments began to place restrictions on smoking in outdoor spaces in the 2000s. By mid-2006 over 700 cities had enacted ordinances placing some restrictions on outdoor smoking.[45] Calabasas, CA, passed the most comprehensive of these ordinances when the City Council banned smoking in all public places, indoor or outdoor, where anyone might be exposed to ETS, in 2006. The ordinance enjoyed widespread public support and received backing from the local chamber of commerce and restaurant association.

The tobacco industry recognized the threat posed by local ordinances at an early stage. In 1986 Raymond Pritchard, Chairman of Brown and Williamson, warned: "Over time we can lose the battle over smoking restrictions as decisively in bits and pieces—at the local level—as with state or federal measures."[46] Efforts to enact state laws that preempt local authority to impose stricter restrictions on public smoking than found at the state level have formed a major part of the industry's strategy for combating this threat to their interests.[47] This strategy had considerable success during the 1990s but has met with some reversals in recent years as states have begun to repeal preemption laws as part of their drive against public smoking. Delaware

Table 11.2   State preemption laws, July 2007

States with Preemption	States with Partial Preemption
Florida (1985)	Michigan (1983)
Oklahoma (1987)	Pennsylvania (1988)
Virginia (1990)	South Carolina (1996)
Iowa (1990)	
Connecticut (1991)	
North Carolina (1993)	
Tennessee (1994)	
Utah (1995)	
South Dakota (1995)	
Oregon (2001)	
Montana (2003)	
New Hampshire (2003)	

Source: Data from American Nonsmokers' Rights Foundation, "History of Preemption of Smoke-free Air by State," www.no-smoke. org (accessed August 6, 2007).

repealed its preemption statute in 2002, Illinois in 2005, and both Oregon and Montana have passed laws that repeal their preemption statutes in 2009. Several other states have repealed preemption provisions that apply to certain settings.[48] By 2007 there were 15 states that preempted, either fully or partially, local authority to regulate public smoking (see table 11.2).

Patterns of Intergovernmental Relations

A complex pattern of intergovernmental relations has been generated by the crusade against public smoking in the United States (see figure 11.4). Some evidence points to a "bottom-up" model of policy development in which local governments play a primary role. Local government action in states such as California, Massachusetts, New York, New Mexico, Oregon, West Virginia, Wisconsin, and Texas has clearly led to the adoption of state laws to control public smoking.[49] Conversely, other evidence points to a "top-down" model of policy development in which the federal and state governments play an important role. First, federal initiatives have undoubtedly stimulated policy action at the state and local levels.[50] Not only have the U.S. Surgeon General's reports prompted state and local restrictions on public smoking, but federal funding and technical assistance have often facilitated state and local government action. ASSIST funding, for example, has proved important in states such as Colorado, Maine, Minnesota, and New Jersey.[51] Second, states such as Delaware, Florida, and Rhode Island that had little experience of local smoke-free ordinances have enacted strict laws to restrict public smoking. States have also used preemption to set limits to local action.

The prominent "bottom-up" aspect of public smoking policy in the United States has produced considerable variation in laws and ordinances. Different populations across the nation have been subject to varying degrees

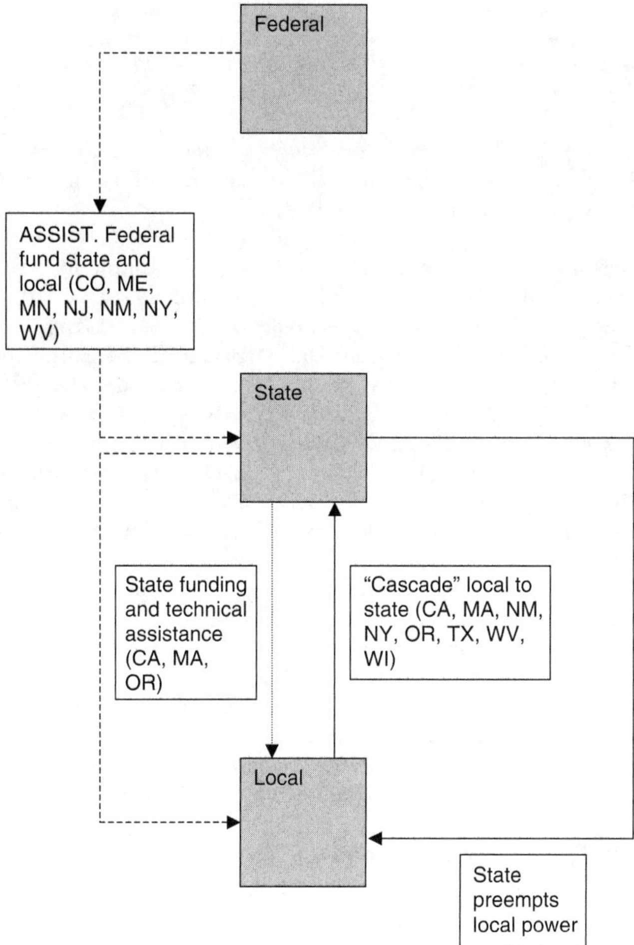

Figure 11.4 The intergovernmental relations of public smoking controls

of protection from ETS despite efforts by the federal government and public health groups to promote "best practices." An important normative question is raised by this variation: should disparities in the provision of a public good such as protecting health be permitted? Two hundred years ago, Thomas Jefferson argued: "Many are the exercises of power to the States wherein a uniformity of proceeding would be advantageous to all. Such are quarantines and health laws."[52] Although state and local governments may be well situated to identify pressing health problems in their communities, the idea that health protection should vary on the basis of geography is difficult to defend. An ideal system would establish national levels of protection from ETS without sacrificing the responsiveness and innovation frequently found at lower levels of government.

Notes

1. James Walton, ed. *The Faber Book of Smoking* (London: Faber and Faber, 2000), 31.
2. Ibid., 49.
3. U.S. HEW, *The Health Consequences of Smoking. A Report of the Surgeon General: 1972* (Washington, DC: Department of Health, Education and Welfare, Public Health Service, 1972).
4. U.S. HEW, *Smoking and Health: A Report of the Surgeon General,* (Washington, DC: Department of Health, Education and Welfare, Public Health Service, Office on Smoking and Health, 1979).
5. U.S. HEW, *The Health Consequences of Involuntary Smoking: A Report of the Surgeon General* (Washington, DC: Department of Health, Education and Welfare, Public Health Service, Office of Smoking and Health, 1986).
6. U.S. HEW, *Smoking and Health: Report of the Advisory Committee to the Surgeon General of the Public Health Service* (Washington, DC: Department of Health, Education and Welfare, Public Health Service, 1964).
7. NIOS, *Environmental Tobacco Smoke in the Workplace – Lung Cancer and Other Health Effects* (Washington, DC: National Institute for Occupational Safety and Health, 1991).
8. U.S. EPA, *Respiratory Health Effects of Passive Smoking: Lung Cancer and other Disorders* (Washington, DC: Environmental Protection Agency, 1993).
9. NIEHS, *9th Report on Carcinogens* (Washington, DC: National Institute of Environmental Health Sciences, 2000).
10. Cal-EPA, *Health Effects of Exposure to Environmental Tobacco Smoke,* (Sacramento, CA: California Environmental Protection Agency, 1997).
11. NCI, *State and Local Legislative Action to Reduce Tobacco Usage,* Smoking and Tobacco Control Monograph No 11 (Washington, DC: National Cancer Institute, 1999).
12. Cal-EPA, *Proposed Identification of Environmental Tobacco Smoke as a Toxic Air Contaminant* (Sacramento, CA: California Environmental Protection Agency, 2005).
13. U.S. HHS, *The Health Consequences of Involuntary Exposure to Tobacco Smoke: A Report of the Surgeon General* (Washington, DC: Department of Health and Human Services, Public Health Service, Office of the Surgeon General, 2006), iii.
14. ANR, "New Report Confirms Hazards of Secondhand Smoke: More Smokefree Laws on the Horizon," *Americans for Nonsmokers Rights,* June 27, 2006 www.no-smoke.org/document.php?id=503. Accessed June 1, 2007.
15. U.S. HHS, *The Health Consequences of Involuntary Exposure to Tobacco Smoke,* 11.
16. Jon D. Andeson, "Parental Smoking: A Form of Child Abuse?" *Marquette Law Review* 77 (1994): 360–384.
17. Allan M. Brandt, "The Cigarette, Risk, and American Culture," *Daedalus* 119 (1990): 167.
18. Stanton Glantz, John Slade, Lisa Bero, Peter Hanhauer and Deborah Barnes, eds., *The Cigarette Papers* (Berkeley, CA: University of California Press, 1996).
19. Roper Organization, "A Study of Public Attitudes Towards Cigarette Smoking and the Tobacco Industry in 1978," 4, available at www.legacy.library.ucsf.edu/tid/jdc70a00. Accessed June 1, 2007.

20. C. M. Fichtenberg and Stanley A. Glantz, "Effect of Smoke-Free Workplaces on Smoking Behaviour: systematic review," *British Medical Journal* 325 (2002): 188.

21. Monique E. Muggli, Jean Foster, Richard Hart and James Repace et al., "The Smoke You Don't See: Uncovering Tobacco Industry Scientific Strategies Aimed Against Environmental Tobacco Smoke Policies," *American Journal of Public Health* 91 (2001): 1419–1423.

22. U.S. HEW, *Reducing the Health Consequences of Smoking: A Report of the Surgeon General* (Washington, DC: Department of Health, Education and Welfare, Public Health Service, Office of Smoking and Health, 1989).

23. Gallup, "Tobacco and Smoking," The Gallup Organization, 2006 www.poll. gallup.com accessed May 29, 2006.

24. Robert C. McMillen and Neil Valentine, "Smoke-Free Public Places and Support for Smoke-Free Legislation among Oktibbeha County Adults," 2005, www.healthpolicy.msstate.edu/publications/sflegislationoc.pdf, accessed May 30, 2007; John Milgrim, "Poll, Data Buttress New York's Anti-smoking Efforts," March 10, 2003, www.pressrepublican.com; NWMCHA, "Survey Shows 82% of Registered Voters Support Smoking Ban in Work Sites and Public Places," Northwest Michigan Community Health Agency, 2004, www.mwhealth.org; M. R. Torabi and C. D. Seo, "Sociodemographic Correlates of Public Perceptions Regarding a Smoking Ban in Bars and Restaurants," *Journal of Drug Education* 24 (2004): 335–350.

25. Gallup, "Tobacco and Smoking," The Gallup Organization, 2006, www. poll.gallup.com. Accessed May 29, 2006.

26. Stanton Glantz, "The Politics of Local Tobacco Control," *Journal of the American Medical Association* 266 (1991): 2110–2117.

27. P. Gambee, Economic Impacts of a Smoking Ban in Bellflower, California (Los Angeles: CA, California Business and Restaurant Alliance, 1991); KPMG, Effect of 1998 California Smoking Ban on Bars, Taverns and Night Clubs (Washington, DC: American Beverage Institute, 1998).

28. Stanton Glantz and L. Smith, "The Effect of Ordinances Requiring Smokefree Restaurants on Restaurant Sales in the United States," *American Journal of Public Health* 84 (1994): 1081–1085, and "The Effect of Ordinances Requiring Smokefree Restaurants and Bars on Revenues: A Follow-Up," *American Journal of Public Health* 87 (1997): 1687–1693.

29. U.S. HHS, *Healthy People 2010* (Washington, DC: Department of Health and Human Services, 2000).

30. A. L. Holm and R. M. Davis, "Clearing the Airways: Advocacy and Regulation for Smoke-free Airlines," *Tobacco Control* 13 (2004): 30–36.

31. K. Bryan-Jones and L.A. Bero, "Tobacco Industry Efforts to Defeat the Occupational Safety and Health Administration Indoor Air Quality Rule," *American Journal of Public Health* 93 (2003): 585–592.

32. L. Girion, "OSHA Drops Plan for Smoke-free Workplace Safety: Public Health Advocates Say They Urged the Agency to Drop the Proposal for Fear It Would Be Watered Down," *Los Angeles Times*, December 19, 2001, 3.

33. NCI, *American Stop Smoking Intervention Study (ASSIST) Evaluation: Questions and Answers* (Washington, DC: National Cancer Institute, 2004) www.cancer.gov/cancertopics/factsheet/assistqa, accessed May 31, 2007.

34. CDC, *Smoking and Tobacco Use: State and Community Resources* (Washington, DC: Centers for Disease Control, 2007) www.cdc.gov/tobacco/tobacco_control_programs/state and community/index.htm, accessed May 31, 2007.

35. Wisottzky, Myra, Melisa Albuquerque, Terry F. Pechacek, and Barbara Z. Park, "The National Tobacco Control Program: Focusing on Policy to Broaden Impact," *Public Health Reports* 119 (2004): 303–310.

36. K. E. Warner, "State Legislation on Smoking and Health: A Comparison of Two Policies," *Policy Sciences* 13 (1981): 139–152.

37. U.S. HEW, *The Health Consequences of Involuntary Smoking*, 267.

38. J. F. Chriqui, M. Frosh, R. C. Brownson, D. M. Shelton, R. C. Sciandra, R. Hobart et al., "Application of a Rating System to State Clean Indoor Air Laws (USA)," *Tobacco Control* 11 (2002): 26–34.

39. S. K. Hammond, "Exposure of U.S. Workers to Environmental Tobacco Smoke," *Environmental Health Perspective* 107 (199): 329–340; M. Siegal and M. Skeer, "Exposure to Secondhand Smoke and Excess Lung Cancer Mortality Risk Among Workers in the `5 B's': Bars, Bowling Alleys, Billiard Halls, Betting Establishments and Bingo Parlors," *Tobacco Control* 12 (1999): 333–338.

40. Heather R. Macdonald and Stanton A. Glantz, "Political Realities of Statewide Smoking Legislation: The Passage of California's Assembly Bill 13," *Tobacco Control* 6 (1997): 41–54.

41. Peter D. Jacobson, Jeffrey Wasserman, and Kristiana Raube, "The Politics of Antismoking Legislation," *Journal of Health Politics, Policy and Law* 18 (1993): 787–819.

42. Richard Kluger, Ashes to Ashes: America's Hundred-Year Cigarette War, the Public Health and the Unabashed Triumph of Philip Morris (New York: Alfred A. Knopf, 1996).

43. U.S. HHS, *The Health Consequences of Involuntary Exposure to Tobacco Smoke.*

44. Martha A. Derthick, *Up in Smoke: From Legislation to Litigation in Tobacco Politics* (Washington, DC: Congressional Quarterly Press, 2005), 22.

45. John M. Broder, "Smoking Ban Takes Effect, Indoors and Out," *New York Times*, March 19, 2006, AI.

46. Raymond Pritchard, "Tobacco Industry Speaks with One Voice, Once Again," *United States Tobacco Candy Journal* (1986), available at www.legacy.library.ucsf.edu/tid/beb85f00.

47. M. Siegal, J. Carol, J. Jordan, R. Hobart, S. Schoenmakin, F. DuMelle and P. Fisher et al., "Preemption in Tobacco Control: Review of an Emerging Public Health Problem," *Journal of the American Medical Association* 278 (1997): 858–863.

48. U.S. HHS, The Health Consequences of Involuntary Exposure to Tobacco Smoke.

49. NCI, *Health effects of Exposure to Environmental Tobacco Smoke, Smoking and Tobacco Control Monograph* No 10 (Washington, DC: National Cancer Institute, 1999).

50. Donley T. Studlar, *Tobacco Control: Comparative Politics in the United States and Canada* (Peterborough, Ontario: Broadview Press, 2002).

51. U.S. HHS, The Health Consequences of Involuntary Exposure to Tobacco Smoke.

52. Bernard J. Turnock and Christopher Atchison, "Governmental Public Health in the United States: The Implications of Federalism," *Health Affairs* 21 (2002): 68–78.

Chapter 12

Abortion, the Judiciary and Federalism in North America

Robert McKeever

Federalism is a protean feature of political life, both in theory and in practice. Its shape-shifting character means not only that federalism varies from country to country and from era to era, but also that it assumes different forms within the same country and era depending on the issue at stake. In the past quarter century, U.S. scholars have identified a movement from "cooperative federalism" to "coercive federalism," though others identify the trend as being toward "opportunistic federalism."[1] Yet federal aggrandizement is usually selective, and in some policy areas the federal government has made little or no attempt to increase its powers at the expense of the states.

Federalism in Canada is less fuzzy than in the United States. Yet although Canadian provinces are considered to have more autonomy than U.S. states, there are areas of policy where the federal mandate is supreme, such as criminal law, and others where a form of cooperative federalism applies, such as health care. While the classical paradigm of Canadian federalism with its sharply delineated watertight compartments of jurisdiction has been overtaken by a modern paradigm of overlapping jurisdictions, both paradigms still operate according to the issue at stake or even the judge presiding.[2]

In short, whatever the broad configurations of federalism in any political system and whatever long-term trends may be evident within any particular system, the application of federalism to any particular issue will vary. In particular, it will vary with the politics of the issue. Parties and interest groups routinely engage in "intergovernmental forum shopping" by which they seek to have policy resolved in whatever level of government is most likely to deliver the result they seek.[3] In that sense, politics shapes federalism as much as federalism shapes politics.

This chapter compares how federalism has interacted with abortion policy and politics in Canada and the United States. The history of abortion in the two countries exhibits both similarities and differences, but what is striking is that the policy outcomes are the same in certain key respects. Above all, the implementation of national abortion policy varies considerably across geographical location and social class in both countries. For good or bad, much of this variation is due to the impact of federalism. This study therefore considers the empirical question of what kind of federalism has been applied to the abortion issue in the two countries. Equally important, it addresses the normative question of what kind of federalism should be applied to the issue, given that in both countries the right to abortion has been declared a fundamental one protected by the constitution.

Federalism and the Origins of National Abortion Policy

The United States

The origins of national abortion policy in the United States are sufficiently familiar to require extensive elaboration here. Prior to 1973, there was *no* national abortion policy. The states were autonomous in this and indeed many other areas of socio-moral policymaking. While some states had liberalized their abortion policies in the previous decade, the majority had maintained highly restrictive policies based upon legislation dating from the nineteenth century.

In 1973, in a decision that took most people by surprise, the U.S. Supreme Court announced what was effectively a sweeping new national abortion policy. In *Roe v. Wade*,[4] it created the constitutional right of a woman to choose to terminate a pregnancy by abortion. Speaking for a 7-2 majority of the Court, Justice Harry Blackmun held that the right to abortion stemmed from the right to privacy. Acknowledging that no right to privacy was explicitly mentioned in the Constitution, he nevertheless argued that the individual's liberty guaranteed by the due process clause of the Fourteenth Amendment included a right to privacy that had been recognized by the Court in a number of prior cases. He then gave reasons why a right to abortion was fundamental to a woman's liberty and privacy:

> This right of privacy ... is broad enough to encompass a woman's decision whether or not to terminate her pregnancy. The detriment that the State would impose upon the pregnant woman by denying this choice altogether is apparent. Specific and direct harm medically diagnosable even in early pregnancy may be involved. Maternity, or additional offspring, may force upon the woman a distressful life and future. Psychological harm may be imminent. Mental and physical health may be taxed by child care. There is also the distress, for all concerned, associated with the unwanted child, and there is the problem of bringing a child into a family already unable, psychologically and otherwise, to care for it. In other cases, as in this one, the additional difficulties and continuing stigma of unwed motherhood may be involved.[5]

So broad was this freedom of choice that only one of the recently liberalized state statutes appeared to meet its requirements. In other words, the *Roe* decision swept away forty-nine state abortion statutes and also the one enacted by Congress for the District of Columbia. The decision was immediately controversial both for the substance of its policy and for the judicial activism that took away the existing autonomy of states to determine their own abortion policies. Justice Byron White, in dissent, condemned the Court's decision for its impact on state values and prerogatives in memorable terms:

> The upshot is that the people and the legislatures of the fifty states are constitutionally disentitled to weigh the relative importance of the continued existence and development of the fetus, on the one hand, against a spectrum of possible impacts on the mother, on the other hand. As an exercise of raw judicial power, the Court perhaps has authority to do what it does today; but in my view its judgment is an improvident and extravagant exercise of the power of judicial review that the Constitution extends to this Court.[6]

Federalism has therefore been a major factor in the abortion controversy in the United States from its very inception. It can safely be assumed that states whose principal objection to *Roe v. Wade* concerned the substance of the policy were emboldened by this particular criticism of judicial illegitimacy to oppose and frustrate the policy that had been handed down.

Another federalism-related aspect of the *Roe* decision was the relatively detailed nature of the policy. Perhaps most famously, the Court instituted a trimester framework within which the relative rights of women, physicians, and the states were balanced. While the states were given greater powers as the pregnancy progressed from the first through the third trimester, at no point were the states granted their traditional power to ban abortion completely. Their greatest powers were over third-trimester abortions, when, the Court decided, the state's interest in protecting potential life became operative since the fetus was now capable of living outside the mother's womb. Even here, however, states could not ban abortions if the mother's health or life would thereby be endangered.

Nevertheless, despite the unusually prescriptive nature of the *Roe* decision, the Court by no means eliminated all avenues of influence by the states. Indeed it explicitly recognized that the states had interests to protect in abortion policy:

> The Court's decisions recognizing a right of privacy also acknowledge that some state regulation in areas protected by that right is appropriate. As noted above, a State may properly assert important interests in safeguarding maternal health, maintaining medical standards, and protecting potential life. At some point in pregnancy, these respective interests become sufficiently compelling to sustain regulation of the factors that govern the abortion decision. The privacy right involved, therefore, cannot be said to be absolute ... We, therefore, conclude that the right of personal privacy includes the abortion decision, but that this right is not unqualified and must be considered against important state interests in regulation.[7]

Some states seized the opportunities afforded by these interests and regulatory powers to thwart the right to abortion. Frequently impelled by pro-life pressure groups and pro-life sentiments, states have mounted a series of antiabortion initiatives consciously designed to undermine the sweeping abortion right announced by the Court. These state restrictions include withholding public funding for abortion, banning specific procedures— such as the so-called partial-birth abortion—and setting preconditions for the performance of abortions. Pertaining to the latter, states have required that minors notify and/or seek the permission of their parents; women notify and/or seek their husband's permission; women read information about abortion that was clearly designed to deter them from going through with the procedure and then to wait at least twenty-four hours before having the operation; and abortions be performed in hospitals rather than clinics.

The Supreme Court thus found itself in an ongoing dialogue with the states over the details and precise parameters of abortion policy, which amounted to an attempt by some states to reclaim much of their former policymaking powers over abortion. The result was a combination of contested federalism, because many states deemed *Roe* an egregious example of unwarranted federal judicial activism, and cooperative federalism, because the Court acknowledged that states had some scope to shape abortion policy. Significantly strengthened by opposition to aspects of the Court's decisions by some national politicians, including presidents, members of Congress, and a growing number of dissenters on the Court itself, the states were in a good position to challenge the authority of the Supreme Court's abortion policy. While they have not yet forced a wholesale retreat by the Court, as they did, for example, over the death penalty issue, they have significantly altered both the policy and its implementation in the years since 1973.

The culmination of this phase of "dialogue" came in 1992 in the form of the U.S. Supreme Court's decision in *Planned Parenthood v. Casey*.[8] A bare 5-4 majority of the Justices rejected the urging of the state of Pennsylvania to overturn *Roe v. Wade* in its entirety. However, the Court simultaneously modified *Roe* and some subsequent decisions in ways that permitted states to have a more powerful role in determining their abortion policies. Thus state regulatory measures would no longer have to meet the near-impossible demands of strict judicial scrutiny, instead having only to avoid imposing an "undue burden" on women's right to opt for abortion. The Court further decided that neither the requirement of "informed consent" nor a mandatory twenty-four hour waiting period after informed consent had been given constituted such an undue burden. In this, the Court reversed its 1983 decision in *Akron v. Akron Center for Reproductive Health*,[9] holding both measures unconstitutional. The *Casey* decision also opened the door a little wider to state control of abortion policy by abandoning *Roe*'s trimester system and accepting that the state's interest in protecting potential life existed from the outset of pregnancy, even if that interest did not become compelling until the fetus had reached viability. On the other hand, it reaffirmed the Court's 1976 decision striking down the requirement of a woman to inform her spouse of her intention to have an abortion.[10]

This constitutional dialogue continues to this day. Thus in 2007, in *Gonzales v. Carhart*,[11] the Court effectively reversed its position on the procedure usually referred to as partial-birth abortion by upholding the federal Partial-Birth Abortion Ban Act of 2003. Just seven years earlier it had struck down as unconstitutional a very similar ban enacted by the Nebraska legislature.[12]

Canada

The development of national abortion policy in Canada displays some similarities with that in the United States, but also some important differences. As in the United States, abortion had been a crime in Canada since the nineteenth century, but a significant reform movement was underway by the 1960s. In contrast to the United States, however, criminal law is a matter for the federal government alone in Canada. It was therefore entirely appropriate that in 1967, Justice Minister Pierre Trudeau introduced into Parliament a major reform of abortion law through the amendment of Section 251 of the Criminal Code that also decriminalized contraception and homosexuality. The bill, which eventually became law in 1969, permitted so-called therapeutic abortions to be carried out in a hospital if approved in advance by a hospital's Therapeutic Abortion Committee (TAC) (typically composed of three doctors, none of whom would actually perform the operation). Abortions performed outside of this framework remained illegal.

This framework did not satisfy proabortion activists and one in particular, Dr. Henry Morgentaler, expressed his opposition by opening a number of clinics in various provinces that performed abortions on demand. In a series of trials in Quebec and Ontario, Morgentaler was prosecuted for performing illegal abortions, which he openly admitted to doing, but juries refused to convict him. In 1984, however, the federal government successfully appealed a fourth acquittal of Morgentaler, who then took his case to the Canadian Supreme Court. Thus in 1988 arose the landmark Canadian case on abortion, *R. v. Morgentaler*.[13]

Morgentaler had taken his case to the Supreme Court before in 1976, but the Court had ruled that it did not possess the authority to strike down the abortion law.[14] In the intervening years Canada had adopted the Canadian Charter of Rights and Freedoms, Section 7 of which guarantees the "right to life, liberty and security of the person and the right not to be deprived thereof except in accordance with the principles of fundamental justice." Morgentaler claimed that the abortion law violated several sections of the Charter, but the Court focused its judgment upon Section 7. In a majority of 5-2 it ruled that Section 251 of the Criminal Code violated Section 7 of the Charter.[15] Before dealing with the substance of the case, Chief Justice Dickson noted that the judicial power had expanded since the 1976 case due to the introduction of the Charter. And while he disclaimed any power to determine policy issues per se, he asserted the new responsibilities of the Court as follows:

> Although no doubt it is still fair to say that courts are not the appropriate forum for articulating complex and controversial programs of public policy, Canadian courts are now charged with the crucial obligation of ensuring that the legislative initiatives pursued by our Parliament and legislatures conform to the democratic values expressed in the *Canadian Charter of Rights and Freedoms*. As Justice McIntyre states in his reasons for judgment, at p. 138, "the task of the Court in this case is not to solve nor seek to solve what might be called the abortion issue, but simply to measure the content of s.251 against the *Charter*." It is in this latter sense that the current *Morgentaler* appeal differs from the one we heard a decade ago.[16]

Chief Justice Dickson then proceeded to argue that S.251 violated the right of security of the person and it did so without respecting principles of fundamental justice. While he stopped short of ruling that there was an absolute right to abortion protected by the Charter, he contended that the uncertainties and delays caused by the procedures set out in the Code caused serious psychological and possibly physical damage to a pregnant woman seeking an abortion:

> At the most basic, physical and emotional level, every pregnant woman is told by the section that she cannot submit to a generally safe medical procedure that might be of clear benefit to her unless she meets criteria entirely unrelated to her own priorities and aspirations. Not only does the removal of decision-making power threaten women in a physical sense; the indecision of knowing whether an abortion will be granted inflicts emotional stress. Section 251 clearly interferes with a woman's bodily integrity in both a physical and emotional sense. Forcing a woman, by threat of criminal sanction, to carry a fetus to term unless she meets certain criteria unrelated to her own priorities and aspirations, is a profound interference with a woman's body and thus a violation of security of the person.[17]

Finally, the Chief Justice did not declare that the federal government could not act on abortion, but he stipulated that any policy undertaken in this regard should comport with the Charter and principles of fundamental justice.[18] Unlike the U.S. Supreme Court, however, the Canadian Supreme Court had no cause to consider the powers of the provinces in the matter, since, as noted above, criminal law in Canada is entirely within the jurisdiction of the federal government.

Some Canadian social conservatives have followed their American counterparts in decrying judicial activism since the adoption of the Charter, but their case lacked validity. Whereas judicial review has always been a more-or-less contentious issue in the United States, particularly regarding its scope, there is little doubt that the adoption of the Charter required a change of judicial role in Canada. Moreover, the relative liberalism of Canadian political culture and some of the explicit guarantees of the Charter's clauses counter any suggestion that the judiciary should employ a static form of judicial review. In the opinion of Lorraine Eisenstat Weinrib, "In sharp and deliberate contrast to the U.S. Bill of Rights, the Charter is unequivocal in departing from the values of a stable, hierarchical, paternalistic and patriarchal society."[19] Inevitably, this entailed an expanded role for the judiciary: "The courts would elaborate, on a case by case basis, a coherent understanding of the content of the various rights guarantees …"[20] This assessment draws support from the unambiguous terms of Section 24 of the Charter: "Anyone whose rights or freedoms, as guaranteed by this Charter, have been infringed or denied may apply to a court of competent jurisdiction to obtain such remedy as the court considers appropriate and just in the circumstances."

Nonetheless, the expanded role of the judiciary did not eviscerate the power of the national and provincial legislatures to defend their policy preferences. Most obviously, the " 'notwithstanding" provisions of Section 33 of the Charter allows the parliament and provincial legislatures to declare in an act that it shall be operative despite provisions of other sections of the Charter. This lasts for five years but may be renewed.

Neither the *Morgentaler* decision nor the abortion debate generally became as hotly contested as *Roe* and abortion politics did in the United States. Exactly why this was the case is a matter of debate. A key factor, according to some analysts, was that the American medical profession and health authorities failed to contain abortion as a medical issue and allowed it to "degenerate into moral conflict."[21] The charge of unwarranted judicial activism was also less potent in Canada than in the United States, because the provinces had no more say in determining abortion policy before the *Morgentaler* case than after it.

That said, the *Morgentaler* decision created a vacuum in the criminal law of abortion that Parliament was implicitly to fill if it wished. Taking up the challenge, Mulroney in 1989 introduced a bill that re-criminalized nontherapeutic abortions and imposed a sentence of up to two years imprisonment on any doctor who performed an abortion on a woman whose pregnancy did not threaten her health. Approved by the Commons, the measure failed to become law because of a tied vote in the Senate in 1991. That was the last time a Canadian national government attempted to introduce a criminal bill governing abortion. Canada thus ranks among the few countries that have no law restricting legal abortion.

It is therefore difficult to categorize national abortion policy in Canada. The Supreme Court invalidated the only modern legislative act to secure a parliamentary majority, but unlike the U.S. Supreme Court in *Roe*, failed to supply even a basic legal framework to replace it. The major political parties have deliberately and publicly taken the decision not to attempt to introduce a new bill and one can only conclude that they are content with the judicially created status quo. During the election campaign of 2006, Conservative leader Stephen Harper joined Liberal leader Paul Martin in promising to keep abortion off the agenda in the next parliament, even in the form of private members' bills. "The Conservative government won't be initiating or supporting abortion legislation," he avowed, "and I'll use whatever influence I have in Parliament to be sure that such a matter doesn't come to a vote."[22]

With no powers to legislate in the field of criminal law, Canada's provincial legislatures have been unable to follow their U.S. counterparts in enacting measures that test the boundaries of national abortion policy. As a result, there has been relatively little law cases in the wake of *Morgentaler*, unlike *Roe*.

Rather than entailing a free-for-all approach, the absence of a criminal law on abortion in Canada has shifted the policy framework for abortion to health care policy. In contrast to criminal law, this policy domain is the joint responsibility of the federal government and the provincial governments. The Canada Health Act provides for full federal funding of medically necessary health services, while the provinces are responsible for delivering those services. In so doing, the provinces must meet criteria such as comprehensiveness, universality, portability, and accessibility. Failure to meet these criteria may result in the federal government withholding funds.

The Federal Government has made it clear since at least 1995 that it regards abortion as a medically necessary service that falls with the ambit of the Health Act of 1984. Together with the *Morgentaler* decision of 1988, this establishes a right to abortion that is legally undeniable and leaves no room for legitimate challenge by the provincial governments. Moreover, in contrast to the United States, subsequent court cases, legislation, or administrative regulations did not undermine federal abortion policy. Among the few legal challenges to the *Morgentaler* policy, the principal one, *Tremblay v. Daigle*,[23] held that a woman did not require the father's consent to an abortion and furthermore that a fetus was not a legal person under Quebec law.

Resistance to National Policy

Abortion is a divisive issue in the United States and Canada, though much more so in the former. With abortion having been declared a fundamental right in both countries, neither states nor provinces can legitimately deny a woman the right to abortion. In practice, however, they have done just that to millions of women. In both countries, there are states and provinces where there is little or no provision for abortion and a range of barriers to the exercise of a fundamental right that effectively eviscerates its enjoyment.

The United States

Finance

States hostile to abortion rights have used a wide array of regulatory devices to hinder or prevent a woman from exercising her constitutional right to abortion. Perhaps the best-known device is withholding funds for abortion for indigent women under joint federal–state Medicaid programs. The passage and repassage of the Hyde Amendment since 1977, and its acceptance by the Supreme Court,[24] has made these funding limitations a central feature of national abortion policy. In allocating their own funds, thirty-two states and the District of Columbia follow the federal standard by funding only those abortions where the pregnancy endangers the mother's life or when it resulted from rape or incest. (Iowa, Missouri, Virginia, and Utah also fund abortions where there is evidence of fetal abnormality and Indiana and Utah do so when there is a serious threat to the mother's health). Seventeen states fund all or most medically necessary abortions, though only four states do so voluntarily (Hawaii, Maryland, New York, and Washington) while the rest do so under court order (Alaska, Arizona, California, Connecticut, Illinois, Massachusetts, Minnesota, Montana, New Jersey, New Mexico, Oregon, Vermont, and West Virginia). Only one state is more restrictive than the federal standard—South Dakota, which refuses to fund abortions resulting from rape or incest. Additionally, four states (Idaho, Kentucky, Missouri, and North Dakota) restrict private insurance plan coverage to those abortions where the mother's life is endangered by the pregnancy.

Medical Restrictions

Many states impose medical conditions on abortion policy that constrain a woman's ability to exercise her right to abortion. Thirty-nine states require abortions to be performed by a licensed physician and eighteen require a second physician to be involved after a certain gestational point, usually viability. Nineteen states require abortions to be performed in hospitals (as opposed to clinics) after a variety of gestational points, ranging from twelve weeks in Massachusetts, North Dakota, and Wisconsin, to the third trimester in South Carolina. These medical regulations make the availability of abortion in a reasonably convenient location dependent upon the existence of hospitals and doctors willing to perform abortions. However, forty-six states permit individuals to refuse to participate in abortions and forty-three states allow public institutions to refuse to perform abortions (though sixteen only extend the right to private ones). In rural areas, particularly in conservative states, willing institutions and individuals are frequently not available, requiring women seeking an abortion to travel long distances, including going out of state. This increases not only the stress level but also the cost of the abortion for the woman seeking it.

Delay Mechanisms

Requirements for informed-consent provisions and the mandatory waiting periods that accompany them further exacerbate stress and financial cost for abortion seekers. At the time of writing, twenty-six states have mandatory counseling regulations and twenty-four have a waiting period rule, usually twenty-four hours after the counseling. Most of these states require information to be provided on alternatives to abortion and the support services available if the pregnancy continues to birth. Some also require patients to be told about fetal pain as a result of abortion, the dangers of developing breast cancer due to abortion, and the serious psychological problems that can result from abortion.

Minors

Finally, there is a semi-separate abortion conflict over the right of minors to have an abortion. Thirty-four states have parental notice and/or consent provisions for minors, and a further nine have introduced them but have had them either temporarily or permanently enjoined by courts.

When these state-imposed constraints on access to abortion facilities are combined with protest and even physical intimidation against both patients and medical staff, it comes as no surprise that the fundamental right to abortion announced in 1973 is not remotely equally available to all women. While middle-class women in most metropolitan areas can exercise their constitutional right with reasonable ease, poorer women in rural, conservative states are frequently confronted by state-created impediments that all but nullify their right to abortion. The significance of this situation should not be underestimated, and it is instructive to speculate upon whether such state regulations would be tolerated in the field of, say, voting rights or even contraception.

Canada

Canada has not experienced anything like the intensity of America's political debate over abortion, but its implementation of abortion policy exhibits some similar patterns and the same asymmetry. In 2001, Laura Eggerston observed:

> In Prince Edward Island, women have nowhere to go to terminate an unwanted pregnancy. In Newfoundland, a woman from an outport on the other side of the island must drive up to twelve hours to have an abortion in St John's. In New Brunswick, she has to get approval from two doctors before she can get a publicly funded abortion in a hospital—unless she can afford the $400 to $700 charged for an abortion in the province's single clinic in Fredericton. In Saskatchewan she must make her way to 1 of only 2 hospitals that will perform the procedure.[25]

Indeed, the evidence suggests that despite a strengthening of abortion rights in Canada since the *Morgentaler* decision, access to abortion has become less equal across the country. As one analyst puts it, "Canadian women face limited and increasingly unequal access to abortion services—even though most legal barriers to such services have been removed."[26]

The Canadian provinces that resist national abortion policy have used similar devices as their American counterparts. Three provinces (Nova Scotia, New Brunswick, and Quebec) refuse to cover the costs of abortions performed in clinics, even though this seems to violate the Canada Health

Act (CHA) that requires coverage of all medically necessary treatment whether performed in hospitals or clinics.[27] Five provinces (Prince Edward Island, New Brunswick, Nova Scotia, Manitoba, and Alberta) exclude abortion, along with cosmetic surgery, from their interprovincial portability benefits, again in apparent violation of the CHA.

Many provinces simply provide few hospitals that perform abortions. At the time of writing, none of Prince Edward Island's seven hospitals perform abortions, while only two of Manitoba's fifty-four hospitals, two of Saskatchewan's seventy-three, and three of Alberta's ninety-nine do so. This lack of hospital provision is often compounded by an absence of abortion clinics. Saskatchewan and Prince Edward Island have none at all, while Manitoba, New Brunswick, Nova Scotia, and Newfoundland have just one each. If forced by this lack of facilities to seek abortions in other provinces, women encounter the further obstacle of provinces that will not cover the costs of clinic abortions for out-of-state patients.[28]

It is evident that the ability of Canadian women to exercise their fundamental right to abortion is severely undermined by provincial-imposed impediments. No less than American women, Canadian women do not share equal rights to exercise their constitutionally protected right to choose abortion.

Federalism and Abortion

One of the most important factors explaining these outcomes in both countries is simply the existence of a system of federalism that allows subnational units of government to thwart national policy, even when that policy is intended to extend constitutionally protected rights to all citizens. That said, it is by no means self-evident that this situation should be considered a failure of federalism or evidence that federalism and constitutional protection of fundamental rights are incompatible. True, Howard Palley and other scholars regard the Canadian experience as a failure of both cooperative federalism and coercive federalism. In a situation the he fairly characterizes as "low policy ambiguity and high policy conflict,"[29] it has emerged that "he federal government lacks the coercive and monetary mechanisms" to enforce national policy. The principal cause, he argues, is that "The political and cultural forces occurring within and among various provinces in the case of national abortion policy have led to a de facto acceptance of provincial asymmetry in an area where the Canada Health Act seems to call for formal symmetry."[30]

Yet the very terms of that analysis indicate the counterargument to Palley's indictment of federalism. In both Canada and the United States, federalism has been considered essential to the purpose of accommodating provincial and state political and cultural forces. It is as much a pillar of Canadian and American democracy as is the concept of constitutional rights. It cannot therefore simply be asserted that the one constitutional principle must automatically give way to the other. Rather, it would seem desirable to at least explore whether in practice, if not in theory, both principles can be accommodated in the making of abortion and, indeed, other policies, where the two collide.

The Normative Debate

Federalism is the bedrock of the political culture of both Canada and the United States. Not only was it a founding principle of the Constitution Act of 1867 and the Constitution of 1787, respectively, it has remained a vibrant and cherished feature of both political systems. Federalism has many virtues in the eyes of its proponents. These include: choice of exit and entry for citizens as states and provinces compete with each other to attract residents;[31] accommodation of widely varying policy preferences and the consequent reduction in political tensions;[32] protection of subcultures;[33] democratic checks on strong central government;[34] and state/provincial capacity to act as laboratories for experimentation with policy.[35] So deeply rooted are these beliefs about the benefits of federalism, they survive even where reality fails to match the normative theory.[36] To its advocates, this is a system of government that underwrites "community, utility and liberty."[37]

Even if the proclaimed virtues of federalism in Canada and the United States were found to be operative, they would not necessarily justify the unequal enjoyment of abortion rights in the two countries. The very essence of a constitutionally protected right is that it is universal throughout the country and is beyond the reach of both local and national majorities. Most famously, in 1957, President Eisenhower federalized the Arkansas National Guard and deployed U.S. Army paratroopers in response to gubernatorial defiance of a federal court order to integrate Little Rock's all-white Central High School. Faced with the indirect forms of resistance to the exercise of abortion rights outlined above, however, national governments have failed to a considerable extent to act decisively to uphold a constitutional right. True, the United States Congress passed the Freedom of Access to Clinic Entrances (FACE) Act in 1994 to combat the worst excesses of the hostile picketing of abortion facilities by antiabortion protesters. Furthermore, the U.S. Supreme Court has also upheld most, though not all, restrictions on excessive picketing of clinics.[38]

Nevertheless, the real barriers to Canadian and American women exercising their constitutional right to abortion stem from legislative and administrative federalism. States and provinces have been granted or have asserted a significant role in abortion policymaking, despite the consequence that a supposedly universal right is anything but that in practice.

Like most aspects of federalism, the tension between the rival claims of federalism and universal rights is an underdeveloped area in terms of normative theory.[39] This is surprising in view of what is at stake. If federalism should indeed trump or at least significantly undermine constitutional rights, an explanation is surely required.

One answer is to adapt the "political safeguards" theory of federalism embodied in Herbert Wechsler's argument that formal federalism was less important in determining the scope of national power in the United States than the politics of federalism. In his assessment, "The actual extent of central intervention in the governance of our affairs is determined far less by the formal power distribution than by the sheer existence of the states and their political power to influence the action of the national authority."[40] In addition to the states' mere existence as political entities, Wechsler emphasized "their crucial role in the selection and composition of the national authority."[41] Inevitably, this makes the Congress highly sensitive to state and local opinion and likely to incorporate aspects of this sensitivity into legislation. Wechsler accordingly concluded that "... it is Congress rather than the Court that on the whole is vested with the ultimate authority for managing our federalism ..."[42]

This empirical analysis slipped easily into a normative theory that the Supreme Court should not attempt to regulate federalism because Congress is better equipped and positioned to fulfill that function. Not only has this normative theory been articulated by some later scholars,[43] it was largely accepted by the Supreme Court from the late 1930s until the 1990s. None of these scholars, it should be emphasized, argued that the political safeguards theory should be applied to constitutional rights cases.[44] Moreover, while the Court seemed to adopt the political safeguards theory in socioeconomic matters, it certainly did not do so on questions of constitutional rights. It is also true that the political safeguards theory came under severe criticism from what might be termed the judicial safeguards school. The Rehnquist Court also rejected it in a number of prominent cases.[45]

Nevertheless, one may ask why the political safeguards theory should not be extended to cover individual constitutional rights. If, as many political scientists argue, constitutional interpretation is in fact policymaking by results-oriented actors disguised in judicial robes, there is no reason to exempt any federalism-related issue from the political safeguards paradigm. In effect, all constitutional adjudication is political and should be subjected to the political processes that prevail in any country, including federalism politics where applicable.

Moreover, in the case of judicially created constitutional rights such as abortion, there is less reason to suppose that the right is supported by the kind of supermajority that the process of constitutional amendment requires in the United States. If, as is the case with abortion, the U.S. Supreme Court circumvented the political process or cut short a developing political debate, it is to be expected that both normatively and empirically that debate will continue into the implementation stage of the judicial policy.

What if we reject both the political safeguards theory and the behaviorist constitutional theory? In other words, if we accept Prakash and Yoo's argument that judicial safeguards are required in *all* areas of constitutional dispute[46] and if we accept that judges take constitutional text and other legal criteria seriously in adjudicating disputes, must we reject any scope for federalism politics where constitutional rights are involved? While the principle of universality in constitutional rights must remain central, are there at least plausible arguments as to why it shouldn't be the sole criterion in both policymaking and policy implementation?

In the first place, it should be remembered that the U.S. Supreme Court has frequently acknowledged, both explicitly and implicitly, that federalism has a part to play in the judicial formulation of constitutional rights. Its stand in this regard reflects a mixture of prudence (or pragmatism) and normative rationale. Pragmatism is required because judicial policymaking, like all other forms of policymaking, is to a considerable extent the art of the possible. Lacking enforcement powers, courts are dependent upon others at various levels of government to implement and administer the policies they seek to have adopted. For this reason, the U.S. Supreme Court has been seen to enter into "constitutional dialogues"[47] with other political actors over rights policies and to deploy a variety of "elements of judicial strategy"[48] in the process. The theory of judicial supremacy in the United States therefore fails to grasp the reality of constitutional interpretation, which is in fact a process in which the states are invited to play a significant part. Once this is recognized, it follows that constitutional rights may not be universally and uniformly enjoyed across the country.

It is also true that the U.S. Supreme Court has often taken the view that constitutional rights should accommodate state and local viewpoints for normative reasons. As the Court said in *Roe*, states have interests in abortion policy that they are entitled to advance. And of course, once policymaking moves to the state level, variation is inevitable. States *may* choose to fund abortions or not, *may* require parental notification in the case of minors or not, and *may* require informed-consent provisions or not.

The U.S. Supreme Court's decisions on abortion are not unique in this respect. For example, in *Miller v. California*,[49] the Court allowed states and localities to define what constitutes obscene materials on the basis of community rather than national standards. As a result, free speech and privacy rights in this policy area vary considerably from state to state and locality to locality. In death penalty jurisprudence, most Justices accept that the definition of the constitutional concept of "cruel and unusual punishment" must include consideration of the variety of views expressed through state statutes.

In the United States at least, it is fair to say that the recognition of constitutional rights must always take federalism values into account, either for pragmatic or normative reasons, or both. Just as the theory of judicial supremacy does not capture the reality of the "constitutional dialogues" that determine the parameters of constitutional rights, the theory of the universality of rights fails to acknowledge that constitutional rights are often universal only in some of their constituent parts. Thus in *Roe v. Wade* and its progeny, the Supreme Court has protected the basic right of women to be free from "undue burdens" in choosing to have an abortion. Beyond that, however, the Court has left it to state politics to determine whether the exercise of that right should be facilitated or discouraged in any given state.

In Canada, the introduction of the Charter of Rights and Freedoms in 1982 is seen to have involved a conscious attempt to avoid the kind of judicial supremacy that theoretically held sway in the United States. As noted above, Section 33 of the Charter—the "notwithstanding" provision—permits both federal and provincial legislatures to override decisions of the Supreme Court. Thus, "… when the judiciary speaks it does not simply tell the political branches what to do and expect them to fall into acquiescence. Rather, judicial decisions are part of a more constructive and equal conversation between judges, legislatures and executives about the appropriate balance between fundamental rights and other important interests."[50]

Nevertheless, a considerable number of scholars considered the purpose of the Charter–and certainly its effect—was to centralize power at the expense of the provinces. In the words of one analyst, critics perceived "the nation-building intentions of the Charter as an attempt by Prime Minister Pierre Elliott Trudeau to transfer citizen loyalty to the national community and to reduce provincial diversity by requiring the provinces to conform to the pan-Canadian values of the Charter."[51] Moreover, a second core feature of this "centralization thesis" is that the goals of the Charter would be advanced through an activist judiciary, spurred on by organized interest groups seeking political reform through litigation.[52]

However, Jacob Levy's detailed empirical study of the Canadian Supreme Court's decisions concluded that the centralization thesis does not stand up to scrutiny. In his assessment, its jurisprudence on the Charter exhibited "sensitivity to federalism."[53] In like fashion, other scholars have seen in Canada a process very similar to that in the United States, where the Supreme Court is both sensitive to federalism values and willing to engage with and accommodate to some degree other political actors who espouse those values.[54]

The U.S. and Canadian Supreme Courts have played a leading role in developing their countries' national abortion policies, but they have not done so on the basis of an absolute judicial supremacy that ignores the wishes of the states and provinces and that tolerates no variation from national practices. Instead they have identified a fundamental right of women that goes to the very core of their liberty and security of person, while allowing state and provincial values to influence the exercise of that right. This embodies a compromise on two core principles of American and Canadian constitutionalism and on a policy issue that others view in absolutist terms. Like all compromises, it blurs lines and fails to satisfy many on both sides of the debate. Nevertheless, the compromise in both countries reflects not only the art of the possible for federal judges, but also a justifiable refusal to sacrifice one core political principle on the altar of another.

Notes

1. See, for example, Robert Albritton, "American Federalism and Intergovernmental Relations," in Gillian Peele, Christopher Bailey, Bruce Cain, and Guy Peters, eds., *Developments in American Politics 5* (Basingstoke: Palgrave Macmillan, 2006), 124–145; Tim Conlan, "From Cooperative to Opportunistic Federalism," *Public Administration Review* 66 (2006): 663–676; John Kincaid,

"From Cooperative to Coercive Federalism," *Annals of the American Academy of Political and Social Science* 59 (1990): 139–152; Paul Posner, "The Politics of Preemption: Prospects for the States," *PS: Political Science and Politics* (2005): 371–374.

2. Bruce Ryder, "The Demise and Rise of the Classical Paradigm in Canadian Federalism: Promoting Autonomy for the Provinces and First Nations," *McGill Law Journal* (1991): 309

3. John Kincaid, "Devolution in the United States: Rhetoric and Reality," in K. Nicolaidis and R. Howse, eds., *The Federal Vision* (Oxford: Oxford University Press, 2001), 151.

4. 410 US 113 (1973).

5. 410 US 113, 153.

6. 410 US 113, 222.

7. 410 US 113, 153–154.

8. 505 US 833 (1992).

9. 462 US 416 (1983).

10. *Planned Parenthood v. Danforth* 428 US 52 (1976).

11. 167 L Ed 2d 480 (2007).

12. *Stenberg v. Carhart*, 530 US 914 (220).

13. (1988) 1 S.C.R. 30.

14. *Morgentaler v. The Queen* (1976) 1 S.C.R. 616.

15. The opinions and voting in the case was complex, but Chief Justice Dixon and Justices Lamer, Beetz, Estey, and Wilson found reasons for nullifying the law, while Justices McIntyre and La Forest found reasons to uphold it. See Christopher Manfredi, *Judicial Power and the Charter: Canada and the Paradox of Liberal Constitutionalism*, 2nd ed. (Oxford: Oxford University Press, 2001), 80–81.

16. 1 S.C.R. 30, 46.

17. 1 S.C.R. 30, 56–57.

18. 1 S.C.R. 30, 54.

19. Lorraine Eisenstat Weinrib, "The Activist Constitution," in P. Howe and P. H. Russell, eds., *Judicial Power and Canadian Democracy* (Montreal: McGill Queen's University Press, 2001), 81.

20. Weinrib, 82.

21. Raymond Tatalovich, *The Politics of Abortion in the United States and Canada* (New York: M.E Sharpe, 1996), 198.

22. www.lifesite.net/ldn/2006, accessed January 17, 2006.

23. (1989) 2 S.C.R. 530

24. *Harris v. McRae*, 448 US 297 (1980)

25. Laura Eggerston, "Abortion Services in Canada: A Patchwork Quilt with Many Holes," *Canadian Medical Association Journal* (March 20, 2001): 847.

26. Howard A. Palley, "Canadian Abortion Policy: National Policy and the Impact of Federalism and Political Implementation on Access to Services," *Publius: The Journal of Federalism* (2006): 569.

27. Palley, 573.

28. Eggerston, 847.

29. Palley, 568.

30. Palley, 568.

31. Jacob Levy, "Federalism, Liberalism and the Separation of Loyalties," *American Political Science Review* 101 (2007): 460.

32. Michael Greve, "Same-Sex Marriage: Commit It to the States," *Federalist Outlook* 20 (March 2004): 2.

33. Ryder, 318–319.

34. Sandra Day O'Connor, "Altered States: Federalism and Devolution at the 'Real' Turn of the Millenium," *Cambridge Law Journal* 60 (2001): 508–510.

35. Louis D. Brandeis, *New State Ice Co. v. Lieberman*, 285 US 262 (1932), 311.

36. Levy, 459.

37. Samuel Beer, *To Make a Nation: The rediscovery of American Federalism* (Cambridge, MA: Belknap, 1993), 386.

38. See, for example, *Madsen v. Women's Health Center*, 512 US 753 (1994) upholding the creation of buffer zones around abortion clinics in the face of a First Amendment challenge by antiabortion activists; and *NOW v. Scheidler*, 510 US 249 (1994) allowing the use of the RICO antiracketeering legislation against antiabortion conspiracies to shut down clinics. However, see also *Scheidler v. NOW* 537 US 393 (2006), barring the use of the Hobbs Act extortion legislation against such efforts.

39. Levy, 459.

40. Herbert Wechsler, "The Political Safeguards of Federalism: The Role of the States in the Composition and Selection of the National Government," *Columbia Law Review* (1954): 544.

41. Wechsler, 546.

42. Wechsler, 560.

43. See for example, Jesse Choper, *Judicial Review and the National Political Process: A Functional Reconsideration of the Role of the Supreme Court* (Chicago: University of Chicago Press, 1980); and Larry Kramer, "Putting The Politics Back Into The Political Safeguards Of Federalism," *Columbia Law Review* (2000).

44. A partial exception was Kramer (ibid., 240) who advocated that judicial review is only warranted once constitutional principles have been settled through the political processes.

45. See, for example, Saikrishna Prakash and John Yoo, "The Puzzling Persistence of Process-Based Federalism Theories," *Texas Law Review* 79 (2001): 1459–1523.

46. Prakash and Yoo, 1476–1477.

47. Louis Fisher, *Constitutional Dialogues: Interpretation as Political Process* (Princeton: Princeton University Press, 1988).

48. Walter F. Murphy, *Elements of Judicial Strategy* (Chicago: University of Chicago Press, 1964).

49. 413 US 15 (1973).

50. Christine Bateup, "Expanding the Constitution: American and Canadian Experiences of Constitutional Dialogue in Comparative Perspective," *New York University Public Law and Legal Theory Working Papers* 44 (2006), 2.

51. Levy, 326–327.

52. Levy, 327.

53. Levy, 325.

54. See, for example, Bateup, 1–66.

Chapter 13

No Child Left Behind: Federalism and Education Policy

Jonathan Parker

After his controversial election threatened to polarize the nation he led, George W. Bush promised to be a "uniter, not a divider" as president. In his first year in office he managed to fulfill this pledge in extraordinary fashion by securing congressional approval of the No Child Left Behind Act (NCLB). Despite a highly charged partisan atmosphere, he enlisted the support of key Democrats—notably Senator Edward M. Kennedy of Massachusetts and Representative George Miller of California, the ranking minority members of the Senate and House education committees. Even more remarkably, he retained the support of his own party in Congress for an education bill that tremendously expanded federal influence and involvement with education at the state and local level.

NCLB is a key element of George W. Bush's domestic political legacy. This chapter examines its significance in both political and historical context. It addresses a number of questions. What impact did the NCLB have on education policy and how innovative were its changes? What is its likely future, facing reauthorization in a Democratic controlled House and Senate under a new president? To what extent did it change the federal government's role in education and domestic policy? Did it significantly change the American system of federalism or merely apply a familiar approach to federal policymaking to a new area?

The significance of NCLB is a matter of debate. Some scholars belittle it as incremental change, noting that the focus on school standards had begun in the 1980s.[1] Others caution that this federal law was the culmination of state reform efforts and was driven by bottom-up pressures as much as by top-down ones.[2] NCLB is rightly portrayed as the end product of over twenty years of policy evolution and development. The most recent generation of the educational standards movement was thrust into public focus by the 1983 publication of *A Nation at Risk*.[3] Efforts to expand accountability continued through the 1990s with federal encouragement. State expansion of testing and accountability policies was crucial for NCLB. However, while state capacity in this area of education made the law possible, it does not explain why it happened or demonstrate its impact.

NCLB's use of very strict mandates and penalties signals a radical departure from previous federal education policy. Bush appeared to have reversed his party's traditional stance on federal education policy and made national leadership in education a Republican issue.[4] However, the bill succeeded by attracting an unwieldy coalition of the left and right across party lines, who were not natural allies.

Conversely, the measure had many critics. States, governors, conservatives, and teachers' unions were united in a loud chorus of complaints against it. Academics and other policymakers also criticized NCLB for failure to implement effectively and enforce fully its own rules, thereby placing unreasonable expectations on states, and for making little progress in boosting student achievement. Conservatives further decried the massive expansion of national power over a local area of responsibility.

Whatever its faults, NCLB is unlikely to be substantially altered or repealed by a new Congress or president. Even its critics have focused on how to amend the bill so it works more effectively. The bipartisan strategy Bush adopted to gain its enactment helped to secure its continued existence even beyond the loss of Republican control in Congress in 2006. There is no widespread partisan coalition in favor of its abolition.

NCLB represents a major shift in federal education policy but continues a familiar trend in federalism. Its use of mandates to compel states to act and incur costs that far exceed what Washington provides them for the purpose puts the onus on state and local governments to pay for the program, a pattern that has characterized much of recent federal policymaking.[5] NCLB marks a radical and significant shift in federal policy that will influence education for the next generation. However, it does not constitute a new approach to federalism. Its sweeping shifts in the context of education policy obscure its more familiar manifestation of federal–state relations and the limitations of this approach. NCLB represents an incremental addition to the direction of federal policymaking that has been occurring for almost half a century. In other words, it is evolution rather than revolution in the context of federalism.

Previous Federal Education Policy

The national government played very little part in education until the second half of the twentieth century. A host of obstacles deterred policymakers from seriously addressing this policy domain until the mid-1960s. Racial segregation in the South meant that the congressional representatives from that region strongly opposed any federal intervention that might threaten that system. The North faced problems stemming from religion and separation of church and state. A strong Catholic presence meant that some Northern congressmen wanted federal aid to go to private as well as public schools so that parochial institutions would also benefit. Others objected to government aid to religion in general and harbored distrust toward the Catholic Church's influence in particular. Finally, conservatives generally opposed the expansion of federal powers in what had always been a state and local responsibility.

The first federal interventions in education began after the Soviet launch in 1957 of the Sputnik satellite, which generated insecurity over the United State's competitive strength in technology. The state of science education was identified as a serious weakness, and a series of curriculum developments were initiated to improve science teaching. Conservatives strongly attacked even this modest effort, but it prevailed in the interest of fighting communism.[6]

This laid the foundation for the incorporation of aid to education into Lyndon B. Johnson's Great Society that was built around two themes: federal promotion of civil rights to tackle racial inequality; and a "war on poverty." The Elementary and Secondary Education Act was enacted in 1965 as part of this new wave of reform. Its most important provision was Title I, aid for disadvantaged children, which was allocated most of the funding. Money was distributed on the basis of the number of disadvantaged pupils in a district, but all districts received some money, which fostered widespread political support. Title 1 funding was minor compared to overall education spending, and the federal role in education funding remained very limited. However, that limited funding was used as leverage to force states to comply with other requirements, called mandates.

The first important mandate involved racial discrimination, which was included in the civil rights bills from 1964 onward. Schools practicing racial segregation and discrimination would be ineligible for federal funding. Congress also utilized mandates to protect children with disabilities. The Education for All Handicapped Children Act of 1975, which became the Individuals with Disabilities Education Act, provided federal aid for educating disabled children, including those with learning disabilities. In return for increased funding, strict regulations stipulated how schools would identify and teach these children. These mandates, which cost far more than the sums provides by Congress, represented a far greater federal intrusion upon state and local governments' authority over education than the relative levels of federal funding suggested.

The National Commission on Excellence in Education report, *A Nation at Risk*, published in 1983, raised concerns over general education standards. The George H. W. Bush administration's attempts to coordinate state efforts on a national scale failed to generate widespread change. President Bill Clinton, a key actor as Arkansas governor and National Governors Association luminary in these earlier efforts, eventually secured passage of the Goals 2000: Educate America Act in 1994. Enacted just before the Democrats lost control of Congress to the Republicans, this created a stronger federal role for sponsoring and coordinating state efforts at standards reform while carefully keeping control over education policy in state hands. It required states to formulate academic standards and assess their students against them. States could set their own standards and there was little national enforcement of these, rendering them largely voluntary. Many were already moving toward development of rigorous state standards, so Goals 2000 simply supported the process without seriously changing the national government's role in education policy.

In the thirty-five years following enactment of the Elementary and Secondary Education Act of 1965, the federal role in education had changed little. Aid was largely limited to disadvantaged children. State and local governments were increasingly regulated in how they treated disadvantaged children, but in the main they retained control over education policy.[7]

The Context of NCLB Gaining Congressional Approval

In the 2000 election, George W. Bush distanced himself from traditionally conservative Republican stands on many domestic issues by declaring himself a "compassionate conservative." He embraced the possibilities of government action as a core part of this slogan, and education would become one of the key policies by which it was defined. Bush's experience as governor of Texas was a formative influence on this approach. Managing the state education system ranks high on every governors' agenda. Minimalist involvement is not an option when the electorate makes the state's chief executive responsible for the quality of its schools. Compelled to engage with education policy as governor, Bush was confident that he could turn it to Republican advantage in national politics despite its traditional association as a Democratic issue.[8] He promoted a detailed reform plan to make states accountable to the national government for educational results, largely based upon his gubernatorial policies. In Texas, Bush had combined standards and accountability, popular with the business community and much of the public, with choice, a more traditional Republican approach. His reform plan in the 2000 campaign took a similar approach but looked to implement it through strong federal leadership and substantial increases in education spending.

This policy mix was not unprecedented for a Republican presidential candidate. Bush's father had professed ambitions to be the "education president." Lamar Alexander, who served as the latter's secretary of education, had made education reform a key issue in his unsuccessful campaigns for the Republican presidential nomination in 1996 and 2000. Neither Bush Sr. nor Alexander had much success in converting the Republican right, whose influence was reflected in the routine inclusion in the national party platform of demands for the abolition of the Department of Education. George W. Bush, however, was a conservative Republican trusted by the right of the party, including its evangelical element. For such a candidate to promote education reform was unusual. Bill Clinton had used education as governor of Arkansas and presidential candidate in 1992 to define himself as a New Democrat who was not beholden to the traditional policies of his party. His successor used it in 2000 to define himself as a compassionate conservative who was different from traditional Republicans.

Even more ambitiously, Bush portrayed his education reforms as a civil rights issue. Previous Republican presidents had followed in the footsteps of Nixon's Southern Strategy. While supporting civil rights as an abstract ideal, they pledged to reduce federal interference in state matters. This coded signal that civil rights would not be vigorously pursued helped to attract white southern voters. Conversely, it played badly in minority communities, reflected in the very low level of African American support for Republicans in presidential elections from the 1960s onward. Nevertheless, Bush had hopes of transcending this racial divide to gain support from blacks who had come to view school choice more positively over time.

The largest American cities had become largely black districts with high poverty levels. Blacks were much more likely to hold a negative view of their local schools and tended to support school choice policies, such as vouchers, charter schools, and parental choice over which public school their children would attend, more than whites.[9] Bush's adroit framing of this issue as a civil rights ideal to reduce the racial gap in student achievement garnered considerable minority support. Attacking the bigotry of low expectations, he hoped to create a wedge issue that could attract support from the Democrats' most reliable voting bloc.

The similarities between the Republican and Democratic positions on education in the election laid the groundwork for a possible bipartisan solution. Since 1994, the expansion of state standards and testing policies made Democrats less opposed to such policies while Republicans were resigned to accept more active federal leadership in education. However, bipartisan compromise was not assured. Holding narrow majorities in both houses of Congress, Republicans would later seek to enact partisan bills on a straight party vote, but the Senate Democrats could employ the filibuster in response.

Bush signaled his desire for a bipartisan bill clearly by submitting only an outline of his reform plan to Congress. The principles it embodied were state testing, corrective action for schools that consistently fail to perform, and the ability of students to transfer out of failing schools through Title I funding (a school voucher program). The blueprint left policy details unspecified in order to facilitate compromise and enactment. Bush also cultivated key minority education committee members, notably Kennedy and Miller, to cement the bipartisan coalition behind the bill.[10] This approach proved crucial for the future of No Child Left Behind after the 2006 elections.

The plan embraced the need for increased federal spending, which pleased Democrats. Requirements for standards and testing were popular among Republicans. Nevertheless, the federal requirements regarding state testing caused unease among both liberals and conservatives. The former suspected that the impact of any testing would fall heaviest upon poor and minority students. The latter distrusted any expansion of federal control over the curriculum. School vouchers probably constituted the most controversial aspect of the whole plan, however. Democratic groups such as teaching unions and most civil rights groups considered any use of public money to fund private school tuition an anathema, while some groups on the Republican right, such as the Family Research Council, claimed they would oppose any bill without vouchers.

Bush's initial voucher proposal also faced opposition from centrist Democrats and even some moderate Republicans. Among the latter was Senator James Jeffords of Vermont, who chaired the Senate Health, Education, Labor, and Pensions Committee. This body initially approved a version of the President's plan that completely eliminated vouchers. The Bush Administration sidelined him by using another committee Republican, Senator Judd Gregg of Hampshire, as its go-between to Senate Republicans. Angered by this and other rebuffs, Jeffords withdrew his Republican affiliation to become an independent. This defection effectively handed control of the evenly balanced Senate to the Democrats, and Senator Edward Kennedy took over as chair of the committee. The bipartisan approach to No Child Left Behind now became a necessity rather than a choice.

Both sides demonstrated a willingness to compromise in order to pass legislation. Bush conceded the voucher issue, and Democrats allowed students in failing schools to receive money for special tutoring instead of tuition vouchers.[11] Like Nixon going to China, only a Republican president could have delivered such an education plan, given the widespread opposition of conservatives to most of the proposals. Bush used his political capital following the election to deliver the votes from his own party. Congressional Republicans wanted to support their new president, and Bush secured their support for a bill they would not have supported otherwise. The bill passed the House by a vote of 384 to 45 and the Senate by 91 to 8. Negotiations were carried out to reconcile differences between the two bills over the amount of federal spending and the accountability programs, but the 9/11 attacks enhanced political resolve to make a success of the bipartisan effort as a symbol of unity. The final conference report passed the House by 381 to 41 votes and Senate by 87 to10.

The Law

NCLB provides increased federal education funding to states with fewer controls on how they spend it. In return states must accept highly prescriptive mandates regarding standards and testing, with serious consequences for schools, districts, and states that do not meet these standards.

Standards and Testing

Each state is required to adopt content with challenging academic standards in the core subjects of mathematics, reading or language arts, and science. These standards must specify what children are expected to know and do. States must also test all students annually in grades 3–8 in mathematics and reading or language arts. Finally, states now have to test students three times by grade 12 in science. These tests must be based upon a state's own academic standards, and each state must define the requirements for reaching proficiency in these standards.

Adequate Yearly Progress

Holding schools, districts, and states accountable for the achievement of all students is the foundation of NCLB. Schools, districts, and states must make Adequate Yearly Progress (AYP) toward the goal of 100 percent academic proficiency for all students by the end of the 2013–2014 school year (ECS 2007). Each state must meet the percentage of students reaching proficiency in their test scores and set yearly targets to raise this percentage each year to reach the final target of 100 percent by 2014. These targets define the requirements for AYP in that state. Both states and districts must reach their own targets for AYP and face serious consequences for failure to do so. However, the main impact of the law is at school level.

For a school to make AYP, students as a whole and all subgroups of students must meet state proficiency targets on their test scores. Subgroups include students from major racial and ethnic groups, economically disadvantaged students, students with disabilities, and students with limited English proficiency. Schools must test at least 95 percent of students, and 95 percent of students in each subgroup to make AYP.

Schools fail AYP if overall scores or a single subgroup does not meet the proficiency targets or fails to reach 95 percent participation. Schools that fail AYP for two consecutive years are labelled "needing improvement." Schools receiving Title I money, which consist of those with a large number of students from low-income households, face an escalating scale of sanctions for each year they fail to make AYP. Once schools are identified as "needing improvement," they must meet proficiency targets for two consecutive years before they are removed from that status.

Sanctions for Failure to Meet AYP

While the AYP requirements apply to all schools, only Title I schools are identified as needing improvement and have sanctions applied. The following table (table 13.1) indicates the succession of sanctions that are applied to Title I schools that fail to meet AYP.

Additional Requirements

States and districts must issue yearly report cards that publish test scores by the state, district, and school level, broken down for each subgroup. This mechanism seeks to ensure the public knows how each school is performing and provide parents with information to weight transfer options to different schools. In addition, every public school teacher must be "highly qualified," which means the state must have certified or licensed that teacher, and they have demonstrated competence in the subjects they are teaching.

Table 13.1   Sanctions for failure to meet AYP

NCLB Status	Action Required
School Improvement I: School Does Not Make AYP for Two Years in a Row	The school must: • Develop an improvement plan • Allow parents to move their children to a school not in School Improvement (school choice).
School Improvement II: School Does Not Make AYP for Three Years in a Row	The school must: • Provide extra services (SES) such as after school programs, tutoring, and summer services, based on budget availability • Continue to offer school choice and provide transportation, based upon budget availability
Corrective Action: School Does Not Make AYP for Four Years in a Row	The school and district must also implement one or more of the following: • Replace staff as allowed by law • New curriculum • Reduce management authority of the public school • Appoint an outside expert to advise the school • Extend the school day or year • Change the school's internal structure
Restructuring I: School Does Not Make AYP for Five Years in a Row	The school, district, and state must plan for one or more of the following actions: • Reopen the public school as a charter school • Replace all or most of the staff, as allowed by law • Turn over the management of the public school to the state, which can use a private provider • Make other governance changes
Restructuring II: School Does Not Make AYP for Six Years in a Row	The school, district, and state must implement the plan developed in Restructuring I.

Funding

In exchange for these new, prescriptive mandates, the Bush administration initially promoted substantial increases in annual federal spending in order to help states make the required changes (table 13.2). The Bush Administration initially raised annual federal education spending by several billion dollars, mostly for Title I programs. However, that growth slowed sharply after the first year of NCLB. Between 2004 and 2007 there was only a 1.6 percent rise in funding without adjusting for inflation. In real, inflation-adjusted dollars, federal discretionary spending on education actually decreased over that period. The federal share of total primary and secondary school spending has not substantially increased from its previous level of 7 percent, leaving the cost of meeting the new federal mandates largely to states and local districts.

Table 13.2 Federal spending on education, FY 2000 to FY 2007

year	Appropriation (billions of dollars)	Percent increase (controlling for inflation)
2000	35.6	
2001	42.2	15
2002*	49.9	15
2003	53.1	5
2004	55.7	3
2005	56.6	−1
2006	57.8	−1
2007	57.7	−3

Note: * 2002 represents the first Bush budget and is also the year NCLB passed.

Source: Data compiled by author from *Education Department Budget History.*

Table: *FY 1980-Present.*

Cumulatively, funding for the Elementary and Secondary Education Act (ESEA), as amended by NCLB, increased by $27.5 billion from FY2002 through 2007, but this was $70.9 billion less than specifically authorized. However, authorization levels only stipulate the amount that can be appropriated by Congress rather than an actual proposed spending level. Democrats accuse Republicans of reneging on an agreement to properly fund NCLB. Republicans contend that funding for the program has been massively expanded and point out that President Clinton also rarely funded education programs to their authorized levels. Both sides are essentially correct. While it is harsh to accuse Bush of shortchanging the program by over $70 billion, it is still true that the federal education budget was cut after FY 2003. Further, the costs to school districts have far outpaced the federal funding offered. It is clear that this massive program of reform was seriously underfunded at the national level, though not necessarily at the levels suggested by the Democrats.

The way in which NCLB has been implemented and the arguments over its funding levels demonstrate a familiar pattern in federalism. Over the past few decades, the tendency in federal policymaking has been to impose mandates or other conditions of aid on state and local governments. The national government rarely pays for all the associated costs, and states usually end up complaining about the financial burden it places on them. The controversy over this practice led to the Unfunded Mandates Reform Act of 1995, but the most common practice of placing conditions on the receipt of federal grants was not covered under the law. NCLB falls into this category, so it is not considered a formal mandate. This pattern of policymaking is familiar even in education circles, for it is exactly the model used in regulating the education of the disabled. The national government developed a complex system of prescriptive mandates stipulating how the disabled should be identified and educated while paying for only a fraction of the states' costs associated with these regulations.

Implementation: An Overview

NCLB represented a dramatic expansion in federal influence on education policy. Its testing and accountability standards made tremendous demands of state education departments. In return, federal spending increased dramatically for a time. Implementation of this sweeping change in policy would be a key battleground. Some on the left of the spectrum, particularly in education circles, viewed the law as a means to discredit the entire public school system. They feared that large numbers of schools would not make annual yearly progress (AYP) and therefore be labeled failing, which would undermine confidence in public education.[12] A common joke among teachers referred to the law as the "No School Left Standing Act."[13] Many observers expected the federal government to relax the stringent expectations enshrined in the law in the face of such widespread opposition.[14]

Many on the right, meanwhile, were shocked that someone they deemed a fellow ideologue was willing to expand federal authority and spending into such a traditionally local policy area. The compromises extracted by the White House on school sanctions, particularly the use of school choice and restructuring through privatization and charter schools, were critical for convincing these skeptics that the tradeoffs were worthwhile.

The coalition assembled behind NCLB was a disparate and unlikely group of allies that were deeply suspicious of one another. Each part of the coalition supported parts of the act but were ambivalent or hostile toward other aspects. The implementation of the law at the federal, state, and local levels required continual balancing of their concerns to make NCLB function.

Rules and Tests

The Bush administration began by drafting strict regulations and guidelines for how the law would be implemented and signaled its intent to cut off funding to states that did not comply.[15] Expansion of testing regimes was a massive undertaking, which some states did not have the capacity to accomplish. Simply designing curriculum standards and creating tests to measure student performance in relation to those standards for every one of the fifty states presented a monumental task. To compound the matter, the stakes were very high, with serious political, administrative, and financial consequences for failure. Finally, the timetable was very short. This combination of factors hardly facilitated a smooth transition.

In 2005, twenty-three states that did not fully implement the law's testing requirements had to administer 11.4 million new tests. The full annual testing requirements, which came into force in 2007, require at least another 11 million tests.[16] By 2006, when the full yearly testing requirements came into force, approximately 26 million students in grades 3–8 and one high school grade had to be tested.[17] By comparison, only 2.6 million people take college entrance examinations, the SAT, and the ACT each year. Ten times this number had to be assessed in 2006 to meet the requirements of No Child

Left Behind.[18] Such an undertaking required careful development and testing of the exams for it to work successfully. Even the SAT and ACT, which have been in place for many years, have had a number of recent public scandals. Scoring errors and reporting delays, which are inevitable given the daunting challenges confronting the testing industry and state testing agencies, undermine NCLB's system of school accountability.[19]

The sheer costs of testing pushed some states into abandoning more qualitative, open-ended questions for cheaper computer-scored multiple-choice questions.[20] In 2003 the Government Accountability Office estimated that testing would cost states $1.9 billion over six years if they relied solely on multiple-choice questions that could be machine-scored. The expense would rise to $3.9 billion for a mix of multiple-choice and open-ended items and to $5.3 billion for hand-scored, written responses.[21] Federal requirements for a new system of testing generated particular opposition in states with fairly rigorous standards already in place. Virginia, Maryland, and Connecticut, for example, were forced to restructure their regimes to fit with NCLB. The lack of federal funding added insult to injury. Connecticut, which had a more rigorous testing system that assessed student writing, was forced to adopt computer-scored multiple-choice tests like other states. It sued in federal court but lost because NCLB is technically a condition of aid rather than a mandate. Meanwhile, Utah's legislature enacted a law prohibiting state and local districts from implementing without adequate federal funding.[22]

Meeting AYP, Proficiency Standards, and Imposing Sanctions

State opposition to testing was overcome in the rush to get tests in place. However, it intensified and expanded as the testing got underway and schools faced state proficiency requirements. The accountability requirements decreed that all schools had to test their students annually and meet state targets for AYP, which rise to 100 percent by 2014. Only Title I schools are subject to the sanctions stipulated in the law, but all schools that do not meet AYP are publicly identified as failing. As the number of schools that did not make AYP rose, the Bush administration came under pressure to relax the enforcement of testing provisions. However, the Department of Education continued to strictly uphold the requirements and refused requests for leniency. Civil rights advocates generally supported this strict approach for focusing attention on every subgroup in a school. The necessity of meeting proficiency targets for the poor, minorities, non-English speakers, and the disabled forced schools to carefully consider the attainment of targets for these groups of students or risk failing AYP.[23]

However, this approach for students with disabilities and English language learners, groups that posed particular problems, proved particularly unpopular with state and local districts. Some schools had a few disabled students with profound problems that could not be solved quickly. Other schools had to teach large groups of recent immigrants with no experience of American schools. Failure to meet state targets for proficiency in either of these two subgroups would mean a school did not make AYP. Some schools with excellent reputations were consequently identified as failing by these measures. On one hand, advocates for students in these subgroups supported the idea that no school could afford to ignore a group or coast on its reputation. On the other hand, the law had not intended to channel scarce resources to such schools because they did not make AYP. By 2004 the Bush administration negotiated more flexible arrangements for states on a case by case basis.[24] States were allowed some leeway over the inclusion of students with disabilities and English language learners in the accountability system. Also, most states were failing to meet the qualified teacher requirements, so the deadlines for this measure were extended.[25]

The consensus of academic research on education over the past half century suggests that most, though not all, of a student's academic success can be attributed to their family circumstances, background, and environment. With limited influence on a young person's life and education, schools cannot compensate for problems in their social or cultural environment. Nonetheless, every school is now judged annually on their ability to reach academic targets that will increase each year to eventually hit 100 percent proficiency. In the face of this seemingly impossible task, many states have moved to ease the task of reaching AYP for schools and thus easier for the state to meet its own targets.

Subgroup Size and Confidence Intervals

States can determine the size of a subgroup in each school that triggers a requirement for schools to report subgroup scores separately. Each subgroup that is reported separately must meet state proficiency targets, which will increase to 100 percent by 2014. Setting minimum numbers for each group is desirable since small group-scores are not statistically reliable. If one or two students fail to take a test, it could cause an entire school to fail. However, if states raise the number of students required to constitute a reportable subgroup, they can reduce the number of schools failing to meet AYP because of that group's scores. Over twenty states have successfully petitioned the government for such exemptions in the past two years. Texas, which was a model for NCLB, does not report separate scores for any of the state's 65,000 Asian students and several thousand American Indian students. Including these scores as part of the overall average makes it easier to make AYP.[26]

In addition, several states use confidence intervals for their targets. A confidence interval is a statistical technique that accommodates for natural fluctuations of test scores due to sampling errors and other factors unrelated to student learning or instruction. It is similar to the plus- and minus margin of error used in opinion polls and represents a range of uncertainty around a given percentage. So long as that target is within the confidence interval, the school makes AYP. This, of course, is an easier standard to achieve. In 2003, twenty-seven states used confidence intervals, but their number increased to forty-one by 2006, with four states increasing the size of their confidence intervals.[27]

Fifty Different Proficiency Standards

NCLB requires all students to reach grade level proficiency in every state by 2014, but leaves individual states to determine what "grade level proficiency" means. As states have more schools failing to reach AYP and must meet even higher targets to raise student proficiency rates, the pressure to change those standards increases. Ironically, the states with the highest standards have been the ones most penalized by NCLB. Rigorous standards meant that it was comparatively harder to meet targets, which led to more schools being labeled "failing." Minnesota, for example, had the best eighth grade scores in the country for math and was at a similar level to the top-ranked countries in the world. At the same time, it had 80 percent of schools on track to be labeled failing according to federal rules.[28] Mississippi, by contrast, has the second lowest passing rate in the country for fourth graders on the National Assessment of Educational Progress (NAEP), a single national benchmarking test administered across every state. However, its students have the highest passing rate in the country on their own state test, which is used to measure proficiency under NCLB. States that set lower standards are therefore rewarded with higher pass rates from their students. As confirmation of this, a study by the Thomas B. Fordham Institute and the Northwest Evaluation Association found that "improvements in passing rates on state tests can largely be explained by declines in the difficulty of those tests."[29]

NAEP data suggests that state assessments overstate the percentage of students reaching proficiency and the rate of improvement.[30] More ominously, a systematic analysis of NAEP national- and state-level achievement of results showed that test scores have remained steady. NCLB did not have a significant impact on improving student achievement or reducing the achievement gap.[31] It is too early to judge NCLB's overall impact on student achievement and other aspects of education. However, evidence that scores on reliable, national tests remained static during such a massive investment in testing and accountability has caused some concern (see figure 13.1).

Impact of Sanctions on Schools

Supporters of NCLB have been frustrated over the reluctance of states, local districts, and schools to employ the sanctions allowed in the law. States have proved very reluctant to use the most sweeping powers for restructuring,

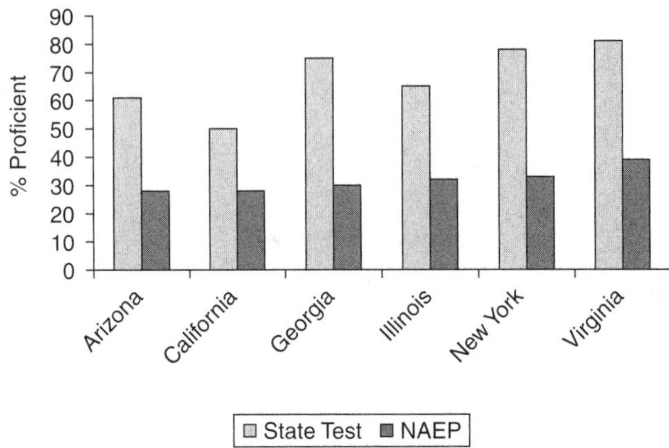

Figure 13.1   Percentage of proficient students meeting or exceeding proficiency standards in state math assessments vs. NAEP

Source: Table compiled from data in Lee, 2006.

which include reorganizing a school, removing teachers and administrators, contracting to private providers, or reconstituting the school as a charter school. To date, about a third of schools adopted less sweeping changes as allowed under the law. About 40 percent of schools took none of the five restructuring actions stipulated by NCLB and 42 percent did not receive the required assistance from districts, though most received assistance from the state. Even when districts did provide support, their interventions tended to be mild. Typically these amounted to extending the school day or year, providing help with data analysis and planning, or appointing an outside expert to advise the school.[32]

The school choice options have also failed to attract many parents.[33] Less than 1 percent of students nationwide opt to transfer out of schools identified for improvement, and only about 17 percent of eligible students take advantage of free tutoring.[34] Two fundamental tensions are particularly evident in this policy. First, states, local districts, and schools can be forced to offer tutoring and choice options to parents, but these will not be taken up in large numbers unless the district actively helps and encourages parents to obtain these services. Second, states, local districts, and schools all face a looming crisis as the targets of NCLB approach 100 percent proficiency by students.

As 2014 approaches, more and more schools will be subject to the severe sanctions stipulated under the law. However, states do not have the capacity to assist the many schools that need help to meet their targets.[35] Schools most likely to be labeled "failing" are concentrated within high poverty, urban areas. Even if the laws were strictly implemented, these struggling districts do not have the capacity, either in staff or resources, to take over or restructure so many schools at once. Further, state departments of education have never undertaken these sorts of activities either. Since none have the capacity to take over large numbers of schools, it is unclear that the NCLB sanctions are enforceable, even if states desired it.

Reauthorization

The bipartisan coalition that enacted NCLB in 2001 has fragmented, but it still remains intact. Bush's strategy of reaching out beyond centrist Democrats helped preserve one of his most significant accomplishments in domestic policy. The 2006 elections brought in a Democratic majority to Congress and elevated two of his chief allies in the passage of NCLB, Representative George Miller and Senator Edward Kennedy, to committee chairmanships over education in the House and Senate. Both were recruited to the cause of standards in the interest of civil rights and expanding education spending. Both have been highly critical of the Bush administration's handling of NCLB since it became law in 2002, and both openly seek to reform the law in response to the chorus of complaints from state and local governments, teachers and their unions, and education researchers. Furthermore, many of the new Democrats elected to the House in the last election ran on platforms highly critical of NCLB.

Congressional discussions over the course of 2007 focused on the extent to which the law should be improved and more fully funded rather than on whether the law should be gutted or its enforcement provisions reduced. It proved impossible to find a middle-ground solution to produce reauthorization, but the law remains extant in the absence of this. A new president and Congress will renegotiate NCLB after the 2008 elections, but the policy options are unlikely to change dramatically. Whatever new agreement is reached, the strong probability is that the measure's focus on testing and accountability will continue.

Conclusion: Implications for Federalism

NCLB constitutes a considerable change, if not revolution, in the field of education. It decisively shifts influence to the national level, despite a host of political obstacles that most commentators thought insurmountable, in a policy area that had successfully resisted such pressures for decades. As two analysts have commented, "NCLB...stands alongside the pioneering compensatory and special education laws enacted in 1965 and 1974.... The crucial aspect of all three pieces of legislation is not so much the money authorized as the policy framework imposed. ... No, it is not the federal dollar contribution but the direction given to all school spending—whether federal, state, or local—that is key."[36] The measure has framed education policy as a debate over standards and accountability, and this framework will continue to shape future developments in education over the next decade regardless of whether the act is strengthened or weakened in its reauthorization.

NCLB has allowed the federal government to set the terms of debate and reform for the next generation. While state and local governments still control education policy, their major efforts are now concentrated upon testing and accountability. Their attention and new policy developments will stay focused on this area because of NCLB. Indeed, it is now difficult to see how any other major reform efforts can be brought forward except in the context that they influence test scores.

From the wider viewpoint of federalism, however, NCLB is not a serious policy revolution. Its initially substantial impact on federal spending for education did not prove lasting. The use of conditions of federal assistance, setting prescriptions as a condition of receiving federal money, to enforce NCLB has been a common tactic in education since the first passage of ESEA in 1965, and it occurred again in the 1970s and 1980s with the education of the disabled. States protest at the systematic underfunding and heavy-handed implementation of the law, and they continue to negotiate with the Department of Education, Congress, and President for leniency. This is nothing new in the field of education policy and more broadly in American federalism.

Far from setting a new direction in federalism, NCLB represents another step in the attempt to centralize policy at the national level through the use of coercive policies to force state and local governments to do the federal government's bidding.[37] Even this centralization is not particularly sweeping if compared to other countries. Education continues to be funded and run at the state and local level. Indeed, in many ways NCLB demonstrates the limits of federal intervention in an essentially decentralized policy area.

Despite attempting a revolution in education policy, which required something of a political revolution to accomplish, NCLB has run into massive difficulties in implementation. Its main goal that all children in the United States will be proficient in reading and mathematics by 2014 is simply unattainable. Two prominent commentators and scholars of education policy, Chester Finn and Frederick Hess note:

> While there is no doubt that the number of "proficient" students can and should increase dramatically from today's 30-ish percent (using the National Assessment definition of proficiency), and while the achievement of children below the proficient level also can and should rise closer to proficiency, no educator in America believes that universal proficiency will, in fact, be attained by 2014, not, at least, by any reasonable definition of proficiency. Only politicians promise such things. The inevitable result is cynicism and frustration among educators and a "compliance" mentality among state and local officials.[38]

Ever a country of optimism, the United States has proposed a utopian goal for its education system that echoes the famous tagline from Garrison Keillor's *Prairie Home Companion*, where "all the children are above average." The problems with implementation highlight the federal government's inability to impose a successful change in education policy on the states and communities without their consent. This inability reaffirms the strength and vibrancy of the American federal system. The highly fragmented system of policymaking and delivery in education makes such central projects exceedingly hard to carry out. NCLB represents an attempt to "overreach" by the federal government that cannot accomplish what it wants to do, no matter how well-crafted the statute or how strictly it is implemented.[39] The main lesson it teaches is that policy success within the intergovernmental context of American federalism is more likely to flow from federal–state cooperation rather than from federal coercion of the states.

Notes

1. Lorraine M. McDonnell, "No Child Left Behind and the Federal Role in Education: Evolution or Revolution?" *Peabody Journal of Education* 80, 2 (2005): 19–38.
2. Paul Manna, *School's In: Federalism And the National Education Agenda* (Washington, DC: Georgetown University Press, 2006).
3. National Commission on Excellence in Education (NCEE), *A Nation at Risk: The Imperative for Educational Reform* (Washington, DC: Government Printing Office, 1983).
4. Patrick J. McGuinn, No Child Left Behind and the Transformation of Federal Education Policy, 1965–2005 (Lawrence, KS: University Press of Kansas, 2006).
5. John Kincaid, "From Cooperative to Coercive Federalism," The Annals of the American Academy of Political and Social Science 509, 1 (1990): 139–152; Timothy Conlan, From New Federalism to Devolution: Twenty-Five Years of Intergovernmental Reform (Washington, DC: Brookings Institution Press, 1998); Paul Posner, The Politics of Unfunded Mandates: Whither Federalism (Washington, DC: Georgetown University Press, 1998), and "The Politics of Coercive Federalism in the Bush Era," Publius 37, 3 (2007): 390–412; David B. Walker, The Rebirth of Federalism (New York: Chatham House, 2000).
6. Diane Ravitch, The Troubled Crusade: American Education 1945–1980 (New York: Basic Books, 1987).
7. NCEE, *A Nation at Risk.*
8. McGuinn, *No Child Left Behind.*
9. Gallup Organization, "Phi Delta Kappan's Thirty-second Annual Survey of the Public's Attitude toward the Public Schools" (2000): 169.
10. S. Crabtree, "Changing His Tune, Kennedy Starts Work with Bush on Education Bill," *Roll Call* (2001).
11. D. Nather, "Compromises on ESEA Bills May Imperil Republican Strategy," *CQ Weekly* (2001): 2009.
12. Linda Darling-Hammond, "Evaluating 'No Child Left Behind,'" *The Nation*, May 21, 2007, www.thenation.com/loc/20070521/darling-hammond
13. Marilyn Cochrane Smith, "No Child Left Behind: 3 Years and Counting," *Journal of Teacher Education* 56, 3 (2005): 99–103.
14. Martin R. West and Paul Peterson, "The Politics and Practice of Accountability," in West and Peterson, *No Child Left Behind? The Politics and Practice of Schools Accountability* (Washington DC: Brookings Institution, 2007).

15. E. Robelen, "Department Levies $783,000 Title I Penalty on GA," *Education Week* (2003).

16. L. Ohlson, "State Test Programs Mushroom as NCLB Mandate Kicks In," *Education Week* (2005).

17. Betty Sternberg, "Testimony before the Commission on No Child Left Behind" (2006)

18. Betty Sternberg "When Less is More," *Education Week* (2004)

19. Thomas Toch, Margins for Error: The Education Testing Industry in the No Child Left Behind Era (Washington DC: Education Sector, 2006)

20. Sternberg, "Testimony before the Commission on No Child Left Behind."

21. Government Accountability Office, Title I: Characteristics of Tests Will Influence Expenses: Information Sharing May Help States Realize Efficiencies (Washington, DC: GAO, 2003).

22. J. L. Sack, "Utah Passes Bill to Trump 'No Child' Law," *Education Week* (2005).

23. Kenneth Wong and Gail Sunderman, "Education Accountability as a Presidential Priority: No Child Left Behind and the Bush Presidency," *Publius* 37 (2007): 333–350.

24. Gail Sunderman, *The Unraveling of No Child Left Behind: How Negotiated Changes Transform the Law* (Cambridge, MA: The Civil Rights Project at Harvard University, 2006).

25. B. Keller, "States Given Extra Year on Teachers," *Education Week* (2005).

26. Frank Bass and Nicole Ziegler Dizon, "States Help Schools to Dodge No Child: Accused of 'Gaming the System,'" *Chicago Sun Times* (2006).

27. Mary Fulton, *Minimum Subgroup Size for Adequate Yearly Progress (AYP)* (Denver: Education Commission of the States, 2006).

28. Darling-Hammond, "Evaluating 'No Child Left Behind.'"

29. James Cronin, Michael Dahlin, Deborah Adkins, and Gage Kinsbury, *The Proficiency Illusion* (Washington, DC: Thomas B. Fordham Institute, 2007). For a similar conclusion, see Laura Hamilton, Brian Stecher, Julie Marsh, Jennifer Sloan McCombs, Abby Robyn, Jennifer Russell et al., and others, *Standards-Based Accountability Under No Child Left Behind: Experiences of Teachers and Administrators in Three States* (Santa Monica, CA: Rand, 2007).

30. Bruce Fuller, Kathryn Gesicki, Erin Kang, and Joseph Wright, *Is the No Child Left Behind Act Working? The Reliability of How States Track Achievement* (Berkeley. CA: Policy Analysis for California, University of California, 2006); Jaekung Lee, *Tracking Achievement Gaps and Assessing the Impact of NCLB on the Gaps: An In-Depth Look into National and State Reading and Math Outcome Tests* (Cambridge, MA: The Civil Rights Project at Harvard University, 2006).

31. Lee, Tracking Achievement Gaps and Assessing the Impact of NCLB on the Gaps.

32. Government Accountability Office, No Child Left Behind Act: Education Should Clarify Guidance and Address Potential Compliance Issues for Schools in Corrective Action and Restructuring Status (Washington, DC: GAO, 2007).

33. Frederick Hess and Chester Finn Jr., *No Remedy Left Behind: Lessons from a Half-Decade of NCLB* (Washington, DC: American Enterprise Institute, 2007).

34. Ron Zimmer and others, *State and Local Implementation of the No Child Left Behind Act*, Vol. 1 (Santa Monica, CA: Rand, 2007).

35. Gail Sunderman and Gary Orfield, "Domesticating a Revolution: No Child Left Behind Reforms and State Administrative Response," *Harvard Educational Review* 76, 4 (2006): 526–556.

36. Martin West and Paul Peterson, "The Politics and Practice of Accountability," in West and Peterson, eds., *No Child left Behind: The Politics and Practice of School Accountability* (Washington, DC: Brookings Institution, 2007).

37. Kincaid, "From Cooperative to Coercive Federalism"; Posner, *The Politics of Unfunded Mandates*.

38. Hess and Finn, No Remedy Left Behind.

39. Michael Petrelli, "The Problem with 'Implementation' is the Problem," in Hess and Finn, *No Remedy Left Behind*.

Index